Language Revitalisation in Gaelic Scotland

Do Fhinn agus do Chiorstaidh

LANGUAGE REVITALISATION IN GAELIC SCOTLAND

Linguistic Practice and Ideology

Stuart Dunmore

EDINBURGH
University Press

Edinburgh University Press is one of the leading university presses in the UK. We publish academic books and journals in our selected subject areas across the humanities and social sciences, combining cutting-edge scholarship with high editorial and production values to produce academic works of lasting importance. For more information visit our website: edinburghuniversitypress.com

© Stuart S. Dunmore, 2019, 2021
Edinburgh University Press Ltd
The Tun – Holyrood Road, 12(2f) Jackson's Entry, Edinburgh EH8 8PJ

First published in hardback by Edinburgh University Press 2019

Typeset in 10/12 Ehrhardt by
Servis Filmsetting Ltd, Stockport, Cheshire

A CIP record for this book is available from the British Library

ISBN 978 1 4744 4311 1 (hardback)
ISBN 9781474443142 (paperback)
ISBN 978 1 4744 4312 8 (webready PDF)
ISBN 978 1 4744 4313 5 (epub)

The right of Stuart S. Dunmore to be identified as the author of this work has been asserted in accordance with the Copyright, Designs and Patents Act 1988, and the Copyright and Related Rights Regulations 2003 (SI No. 2498).

Contents

List of Figures	viii
List of Tables	ix
Foreword	x

1 Gaelic Scotland: Bilingual Life in the Twenty-First Century?   1
   Introduction   1
   1.1   Gaelic language and culture in Scotland   3
   1.2   Theoretical foundations: Language revitalisation and the role of education   10
   1.3   Concluding remarks and book structure   16

2 Language, Culture and Identities: Theoretical Perspectives   17
   2.1   Theorising the relation of language, culture and identities   17
        2.1.1   Language and ethnic identity: (Socio)linguistic, anthropological and sociological perspectives   18
        2.1.2   The symbolic value of language   21
        2.1.3   Essentialist perspectives on language and identity   22
        2.1.4   Language and nationalism   23
   2.2   Language ideologies   25
   2.3   Language socialisation   27
   2.4   Education and the role of immersion schooling   29
        2.4.1   Language acquisition and immersion education   29
        2.4.2   Immersion education and language attrition   32
        2.4.3   Principles from overseas: Immersion revitalisation education in Europe, North America and Australasia   34
   2.5   Concluding remarks on language, culture and immersion education   41

3 Exploring Outcomes of Gaelic-Medium Education: Research Design and Analysis   43
   3.1 GME: Past, present and prospects for revitalisation   44
       3.1.1 The development of GME in Scotland 1872–1985   44
       3.1.2 Expectations and experiences of GME: 1980–90   47
       3.1.3 Limitations of GME in Gaelic language revitalisation   49
       3.1.4 Concluding remarks on GME as education system and research site   53
   3.2 GME in its first decade: Sample design and analysis   53
       3.2.1 Defining the informant universe   54
       3.2.2 Questionnaire design and analysis   56
       3.2.3 Ethnographic interviews in the 'field'   57
   3.3 Analytic methods   58
       3.3.1 Research design: Mixed methods and data triangulation 58
       3.3.2 Analysing language and culture in interaction: The ethnography of speaking   59
       3.3.3 Transcription: Approach and application   62
       3.3.4 Coding and analysis procedure   63
   3.4 Concluding remarks   64

4 Linguistic Practice, Gaelic Use and Language Socialisation: Findings from Qualitative and Quantitative Analyses   65
   4.1 Gaelic language practices: Discourses of (dis)use   65
       4.1.1 'High' reported use of Gaelic and the role of Gaelic employment   66
       4.1.2 Intermediate to limited use: Family and peers?   67
       4.1.3 Low use of Gaelic   69
       4.1.4 Language practice I: Gaelic as a 'secret code'   72
       4.1.5 Language practice II: Code-switching and 'informal' Gaelic 73
   4.2 Gaelic language socialisation   76
       4.2.1 Gaelic language socialisation at home   76
       4.2.2 Socialisation at home by one Gaelic-speaking parent 78
       4.2.3 No Gaelic at home   80
   4.3 GME and Gaelic socialisation   83
       4.3.1 Role of GME in Gaelic language socialisation   83
       4.3.2 GME: Socialisation in Gaelic culture?   85
       4.3.3 Negative affect in school language socialisation   87
       4.3.4 Gaelic language socialisation experiences: Some conclusions   89
   4.4 Language use, GME and Gaelic socialisation: Statistical analysis   89
       4.4.1 Social background variables   90
       4.4.2 Reported abilities in Gaelic   94
       4.4.3 Overall Gaelic language use   96

		4.4.4	Family Gaelic use, socialisation and intergenerational transmission	97
		4.4.5	Social use of Gaelic: Conversation, technology and (social) media	102
	4.5	Concluding remarks and data triangulation		107

5 Underlying Language Use: Gaelic Language Ideologies and Attitudes — 108
  5.1 Ideologies of Gaelic I: Language use — 109
    5.1.1 Discourses of regret/'guilt' — 109
    5.1.2 Intergenerational transmission and Gaelic use — 111
    5.1.3 'Judgement' and 'snobbery' in the Gaelic community — 113
    5.1.4 Disuse, loss and 'having' Gaelic — 115
    5.1.5 'Opportunity' and choice in Gaelic use — 118
  5.2 Ideologies of Gaelic II: Language and identities — 121
    5.2.1 Gaelic and personal identity — 121
    5.2.2 Gaels? – *Gàidheil*? Gaelic identity, culture and heritage — 123
    5.2.3 National or regional language: 'Highlands and Islands' identity? — 126
    5.2.4 Albais/Scots language: A rival linguistic identity? — 129
    5.2.5 Gaelic and Scottish identity: Language, nation and culture — 131
  5.3 Gaelic Language Attitudes — 136
    5.3.1 Identities and attitudes — 136
    5.3.2 Attitudes to Gaelic language and community — 138
    5.3.3 Attitudes to GME — 139
  5.4 Concluding remarks and triangulation of language ideologies and attitudes — 140

6 Bilingual Life After School? Linguistic Practice and Ideologies in Action — 141
  6.1 Language use among Gaelic-medium educated adults: Past, present and future prospects — 142
    6.1.1 Present Gaelic language use — 142
    6.1.2 Language abilities — 145
    6.1.3 Language socialisation — 146
  6.2 Language ideologies and attitudes: Factors underlying linguistic practice — 147
    6.2.1 Ideologies of Gaelic language use — 147
    6.2.2 Gaelic and sociocultural identities — 149
    6.2.3 Attitudes to GME — 151
  6.3 Conclusions: Bilingual life and the relationship of linguistic practice and ideology — 151

Bibliography — 155
Index — 179

Figures

4.1	Percentage of GME students in Highlands and Islands, 1985–2000	91
4.2	Reported Gaelic language abilities	94
4.3	Language use at work or university	97
4.4	Language use at home	97
4.5	Language use with mother	99
4.6	Language use with father	99
4.7	Language use with partner/spouse	100
4.8	Language use with son/daughter	101
4.9	Language use with brother/sister	101
4.10	Conversation with all friends	102
4.11	Conversation with Gaelic-speaking friends	103
4.12	Communicating with Gaelic-speaking friends – phone	103
4.13	Communicating with Gaelic-speaking friends – SMS/text	104
4.14	Communicating with Gaelic-speaking friends – social media	104
4.15	Listening to music/radio	105
4.16	Watching television	105
4.17	Reading books	105
4.18	Using social media	106
4.19	Using other internet	106

Tables

1.1	Gaelic speakers in Scotland 1806–2011	8
3.1	Growth of GME 1985–2005. Primary GME provision by area	47
3.2	Primary pupils in GME 1985–95	54
4.1	Interviewees' home linguistic backgrounds by current Gaelic use	76
4.2	Occupational class	90
4.3	Continuation with GME at secondary school	92
4.4	Continuation with Gaelic study	92
4.5	Reported socialisation in Gaelic	93
4.6	Language ability after school	93
4.7	Change in Gaelic language practices since leaving school	94
4.8	Competence in Gaelic	95
4.9	Competence in English	95
4.10	Frequency of Gaelic use	96
4.11	Reported Gaelic ability among family members	98
4.12	Reported Gaelic use, socialisation and ability. Spearman's rho correlations	98
4.13	Family Gaelic use – linguistic and social variables. Spearman's rho correlations	102
4.14	Social (/-media) use, social and linguistic variables. Spearman's rho correlations	107
5.1	National identity	136
5.2	Attitudes to Gaelic and Scottish identity	137
5.3	Attitudes to Gaelic and personal, cultural and national identities	138
5.4	Attitudes to the Gaelic community	138
5.5	Attitudes to GME and intergenerational transmission	139

Foreword

Gaelic-Medium Education as Revitaliser: A Pointer for Future Prospects?

Gaelic is the original language of the Scots, and it is still spoken. This is why Gaelic matters: it is foundational in Scottish culture as one of the defining attributes of the Scotti, the people who eventually developed into the Scottish nation of today. Recent decades have witnessed a change of fortunes for the language. It has been recognised, first as an official language of the United Kingdom (2003), and subsequently as an official language of Scotland (2005). A statutory language development authority, Bòrd na Gàidhlig, was subsequently created (2006), and a Gaelic media and broadcasting authority, MG Alba, with a Gaelic-medium television station, BBC Alba, was established (2008). The language has longer-standing official recognition, however, with statutory members on the Crofters' Commission (from 1886) and the Scottish Land Court (established 1911); in education acts (from 1918), first as a school subject and later as a medium of education (from the earlier and mid-twentieth century, respectively); and in Gaelic-medium education (GME) as such (from 1985).

There has thus been a full generation or more since the beginnings of GME, and Stuart Dunmore's study of its first generation of (mainly) new speakers is therefore timely. Since a question on Gaelic speaking ability first appeared in Scotland's population census (1881), the language has been in conspicuous overall decline in terms of both numbers, and area where the language features as local community speech. Ostensible increases in numbers (1891, 1971) were chiefly due to changes in the wording of the census question. Recent censuses (2001, 2011), however, have witnessed some growth in the numbers of Gaelic speakers amongst young people, which is now beginning to overcome the loss of speakers (mainly) through death.

From its inception, Bòrd na Gàidhlig has made GME one of its principal strategies for language revitalisation, and has pushed strongly for further development of the sector, both in the Highlands and Islands 'Gaelic-speaking areas', and in urban, Lowland Scotland – this despite some admonition from the late Joshua Fishman (father of the sociology of language) not to place too much reliance on 'education and other higher order "props"' (1991: 380, 391). The Bòrd has also been involved in the formulation of a National Gaelic Language Plan, and similar schemes potentially for all Scottish official authorities, Gaelic-medium broadcasting, research on Gaelic language in the community, and much else, as well as Gaelic educational policies. Its language plans are reviewed on a five-yearly basis. Some overall scrutiny and review of the effectiveness of its policies are now due, together with those of its non-statutory predecessor (from 2003).

Stuart Dunmore's study provides a perspective on an important aspect of these policies: namely, whether the Bòrd's educational policies have had any real effect on language revitalisation, and brought about any real prospect of a longer-term future for the language in Scottish society and culture. The study thus purposively sought a representative sample of the first generation of GME-educated ex-pupils, now adults, some with children of their own. The subjects were asked about the significance of Gaelic in their present lives: whether they still speak it, whether and how they use it, what significance they place upon it, how it relates to their own identities, what their own attitudes to GME are, and the likelihood of their own children acquiring the language. These are crucial questions for Gaelic language planners at the present time, and the study considers the future prospects for the language in the light of its findings, bearing in mind that respondents are likely to have been more favourably inclined towards the language, and possibly too more successfully acquisitive of it.

The final chapter on the bilingual life of ex-GME pupils after school is thus a crucial pointer to the future role of Gaelic in Scottish society. In reviewing other studies that had observed the language abilities, usages and attitudes of GME pupils and former pupils, Dunmore's present work details the weaknesses of Gaelic in all these respects. The quoted objective of D. J. MacLeod (2007, 2009), regarding the prospects for the GME system creating 'a new generation of Gaelic-speakers', and for a revival evidenced by their children being 'raised as mother tongue Gaelic speakers', is thus still far from being demonstrated by the present findings, despite census data on increases in reported Gaelic language abilities amongst young people. The clear implication is that Gaelic language planners need to take a hard, unblinkered look at the realities demonstrated in this study. It might be salutary for consideration to be given as to what it would take to develop the system to enable MacLeod's 'new generation of Gaelic speakers', or at least to develop it to the levels of performance noted by the corresponding immersion systems for Welsh and Irish. Could that even be a possibility for the Scottish education system? What, then, is envisaged by Gaelic language planners as a realistic, feasible and achievable future role for the language? A new, revitalised Gaelic-speaking generation? A Gaelic-using network linked by new media? A cultural coterie in its own cocoon?

Stuart Dunmore's present study thus presents vitally important data on crucial current language-planning questions, and by extension develops an agenda for new directions in policymaking. In doing this, he has undertaken a landmark study in the field, which has very amply fulfilled the purpose of the Soillse project (from 2010, to create an ongoing contingent of advanced language researchers to support Gaelic language planning), of which he was amongst the first cohort

Dunmore's study reports at a time when the fortunes of Gaelic are challenged by formidable social, economic and political changes in wider society. The recently improving provisions of infrastructure, cultural support, and new opportunities for the language come at a very late stage in its history, and had they been implemented much earlier, they might, in all fairness, have given the language and its speakers a much firmer base on which to maintain its culture and place in what I have called 'runaway language-shift'. This will call for its own study of external forces. What Stuart Dunmore has provided here, however, is the corresponding, penetrating and long called-for study of the internal motivations and attitudes of the new ex-GME generation, in which, importantly, we hear the actual voice of that generation itself. I am delighted to commend this study as an essential read for all those interested in the future prospects of Gaelic in Scotland, and to language planners and policymakers in particular.

Kenneth MacKinnon
Ferintosh, the Black Isle, April 2019.
Honorary Professor (Gaelic Studies), University of Aberdeen;
Reader Emeritus (Sociology of Language), University of Hertfordshire

1

Gaelic Scotland: Bilingual Life in the Twenty-First Century?

Introduction

Language decline and revitalisation are matters of increasingly urgent political concern internationally. Whilst bilingual education occupies a prominent position in policy to stem the loss of minoritised languages, various scholars have suggested that the long-term impact of such education on language revitalisation initiatives may be undermined by a complex assortment of sociolinguistic and psychological factors. Yet while the limitations of formal education for revitalising minority languages have been widely theorised, empirical research on long-term outcomes of minority language-medium education has been relatively scarce. This monograph seeks to contribute to filling this important lacuna by empirically assessing long-term outcomes of Gaelic-medium education (GME) in Scotland. This opening chapter will contextualise the key themes of the book within the sociological and historical setting of Gaelic in Scotland (1.1), and introduce the crucial issue of language revitalisation and the role assigned to bilingual immersion education in current initiatives to maintain and renew minority languages (1.2). Lastly, section 1.3 will outline the overall structure of the book, with a view to situating the wider study against this conceptual backdrop.

Gaelic has been spoken in Scotland for over 1,500 years, and was used over a major part of northern Britain – spoken throughout but not confined to the borders of present-day Scotland – in the medieval period (Dumville 2002; Woolf 2007; Ó Baoill 2010; Clancy 2011; Márkus 2017). Yet the language has now been in a state of decline for almost a millennium. From the twelfth century the ascendancy of a Norman French-speaking aristocracy combined with the increasing economic importance of the market burghs – where varieties of the Northumbrian 'Inglis' language predominated – effected a gradual transition among Scots in lowland areas from membership of a Gaelic-speaking, kinship-oriented society to an Inglis-speaking, feudalist one (Barrow 1989). Gaelic was increasingly replaced by Inglis as the language of social prestige and vernacular speech in most lowland districts, and from c.1500 the latter became increasingly known there as 'Scottis' (modern 'Scots'), while the social terrain of Gaelic became increasingly restricted to the mountainous Highlands and Islands (M. D. MacGregor 2009). One consequence of this dynamic was an increased ideological association of Gaelic with the Highlands and Islands, while Scots, and later English, became majority languages in the more densely populated Lowlands. From the mid-sixteenth century the extirpation of Gaelic and Highland culture became an explicit policy of the Scottish and, later, the British state (Withers 1984, 1988; MacKinnon 1991, 1993; MacGregor 2006).

MacKinnon (1993) notes that by the early nineteenth century, the proportion of Scotland's population able to speak Gaelic was 18.5%; this had fallen to 6.3% by the end of that century, largely as a result of processes of land reorganisation and mass displacement that became known as the Clearances (Withers 1984; Richards 2007). This was compounded by the passing of the Education (Scotland) Act 1872, which made no mention of Gaelic (McLeod 2005; Dunbar 2006; MacLeod 2007). Responsibility for education in the Highlands, which had previously been administered by third-sector and church organisations, was transferred to local school boards, and in areas where schools had previously made provision for Gaelic its use consequently declined (Durkacz 1983; MacKinnon 1993; Macleod 2010). While Gaelic was used sporadically in education in different areas during the twentieth century (O'Hanlon 2012; O'Hanlon et al. 2012), the proportion of its speakers in Scotland continued to decline, falling to 1.6% by 1981 (MacKinnon 1993). GME, as it exists today, emerged from the grass-roots efforts of primarily Gaelic-speaking parents who were chiefly concerned for their children's Gaelic language acquisition, but was quickly augmented by hundreds of non-Gaelic-speaking children (Comunn na Gàidhlig 1989; Fraser 1989).

Present-day GME in Scotland (see Her Majesty's Inspectorate of Education 2011) started in 1985, when two classes offering instruction through the medium of Gaelic opened within primary schools in Glasgow and Inverness. GME grew rapidly throughout the first decade of its availability, and 1,258 students were enrolled in the system by 1995 (MacKinnon 2005: 7–8). This book examines outcomes of the system in terms of the manner and degree to which former pupils who started in GME during this period continue to use Gaelic in their daily lives, and provides an assessment of their language ideologies and attitudes.

The 2011 census showed a diminution in the decline of Gaelic speakers in Scotland, and for the first time marginal growth of 0.1% was recorded in the national proportion of speakers under the age of 20 (National Records of Scotland 2013a). Crucially, this growth was interpreted by policymakers such as Bòrd na Gàidhlig – the statutory agency charged with the promotion of Gaelic – as evidence of the role of GME in revitalising the language (Bòrd na Gàidhlig 2013, 2014). For example, in 2014 Bòrd na Gàidhlig's then chief executive, John Angus MacKay, claimed of the 2011 census results that:

> the number of Gaelic speakers in Scotland has almost stabilised since the census of 2001. This is mainly due to the rise in Gaelic-medium education . . . [and] shows that within the next ten years the long term decline of the language could be reversed. (Bòrd na Gàidhlig 2014)

Yet the census figures give only a limited picture of the actual language practices of reported speakers, the extent to which they use Gaelic, and their beliefs, feelings and attitudes regarding the language, a shortcoming typical of census data, regardless of geographical location. Internationally, little research appears to have been done on the life trajectories of adults who received a bilingual education: that is to say, on the long-term effects that systems of bilingual education may have on such individuals' relationship to the minority language after formal schooling is 'over and done with' (Fishman 2001b: 470).

The first students to receive GME at primary school are now in their late twenties to mid-thirties, and prospects for the maintenance and intergenerational transmission of Gaelic by this group have not previously been examined. As a response, the principal research questions of the investigation outlined in this book comprise the following:

- What role does Gaelic play in the day-to-day lives of former Gaelic-medium students who started in GME during the first decade of its availability? How and when do they use the language?
- What sets of beliefs and language ideologies do these Gaelic-medium-educated adults express in relation to Gaelic?
- How do these beliefs and ideologies relate to their actual language practices, to their attitudes concerning the language, and to future prospects for the maintenance of Gaelic?

Through a combination of qualitative and quantitative research methods, this book provides an assessment of these overarching questions among a sample of 130 Gaelic-medium-educated adults. A thematic ethnography of speaking methodology is employed to analyse qualitative data from interviews with forty-six Gaelic-medium educated adults, whilst 112 responses to an online questionnaire on language use and attitudes are evaluated through correlational statistical analysis. Results are discussed with reference to extensive research literatures on the nexus of language, culture and identity, language revitalisation in the international context, and the limitations of GME in relation to the revitalisation of Gaelic. The first section of this introductory chapter (1.1) will introduce the current sociolinguistic situation of Gaelic in Scotland. In section 1.2, I introduce and conceptualise current ideas on language revitalisation, drawing particular attention to Fishman's ideas concerning reversing language shift (RLS), and some of the major critiques of his theories. Finally, section 1.3 sets out the overall structure of the book.

1.1 Gaelic language and culture in Scotland

Gaelic speakers constitute a marked linguistic minority in modern Scotland. In the 2011 census, 57,602 people over the age of 3 were reported as being able to speak Gaelic, approximating to 1.1% of the total population of Scotland (National Records of Scotland 2013a). This figure amounted to 1,050 fewer speakers than were recorded in the 2001 census, a 2.2% decline in speaker numbers from ten years previously (as against a decline of 11.1% between 1991 and 2001). Language shift is an increasingly common phenomenon in the international context; as the late Joshua Fishman (1991, 2001b, 2013) consistently observed, countless minority language communities across the world are currently attempting to maintain and revitalise their traditional modes of communication and cultural practice against an oncoming tide of global language loss. Various scholars have critiqued the notion of 'endangerment' in discourses of language minoritisation and shift, however, particularly problematising the nature of narratives that have come to predominate in certain contexts of language revitalisation (see chapter contibutions in Duchêne and Heller 2007, for example). Similarly, Costa (2017) has recently argued that rationales for revitalisation movements may not, in fact, stem principally from linguistic concerns, but rather reflect broader sociocultural phenomena in late modernity.

Over 90% of the world's estimated 7,105 languages are thought to be spoken by fewer than 1 million first-language speakers, with almost 50% spoken by fewer than 10,000 (Phillipson and Skutnabb-Kangas 2013: 496–7). Not all small languages are considered to be 'endangered', however. The *Ethnologue* listing of world languages identifies 906 of a total of 7,105 languages to be 'dying' at present (12.6%), with a further 1,481 (21%) thought to be 'in trouble'. Some 377 languages are reported to have become extinct since the first *Ethnologue* estimates were made in 1950, a global language loss rate of 6 per year (Ethnologue 2017). Some scholars have been considerably more pessimistic than this figure would suggest, however, estimating that as many as 50% of the world's languages are no longer being 'reproduced' among children, and that a further 40% are threatened or endangered at present (Baker 2011: 44). On this basis, Krauss (1992) suggested that, by the end of the current century, as many as 90% of the world's languages could be either extinct or moribund. Language endangerment is a concern of increasing importance to scholars, activists and institutions of various kinds (Nettle and Romaine 2000). The United Nations, for example, has acknowledged the value of linguistic diversity through its educational, scientific and cultural organisation UNESCO (2003a, 2003b), a position that Nic Craith (2007: 180) has linked to a greater appreciation and promotion of cultural diversity among international organisations generally.

The figure of 57,602 reported Gaelic 'speakers' in the 2011 census may go some way to providing an estimate of the size of the Gaelic speech community in Scotland. As Romaine (2000: 36) points out, however, census data will often generate 'quite a different perspective' on questions of language use to that which might emerge from more fine-grained ethnographic or statistical analyses. It is essential to bear in mind the distortions that 'self-reporting' can have on data regarding language competence in surveys such as the national census, whether through over-reporting of language skills by individuals of limited proficiency, or under-reporting of skills by speakers lacking confidence (Wray and Bloomer 2006: 166–7). Romaine (2000: 41) notes, in any case, that in many instances 'it may not be clear to community members themselves who is or is not a proficient speaker' in minority language contexts.

Gaelic has now been in a state of language decline in Scotland for close to a thousand years. The generally accepted account holds that Gaels (Old Gaelic: *Goídil*; Latin: *Scotti*) from the kingdom of Dál Riata in north-eastern Ulster had established settlements and maintained close contact with communities in Argyll (from Old Gaelic: *Airer Goídel*, 'coastline of the Gaels') from at least the beginning of the sixth century (Ó Baoill 2010; Clancy 2011; Márkus 2017). The Gaels (or 'Scots') extended their political and cultural influence across the mainland of northern Britain over the next 500 years, their language expanding as they did so at the expense of Pictish and Brythonic varieties that had previously been spoken within that territory (Dumville 2002). Ó Baoill (2010: 8) has observed that the decline of the Picts, and their language and society, from written records by the end of the ninth century reveals the extensive scale and degree of Gaelicisation (or 'Scotticisation') that occurred during the early medieval period, though Woolf (2007: 17) has cautioned that 'textual evidence for social history of Scotland is appallingly slight' for this period. Nevertheless, the preponderance of Gaelic place names over much of southern Scotland and even into northern England indicates the furthest extent of the Gaelic Kingdom of Alba in the early medieval era. Notably, however, Gaelic names are sparsest in south-eastern districts, which had been predominantly settled by Anglian peoples whose language – 'Inglis' – became established in that region, while the Gaels continued to expand their kingdom from the west (Barrow 1989; Woolf 2007; Clancy 2011).

The institutions of the Kingdom of Alba appear to fade rapidly from historical record around the early years of the twelfth century, increasingly being replaced by the families and institutions of the ascendant Anglo-Norman nobility (Barrow 1989: 70; MacKinnon 1991: 34). Subsequently, the combination of a French-speaking aristocracy and the increasing importance of the market burghs (where Northumbrian 'Inglis' varieties predominated) to Scotland's economic development effected what Barrow (1989: 70) has described as 'a gradual transition from membership of a Gaelic-speaking essentially kin-based society to that of a Scots-speaking feudal society'. In the later Middle Ages, Gaelic was increasingly replaced by 'Inglis' as the language of social prestige and vernacular speech in lowland districts, the latter becoming increasingly known as 'Scottis' from *c.*1500, while Gaelic was referred to as 'Erse' ('Irish'; M. D. MacGregor 2009: 37). This dichotomy is partly paralleled in the Gaelic distinction between the Highlands (*Gàidhealtachd*; approximately, 'Gaelic-speaking area') and Lowlands (*Galltachd*, 'foreign area'). To both groups, then, the Highland/Lowland divide first expressed itself in terms of a primarily (ethno-)linguistic distinction, and as a result of language shift (MacKinnon 1991; Withers 1984, 1988).

After the mid-sixteenth-century Scottish Reformation, hostility to Gaelic on the part of the crown became connected to policy to extirpate rebellious and resistant elements from the kingdom. Developments throughout the seventeenth century, starting with the 1609 Statutes of Iona, are regarded by Withers (1988: 157–8) as constituting an early wave of processes of 'improvement' and Anglicisation that instigated language shift to English in the traditional strongholds of the Gaelic language within the Highlands and Islands. The Statutes consisted of a series of measures aimed at undermining the effective autonomy that Highland and Island chiefs exercised over the region. Crucially, the Gaelic chiefs' heirs were required subsequently to be educated in Lowland schools, with the express intention that they should henceforth be able to speak, read and write the English language (MacGregor 2006: 145).

As a consequence, the centuries-old link between the clan chiefs, their tenant vassals (tacksmen) and subordinate followers was severely disrupted. Processes of cultural transformation had therefore begun even a century before the onset of more explicit moves toward 'improvement' in the eighteenth century. Policy in this connection was linked in large part to notions of civilisation and enlightenment, particularly after the 1707 Union (Withers 1984, 1988). A central concern of philosophical enquiry in the eighteenth century, reflected in the thoughts and writings of philosophers such as Rousseau, Herder and von Humboldt, was the relationship of reason and culture as the distinguishing features of humanity – and the absolute centrality of language to these notions (Glaser 2007: 37). The Romantic, Herderian view of the nation drew upon the notion of a people's 'shared spirit' (*Volksgeist*), which was chiefly manifested in their language and culture (Reicher and Hopkins 2001: 8). Yet, crucially, the conception of language that Romantic philosophers privileged in their enquiries pertained to varieties that were perceived to be of benefit for wider communication, such as French, German and English (see section 2.1, below, on Romanticism, language and identity). The English philosopher John Stuart Mill insisted, for instance, that:

> Nobody can suppose that it is not more beneficial to a Breton, or a Basque of French Navarre, to be brought into the current of ideas and feelings of a highly civilised and cultivated people . . . than to sulk on his own rocks, the half-savage relic of past times . . . . The same remark applies to the Welshman or the Scottish highlander [sic] as members of the British nation. (Mill 1991 [1861]: 431)

Gaelic was perceived to be a barrier to the economic, moral and cultural development of Highlanders, and its extirpation (and replacement with English) was increasingly regarded by the ruling elite as a necessary goal of improvement (Withers 1988: 58). Additionally, Withers (1988: 58) identifies the Society in Scotland for Propagating Christian Knowledge (SSPCK) as an important instrument in this regard during the eighteenth and nineteenth centuries, as the dominant educational institution at work in the Highlands, an explicit goal of which was to civilise the region through the propagation of English and Protestantism. Processes and ideologies of improvement in the Highlands came into fierce conflict with notions of *dùthchas* ('heredity', 'tradition', 'heritage') and Highland(/Gaelic) understandings of what society was, and how it had always operated (MacKinnon 1991: 64–5). In particular, the cultivation of industry in the Highlands was actively encouraged by Enlightenment thinkers such as Adam Smith, who denounced traditional Highland society as an example of all that was worst about patriarchal, feudal society (Withers 1988: 58).

Landowners became increasingly concerned with economic reorganisation, in the belief that harnessing markets and cultivating industry would impart civilisation and cultural development in Highland Scotland (Withers 1988; Macleod 2010). The landed gentry, increasingly absorbed within the British aristocracy, took an ever greater interest in production and profit on their estates, exacting higher rents from tenants and developing the large-scale pastoral farming of sheep and cattle (Glaser 2007: 65). Faced with increasing economic pressures and loss of traditional livelihoods, Highlanders began to emigrate as early as the 1730s (Devine 1994: 16). Harvest failures in the late eighteenth and early nineteenth centuries exacerbated hardships for middle-class tacksmen and rural workers alike, and drove ever greater numbers to emigrate to the urban Lowlands, England or the New World (Glaser 2007: 65). Hunter (1976) has estimated that in 1803 alone up to 20,000 people may have left the Highlands for North America. Highlanders were increasingly encouraged or compelled to emigrate, in a process of land reorganisation and mass displacement that has become known as the Clearances (Withers 1984; Glaser 2007; Richards 2007).

McLeod (2005: 178) has stated of the relationship between the Clearances and language shift in the Highlands and Islands that 'the dislocation and disruption caused by clearance . . . seem to have contributed to longer-term trends by which Gaelic was devalued and gradually abandoned'. The activities of the SSPCK and Gaelic Schools Societies in connection with their use of Gaelic for elementary tuition (in effect, to promulgate English) tended to reinforce general trends toward bilingualism in the Highlands (Durkacz 1983: 219–22; MacKinnon 1991: 64; see section 3.1, below). Responsibility for education that had previously been administered by SSPCK, Church and Gaelic Schools Societies was transferred to local school boards with the passing of the Education (Scotland) Act 1872, which made no mention of Gaelic (MacLeod 2007; Macleod 2010; McLeod 2005). Where schools had made provision for Gaelic prior to 1872, its use declined as a consequence of the Act (Durkacz 1983: 223–4; MacKinnon 2009: 588), although the 1918 Education (Scotland) Act required education authorities to make adequate provision for Gaelic to be taught 'in Gaelic-speaking areas' (MacLeod 2007: 1). Events in the next decades would further contribute to this decline, and the First World War in particular had a major, deleterious effect on Gaelic-speaking communities in the Highlands and Islands. Macleod (2010: 29) notes that the especially high proportions of young men from these communities who never returned from the trenches rapidly hastened the decline of Gaelic in Scotland.

Although a 'complete social history' of Gaelic in the twentieth century is currently lacking (Macleod 2010: 30), various researchers have traced initiatives related to the revitalisation of Gaelic from the 1960s developing in tandem with the ongoing decline of Gaelic in Highland and Island communities (MacKinnon 1977; Dorian 1981; Macdonald 1997; Oliver 2002; McEwan-Fujita 2003, 2010c). In particular, Macdonald (1997: 6) has referred to greater institutionalised provision for Gaelic since the early 1980s, as well as a general 'growth of interest' in the language in Scotland, as a 'Gaelic renaissance'. McLeod (2014: 6) relates this growth to both greater perception of Gaelic 'as a national language', and 'the increasing emphasis on Scottish political and cultural distinctiveness in general', particularly since 1999.

In spite of developments related to the Gaelic renaissance in the late twentieth century, the language enjoyed no formal legislative protection prior to the Gaelic Language (Scotland) Act 2005 (Dunbar 2006). Gaelic development agency Comunn na Gàidhlig had campaigned for legislative support for Gaelic since the passage of the Welsh Language Act 1993, which stipulated that Welsh and English should be treated on 'a basis of equality' in Wales (Jones and Williams 2009: 697). In post-devolution Scotland, the MacPherson Taskforce was set up in 1999 to look into possible legislation for Gaelic, followed by the establishment in 2001 of the Ministerial Advisory

Table 1.1 Gaelic speakers in Scotland 1806–2011

Date	Total Gaelic speakers in Scotland	% of total Scottish population
1806	297,823	18.5
1891	254,415	6.3
1951	95,447	1.9
1981	79,307	1.6
1991	65,978	1.3
2001	58,652	1.2
2011	57,602	1.1

Group on Gaelic (MAGOG; Dunbar 2006: 16). The MAGOG recommendations included the establishment of a Scottish Executive unit dedicated to Gaelic affairs, along with a language board, and the formulation of a language act conferring official status; the broad recommendations of the MAGOG were followed up in 2005, when the Act was passed unanimously in the Scottish Parliament (MacKinnon 2009: 644). The Act established the national language promotion agency Bòrd na Gàidhlig on a statutory basis, requiring it to produce a National Gaelic Language Plan every five years, and conferring upon it the authority to require public bodies to produce Gaelic language plans. The Act stipulated that this work be undertaken with a view to securing the status of Gaelic as 'an official language of Scotland commanding equal respect with the English language' (Walsh and McLeod 2008: 35).

McLeod (2014: 6) states that this expression of the language's position in society constitutes the 'most significant formal statement of Gaelic's status as a national language'. Yet the wording of the phrase 'equal respect' has come under criticism on the grounds that it has no clearly defined legal meaning (Walsh and McLeod 2008: 35) and the legal requirements involved in securing 'equal respect' were intended to be less demanding than those in the Welsh Language Act's 'basis of equality' (ibid.). Dunbar (2006: 17) argues that it is rather unclear where the status of 'equal respect' derives from, since it is by no means obvious that the Act itself confers such status. He regards this as an important failing, since it is by means of this sort of statutory legislative provision that status is ordinarily conferred on ('national') languages (ibid.). The 2005 Act is nevertheless seen as a 'historic step forward for the language' (Walsh and McLeod 2008: 35), even though in international terms it is a 'relatively weak' enactment (ibid.).

Crucially, while the availability of service provision through the language has an important role to play, Walsh and McLeod (2008: 24) argue that the goal of stimulating language use relies ultimately on the intrinsic motivations of speakers to do so, often involving 'aspects of identity and ideology'. While the Gaelic language has long been regarded as a facet of an expressly Highland identity, positive attitudes to the language's place in Scottish identity more generally have been revealed in surveys undertaken in recent years. For example, the 2012 Scottish Social Attitudes Survey found that 76% of a representative sample of the Scottish population (N=1,180) regarded Gaelic as 'very important' (30%) or 'fairly important' (46%) to Scottish culture and heritage (Paterson et al. 2014: 10). Similarly, 87% of participants (N=1,229) felt that Gaelic should be encouraged, either 'throughout Scotland' (32%) or in areas 'where it is already spoken' (55%; Paterson et al. 2014: 11; see also Bechhofer and McCrone 2014).

On the basis of these findings, Paterson et al. (2014: 18) conclude that Gaelic is regarded as a 'core part of Scottish life and identity' (see section 5.2.4, below). Macdonald (1997: 256) similarly observes, on the basis of anthropological fieldwork conducted from 1983 to 1986, that Gaelic had 'come to be accepted as a symbol of Scotland's distinctiveness', as a result of shifting perceptions linked to the Gaelic renaissance, and the effects of the increased visibility of Gaelic in Scottish popular consciousness. Gaelic speakers have therefore found themselves to be increasingly regarded as the repository of an important national resource (Macdonald 1997: 63), and the bounded and quasi-ethnic understanding of Gaelic as the language of the traditional Highlander is seen to have weakened (Oliver 2002, 2006). In the 2011 census, 48% of all Gaelic speakers were recorded outside of the traditional heartland areas in the Highlands and Islands (National Records of Scotland 2013a). Yet the historic perception of the Highlands and Lowlands as distinct ethnocultural zones still persists in certain quarters (Macdonald 1999: 106; Glaser 2006: 170), and Macdonald (1997: 131–2) notes that the link between the language and a specific sense of place remains strong in heartland communities.

On the basis of ethnographic research conducted among school pupils in Skye and Glasgow, Oliver (2002, 2005, 2006) observes that conceptions of Gaelic as a bounded language indexing an identity that is restricted, in both geographical and cultural terms, to areas where the language is widely spoken had weakened in the later twentieth century, giving way to broader understandings of the language's relevance at a national level. The contrast is defined by Oliver (2005: 5; following Fishman 1972) in terms of *Gemeinschaft* and *Gesellschaft*, conceived of as a distinction between 'community' and 'society'. Yet Oliver (2006: 161) elaborates that the evolution of the *Gesellschaft* approach is often inhibited by the persistent association of Gaelic with the 'traditional', and asserts that the language is more frequently perceived as a marker of a specifically Gaelic identity than of Scottish identity in a wider sense (Oliver 2005: 9; Oliver 2006: 162). In recent decades, increasing numbers of people from a range of different cultural backgrounds have chosen to learn Gaelic, and the language's role as a marker of identity among different Gaelic speakers today is seen to be far from straightforward (Glaser 2007: 247; McLeod et al. 2014: 27).

The hybrid nature of many learners' identifications with Gaelic has often tended to be treated with a mixture of suspicion and scepticism in traditional (*Gemeinschaft*) contexts in the Highlands and Islands (MacCaluim 2007: 78–82), whilst being regarded as an advantage in the formation of emerging *Gesellschaft* identities in the *Gàidhealtachdan ùra* (new Gaelic-speaking communities) of the urban Lowlands (Glaser 2007: 258). At the same time, however, some have questioned the importance of the language to either Scottish or Highland identity (Rogerson and Gloyer 1995). Nevertheless, Dorian (2011: 468) has argued that revitalisation efforts on behalf of Gaelic have led to the 'revalorization of a language that was once disdained', with knock-on benefits for the psychological wellbeing and 'self-regard' of traditional speakers.

In spite of these benefits, Dorian (2011: 468) states that the long-term success of efforts to revitalise Gaelic remains to be seen; losses to speaker numbers that result from older speakers dying 'still far outstrip gains in new speakers via home transmission and Gaelic-medium schools', she argues, concluding that 'the relatively favourable current position of Gaelic is very precarious'. On this point, Edwards (2013: 13) has argued that a qualitative distinction may be required between bilingual speakers in Gaelic 'heartland' areas and those 'in Glasgow . . . or Edinburgh [who] have more formally set themselves (or been set) to become bilingual'. He argues that classifying speakers within these two groups 'under a single "bilingual" rubric'– irrespective of language practices and abilities – 'might give a rather inaccurate picture of the state of health of . . . Gaelic' (Edwards 2013: 14). Indeed, Bòrd na Gàidhlig's (2014) claim that an apparent diminution in the decline of Gaelic speakers in the 2011 census 'is mainly due to the rise in Gaelic-medium education' – and its statement that 'within the next ten years the long term decline of the language could be reversed' – must be carefully considered in light of current theory on language revitalisation.

1.2 Theoretical foundations: Language revitalisation and the role of education

Dunbar (2001: 234) states that a chief concern for linguistic minorities in contexts of language shift is often 'the maintenance of their minority linguistic group identity', in addition to that of their 'distinctive language community'. The relationship between language and ethnic identity lies at the core of Fishman's (1991, 2001b, 2013) model for the maintenance and revitalisation of threatened languages, or 'reversing language shift' (RLS; see section 2.1). Whilst his ideas and theoretical stance have been critiqued by scholars in various fields (see, for example, Baker 2011; Edwards 2009, 2010a; Romaine 2006; Williams 1992), Fishman's theories continue to influence much discussion of language revitalisation. He states that RLS efforts often have 'a stress on real and putative ethno-kinship . . . and identity (re)formation' (Fishman 1991: 383). Crucially in this respect, Fishman (1991: 394) argues that relevant group boundaries must be maintained; the revitalisation of minority ('Xish') language and culture, he argues, rests largely on the 'premises that Xmen are not Ymen and that Xish culture . . . is not Yish culture'. It is seen as imperative that 'ideological clarification' of these fundamental premises 'must not be skipped over' if RLS initiatives are to succeed (Fishman 1991: 394; see section 2.1, below, on contemporary notions of language and identity). Dauenhauer and Dauenhauer (1998: 62) have argued that since such prior ideological clarification is in fact rarely achieved as a first step to revitalisation initiatives, considerable disparities often develop between speakers' explicit goals in favour of RLS on the one hand, and deep-seated beliefs and feelings that continue to contribute to language decline on the other.

Subsequent to the theoretical 'prior ideological clarification' of group boundaries and rationales for RLS among 'Xmen' or 'Xians' (the traditional and ethnically defined minority community), Fishman's (1991: 395) paradigm is based on winning back linguistic domains for the threatened 'Xish' language one at a time. The first stages of his model, the 'Graded Intergenerational Disruption Scale' (GIDS), involve the 'reassembly of Xish' (through corpus planning and so on) to whatever extent is necessary, and the attainment of diglossia, through concerted efforts at the 'home–family–neighbourhood' level to re-establish intergenerational transmission (Fishman 1991: 395). Fishman's most recent formulation of GIDS, which is designed to be read from the bottom up, is as follows (2001b: 466; emphasis added in bold):

1. Educational, work sphere, mass media, and (quasi-)governmental operations in Xish at the highest (nationwide) levels.
2. Local/regional mass media and (quasi-)governmental services in Xish.
3. The local/regional (that is, supra-neighbourhood) work sphere, both among Xmen and among Ymen.
4a. Public schools for Xish children, offering some instruction via Xish, but substantially under Yish curricular and staffing control.
4b. Schools in lieu of compulsory education and substantially under Xish curricular and staffing control.
B. *RLS efforts to transcend diglossia, subsequent to its attainment*
5. Schools for Xish literacy acquisition, for the old and/or for the young, and not in lieu of compulsory education.
6. **The intergenerational and demographically concentrated home–family–neighbourhood–community:** *the basis of Xish mother-tongue transmission.*
7. Cultural interaction in Xish primarily involving the community-based older generation (beyond the age of giving birth).
8. Reconstructing Xish and adult acquisition of Xish as a Second Language.
A. *RLS to attain diglossia (assuming prior ideological clarification)*

Stage 6 of Fishman's GIDS, with its emphasis on the transmission of Xish within the home–family–neighbourhood sphere, is regarded as the absolute focus and 'dynamic fulcrum' of his theory; if this stage is not 'attained and vigorously retained', all efforts concentrated at higher levels will be effectively undermined in bolstering the maintenance of Xish (Fishman 2001b: 485). Crucially, Fishman (2001b: 470–1) stresses RLS interventions based in the school (stages 4b–4a) 'will fail unless the minority language has a society in which it can function, before school begins, outside of school, during the years of schooling and afterwards, when formal schooling is over and done with'. Indeed, he states categorically that '[w]ithout intergenerational mother tongue transmission . . . no language maintenance is possible. That which is not transmitted cannot be maintained' (Fishman 1991: 113).

Yet Fishman's views have subsequently been critiqued by a wide variety of theorists across various disciplines, including linguistics, sociology and psychology. Sociolinguist Suzanne Romaine (2006: 443), for instance, has commented that it may be necessary, in light of the enduring fragility of home transmission in many instances of language shift, to 'reconceptualize what it means for a language to be maintained and survive without intergenerational mother tongue transmission'. John Edwards (2010a: 67) has concurred with this view, observing that the maintenance by bilingual speakers of 'one language for home and hearth, another for the world beyond one's gate' is often extremely difficult in situations of language shift.

Elsewhere, Romaine (2000: 54) has agreed in principle with Fishman's theoretical premise, observing that it is the 'inability of minorities to maintain the home as an intact domain for the use of their language' that has often proved decisive in language shift. Similarly, Nettle and Romaine (2000: 189) highlight that emphasising bottom-up initiatives to secure intergenerational transmission in the home is indeed the most crucial goal of language maintenance, rather than (as has often been assumed) persuading policymakers and governments to act on behalf of the threatened language. These observations parallel Fishman's emphasis on the difficult task of focusing on 'lower-order' goals – such as securing Xish as the language of the home – and the failure to do so contributing in large part to the failure of RLS (Fishman 1991: 406). Yet it is chiefly in relation to diglossia, and Fishman's approach to winning back domains on a 'low-to-high' basis, that Romaine (2006, 2013) has critiqued this model.

Diglossia is said to have been attained when each linguistic variety in a multilingual community has a specific function, and is often regarded in sociolinguistic literatures to reflect a relatively stable situation (Romaine 2000: 46). Romaine (2000: 46–8) observes that a classic example of the paradigm (which can be extended to discrete 'languages' functioning in this way in multilingual societies) is the differentiation of domains occupied by 'colloquial' Egyptian Arabic (the 'lower' [L] variety that dominates in the home) and 'standard' Arabic, the language of formal and public communication and of writing (the 'higher' [H] linguistic domains). Romaine (2000: 55) states that some minority languages 'may never emerge from diglossia', but may equally be in no danger of language death, as long as functional differentiation has been firmly established. Fishman (1991: 406) stresses that even where higher-order domains within the spheres of education, work and the media are secured for the minority language, 'they must be translated into the lower-order processes' of use in the home, and intergenerational transmission. Cultural autonomy within the 'institutions of modernity', he argues, will do little for the minority language that has not been reproduced organically in the home (Fishman 1991: 406).

Yet Romaine (2006) has questioned the utility of this approach for restoring minority varieties to the condition of being fully sufficient for interaction. She stresses that conceptions of languages in bilingual communities are often 'ideologically linked to and entangled with other dualities' that contribute to and reinforce patterns of language shift (Romaine 2006: 445). This point emphasises the importance of language ideologies in situations of language shift (discussed further in section 2.2, below); respective competing varieties may be ideologically associated with modernity or the past, tradition or wider functionality. Edwards (2010a: 57) identifies various related dichotomies that have been theorised to encapsulate the tension between the 'benefits and disadvantages of mobility', whether parochialism versus intercourse, roots versus options, tribalism versus globalism, or even *Gemeinschaft* versus *Gesellschaft*.

Following Fishman's logic, Romaine (2006: 445) cautions that by seeking to reinforce the ideological associations of a minority variety with the traditional and parochial domains of the home–family–neighbourhood, activists on behalf of language revitalisation might ironically reinforce ideologies that contributed to instigating language shift in the first instance. In any case, Romaine (2013: 454) has also argued, appropriate language use within proper domains often becomes complicated in bilingual contexts, so that 'domains become unclear and setting and role relationships [in social interaction] do not combine in the expected way'. Monica Heller (2007b: 9) has argued that whilst on the one hand Fishman's theoretical approach appears to view domains as 'primarily connected to social activities' that are often institutional or connected to power and social status differences, it nevertheless tends to underplay the importance of such considerations.

As Romaine observes (2013: 463), 'conflicts involving language are not really about language, but about fundamental inequalities between groups'. Pierre Bourdieu (1991: 57) argued that 'those who seek to defend a threatened language . . . are obliged to wage a total struggle. One cannot save the value of a competence unless one saves . . . the whole set of political and social conditions of production'. Edwards (1984b: 304; 2004: 452; 2010a: 4) has consistently argued on this point that community language decline and attrition are symptoms of social contact and unequal power distribution, and as such, are extremely difficult to tackle in isolation, without at least in some manner unpicking the existing social fabric. Yet language maintenance efforts, he argues, generally have an emphasis on social evolution, not revolution (Edwards 2010a: 24). One of Fishman's chief detractors in this regard has been Glyn Williams (1992), who critiqued Fishman's theories as being essentially conservative in nature, downplaying the importance of differential power relations and political struggle by the minority group, whilst emphasising consensus, integration and cohesion in the pursuit of minority language rights. Indeed, rather than advocating a radical approach to redistributing power for minority language communities, Fishman (1991: 387) insisted that minority language activists are in fact 'change-agents on behalf of persistence'.

A further, related criticism of Fishman's model offered by Edwards (1984b: 304) is that shifts in language use 'reflect powerful social changes, most of them economic. Appeals for revival or restoration', he argues, 'will not be successful if they are based essentially on cultural grounds.' In Fishman's (2001a) follow-up to *Reversing Language Shift*, Ó Riagáin (2001) argues on the basis of the Irish experience that economic incentives are often needed to persuade parents that intergenerational transmission is worthwhile, and to provide a rationale for using the language themselves. In this regard, Brian Barry (2001: 75) argues that whilst linguists and anthropologists 'may well have professional regrets' if a given language or culture declines, this in itself is 'surely not an adequate basis on which to force people to perpetuate the language . . . against their own judgement as to where the advantage lies'.

Barry's emphasis here on speakers' 'own judgement' may again downplay the importance of power relations in minority language contexts, and how these can cause people to understand their options in certain ways. Alexandra Jaffe (2007b: 51) remarks that 'the term "language shift" itself de-emphasizes language practice and human agency', suggesting that judgement and choice in minority language use often are important. From a sociolinguistic perspective, and based on observations from years of extended fieldwork in Corsica, Jaffe (2007b: 51) argues that 'the very notion of language shift . . . is linked to ideological constructs': both that regarding 'language' as a fixed entity, and that of 'shift' as 'a community transferring its allegiances and completely transforming its practices'. In reality, she suggests, the picture is often considerably more complex.

An additional critique that Edwards (2010a: 34) has levelled against Fishman is that the latter 'implicitly and explicitly endorses a view of applied linguistics as both scholarship and advocacy', arguing that in fact the two 'do not always make happy partners' (2010a: 5). Researchers debated best practice in relation to minority languages in the journal *Language* over twenty years ago. In a series of exchanges, Peter Ladefoged (1992) advocated a more detached, scholarly approach whilst Nancy Dorian (1993) responded that researchers of language revitalisation necessarily influence the communities they study, regardless of their stance, and as such, have a responsibility to advocate on their behalf. Dorian's stance is explicitly promoted by some scholars (for example, Fishman 1991, 2001a, 2001b; Nettle and Romaine 2000; Skutnabb-Kangas 1988, 2000). In part, this approach was informed by the 'ecology of language' paradigm formulated by Einar Haugen, which conceived of society – by analogy with biological diversity – as the 'true environment' of language, which could in turn be more or less hospitable to linguistic diversity (Haugen 1974: 325). In one prominent example of the linguistic ecological paradigm, Romaine (2008: 19) argued that since linguistic and cultural distinctiveness have often served as 'the basis for defining human identities . . . they are vital parts of local ecologies'. Edwards (2009: 238) has objected to such views on the basis that they tend to lack 'a strong logical base' since, ultimately, 'language is not organic', and never actually lives or dies (2009: 232).

As Ó hIfearnáin (2013a: 349) observes, the various critiques of Fishman's (1991, 2001a, 2001b) theories do not recommend abandoning intergenerational transmission as a focal point for language revitalisation, but rather emphasise that the notion is still rather poorly theorised, and understood inadequately by researchers and activists for either to support it sufficiently. Various other models have been proposed to aid linguistic revitalisation since Fishman's (1991) paradigm was published. Edwards's (2010a: 100) own thirty-three-item typology for the classification of minority languages draws on eleven overarching disciplinary perspectives (from demography to linguistics, psychology and media) and the three criteria of speaker, language and setting, to provide what he regards as a richer conceptual starting-point for the analysis of minority language health than the 'Richter scale' of Fishman's GIDS.

In somewhat less precise terms, David Crystal's (2000: 141) *Language Death* theorises that an endangered language 'will progress':

- if its speakers can increase their prestige within the majority community, and simultaneously maintain a strong group identity that can resist the influence of the dominant culture;
- if its speakers can increase the domains of use for their language;
- if its speakers have a critical mass in demographic terms at the community level;
- if the language has a presence in schools and literate speakers; and
- if it can be used in electronic communication.

Miquel Strubell (1999) hypothesised that governments and policymakers can support minority language maintenance through the provision of services in the threatened language, thereby extending the potential number of sociolinguistic domains available and stimulating greater language use. Strubell's (1999: 240–1) 'Catherine wheel' model theorises that competence in a minority language leads to greater use of it, which in turn stimulates demand and provision for services and products in the language, leading to greater language learning and increasing competence, and so on. Edwards (2004: 457; 2009: 62) has argued that securing 'domains of necessity' – those pertaining to the home, certainly, but also those of the school and workplace – is absolutely critical for language maintenance efforts, since each of these is tied closely to 'the most central aspects of people's lives'.

In a defiant rejoinder to some of the critiques discussed above, Fishman (2013: 486–7) re-emphasises his earlier observations on the role of formal education in RLS, insisting that whilst schools 'can serve to further motivate and protect Stage 6, [the latter] must be alive and well for such motivation and protection to emerge'. In comparison with prevailing socio-economic circumstances two decades previously, Fishman (2013: 487) considers various processes linked to 'postmodernisation' to have 'served to render the school–home continuity relationship more tenuous than ever before' (see Duchêne and Heller's 2012 considerations relating to bilingual practices in 'Late Capitalism'). Activists on behalf of language revitalisation 'may safely focus on the school, on the place of worship, or on the workplace', Fishman (2013: 493) argues, 'if specific non-mother-tongue functions are being aimed at' (ibid.); yet none of these constitutes a substitute for the key focus of home–family–neighbourhood processes by which children are primarily socialised in a language. He further suggests that the inadvisability of supposing otherwise is revealed in the Irish experience of RLS, and the perceived focus on formal schooling in revival efforts there (Fishman 2013: 497).

Partly in response to the apparent extent of intergenerational disruption in Scotland generally (see Mac an Tàilleir 2010; National Records of Scotland 2013a), and even in the Western Isles communities where Gaelic is most widely spoken (Munro et al. 2010), increasing attention has been paid in the development of national language policy to GME as a means of developing the language (Bòrd na Gàidhlig 2012b, 2018). GME was 'prioritised' as a development area in the second *National Gaelic Language Plan 2012–2017*, which aimed to double the annual intake of pupils entering the system to 800 by 2017 (Bòrd na Gàidhlig 2012b: 22). Whilst it is still unclear (if highly unlikely) that this target was attained by the end of 2017, the focus on GME as a key means of generating greater numbers of Gaelic speakers and users was carried over in the Bòrd's *Draft National Gaelic Language Plan 2017–2022*, a consultation on which was undertaken in Spring 2017, before eventually being published the following year as the third *National Gaelic Language Plan 2018–2023* (Bòrd na Gàidhlig 2017, 2018). Crucially, however, scholars have continued to caution against excessively prioritising immersion education as a strategy toward this end. Ó hIfearnáin (2011: 104), for example, states that while the 'emphasis on immersion [education] as the most effective way to create new speakers' in diverse contexts of language shift is understandable, in the international perspective 'it is rare for schooling to lead to revitalisation or revernacularisation'.

1.3 Concluding remarks and book structure

There are a variety of paradigms and principles present in the literature that are important to bear in mind for the purposes of this book, including the implications of social variables such as identity, language socialisation and ideology for language use, and the limitations of bilingual immersion education in realising the objectives of language revitalisation. In the following chapters, I will firstly situate and contextualise the monograph in the wider fields it is situated within (Chapter 2), and introduce the specific context and research design of the study it draws upon (Chapter 3). In Chapter 2, I build on the review of theoretical literatures introduced in this chapter, examining the notional relationship of language and identities (section 2.1), as well as conceptualising the theoretical notions of language ideologies (2.2) and language socialisation (2.3), and, lastly, reviewing research literatures on language acquisition and attrition in immersion education, and contextualising this system within various settings internationally (section 2.4).

Section 3.1 provides a succinct overview of GME in Scotland, outlining the system's growth and the expectations of parents and practitioners within the system in its earliest years, and situating the present research within the wider experience of GME in Scotland. Section 3.2 summarises the overall design of the research, which makes use of both quantitative and qualitative methods. Semi-structured interviews and an online questionnaire are employed to examine language use and attitudes, and to facilitate data triangulation of research results. In section 3.3 I outline and describe the pool of participants among whom the research is conducted, and describe various methods used to contact this group, and to analyse the quantitative and qualitative datasets. The method of transcription, qualitative analysis and the methodological framework adopted will be described and explained in relation to the data. Attention will additionally be drawn to the data-collection process in the field before tracing the development of GME in Scotland and considering the major findings of research that has been conducted on various aspects of the system to the present day (section 3.3)

Chapter 4 provides a qualitative analysis of interviewees' Gaelic language use (4.1), socialisation experiences in the home and community (4.2), and within the school setting (4.3), and additionally examines the interrelationship of these variables from a quantitative, statistical perspective (4.4). The holistic approach adopted, employing correlational statistical tests to investigate the relationships between non-parametric variables and thereby cross-check and contextualise results from the qualitative analyses, lends important empirical depth to the analysis. Chapter 5 analyses the language ideologies that informants conveyed (both explicitly and implicitly) in interviews, drawing on the overarching themes of Gaelic language use (5.1) and social identities (5.2) before exploring the relationship between language ideologies and attitudes (5.3). Finally, Chapter 6 draws together conclusions from the preceding, empirical chapters, and relates these findings back to the theoretical literatures discussed in Chapters 1–3 to make recommendations for policymakers, language advocates and educators.

2

Language, Culture and Identities: Theoretical Perspectives

Various analytic perspectives have been brought to bear on the interrelationship of language, culture and identity within relevant research literatures in sociolinguistics and the sociology of language, social psychology and linguistic anthropology. This chapter is structured into five overarching sections: firstly, section 2.1 will set out the wider theoretical framework surrounding the nexus of language and social life (section 2.1.1). In particular, this section will seek to define a conceptual framework for drawing together the interplay of language, culture and sociocultural identity before addressing the symbolic value that languages are thought to possess (section 2.1.2), essentialist conceptions in this respect (2.1.3), and relatedly, the relationship between language and nationalism (2.1.4). Section 2.2 introduces the concept of language ideologies, and conceptualises theoretical understandings of how speakers' culturally constituted beliefs and feelings about language, as revealed in interaction, can be seen to impact upon the ways a linguistic variety is used by its speakers from day to day. Section 2.3 addresses language socialisation, with a view to considering how the issues discussed previously might be reflected in the retrospective accounts and responses of participants. Lastly, section 2.4 focuses on how bilingual (immersion) education may interact with considerations of language and identity, ideologies and socialisation in diverse settings internationally, in order to conceptualise how these matters can help to frame and inform the present monograph (section 2.5).

2.1 Theorising the relation of language, culture and identities

Over the past fifty years, researchers in the fields of sociolinguistics, linguistic anthropology and the sociology of language have established that the interplay of language, culture and society is both complex and context-specific. As an initial point of departure, Romaine (2000: 26) has stated that although there is 'no necessary one-to-one relationship' between language and society, there are unlikely to be any contexts in which the two have no impact on one another. Yet the meanings of either of these terms are far from universally agreed upon in contemporary scholarship. Others, such as Makoni and Pennycook (2007), have argued that the popular notion of language as a bounded, finite and standardised entity ultimately stems from state attempts to legitimate and consolidate political power and control linguistic practices, and they advocate a less rigid approach to conceptualising language. In this regard, García (2009: 40) has stated that commonly held, persistent 'assumptions' about what language is must be constantly challenged in light of how speakers use language within its social context. Similarly, Heller (2007b: 9) has argued that the very concept of language cannot be defined without reference to the speakers who use it and the social context in which they do so, since empirical studies in sociolinguistics and anthropology have consistently shown that language is an inherently social notion. A more fluid conception of 'language' foregrounds speakers' actual linguistic practices, taking account of research on multilingual speakers' flexible use of multiple linguistic resources across disparate sociocultural contexts (see, for example, García 2009; García and Wei 2014).

Heller (2007b: 9) has noted that research on bilingualism has increasingly encouraged researchers to query 'the nature of language itself', and considerations of this kind were clearly at the forefront of theorists' and researchers' considerations when the field of sociolinguistics first developed over fifty years ago (see Fishman 1972; Trudgill 1974). Fishman (1972: 153–4), for instance, challenged what he regarded as a tendency on the part of many psychologists and sociologists to view bilingualism as an 'unnatural' and transitory occurrence, arguing instead that bilingualism was both widespread internationally and likely to remain so in the future. In the same period, Haugen (1974: 325) sought to integrate and conceptualise linguistic diversity within its societal 'environment' as part of his 'ecology of language' paradigm.

Linguistic anthropologists frequently position their work on language and culture within three theoretical frameworks, respectively concerning the interrelationship of language and identity (Kroskrity 2000a, 2000c; Echeverria 2003), language ideologies (Kroskrity 2000a, 2004; Silverstein 2000) and language socialisation (Friedman 2010; McEwan-Fujita 2010a). While the three frameworks have distinct research traditions, there is considerable overlap between them. I will return to this third notion in section 2.3, below, but draw attention firstly to the large and multidisciplinary research literature on language and identity, before examining relevant literature concerning language ideologies (section 2.2). for the immediate concerns of this book, the school constitutes one of a wide variety of contexts in which social and linguistic identity is formed and moulded across an individual's lifespan (Woolard 2007: 617–19). Correspondingly, identity may play an extremely important role in bilingual education and students' socialisation in and acquisition of language (García 2009: 82; see section 2.3, below).

2.1.1 Language and ethnic identity: (Socio)linguistic, anthropological and sociological perspectives

Edwards (2009: 15) has noted that studies of identity within the human and social sciences have come increasingly to the fore in recent decades, partly as a consequence of psychological models of the self in the twentieth century, and the subsequent impact of these considerations on popular understandings of identity and personhood.

Similarly, Glaser (2007: 30) has observed that the possession of identities has become an essential concomitant of an individual's social and psychological existence in contemporary society. She notes a mid-twentieth-century shift in theoretical orientations to identity, from examinations of personal identity based primarily within psychology, toward social scientific approaches that tended to privilege considerations of 'symbolism and imagination' (2007: 32; see Anderson 1991; Reicher and Hopkins 2001). Whereas personal identity draws on distinguishing features at the level of the individual, social identity is therefore based on differences and similarities across groups. La Fontaine (1985) and Krombach (1995) theorised that these processes draw on notions of 'otherness', viewing identity formation as the result of overcoming internal and external differences in social life. Taylor (1989: 376) commented that 'expressive individuation' – that is, the affirmation and expression of one's personal individuality in society – had become one of the most ubiquitous characteristics of contemporary (Western) culture.

A large theoretical literature on the interrelationship of language and identity demonstrates its complexity, and ongoing debate as to the nature of the nexus is lively (see, for example, Fishman 1991, 2001b, 2010, 2013; Eastman 1984; Edwards 1984a, 1984b, 2009, 2010a, 2013; May 2012). In the most straightforward terms, Joseph (2004: 20) has stated that language and identity are 'ultimately inseparable', since 'language is central to the human condition'. Language has similarly been viewed as central to the ethnic and national groups into which human society is organised. Edwards (2009: 162) suggests the following as a definition of ethnic identity: 'allegiance to a group ... with which one has ancestral links'. As (first) languages are often inherited in a similar way to ethnicity, May (2012: 135) notes that a large body of evidence suggests that language remains significant in many instances, whilst not generally regarded as an 'essential', 'primordial' or 'determining' feature of ethnic identity.

Indeed, Williams (2008: 74) has stated that as a major component of group identity, language has become 'one of the most sensitive issues' in contemporary societies. Much anthropological and linguistic thought in the first half of the twentieth century was dominated by the Sapir–Whorf Hypothesis, which, building on the ideas of Franz Boas, proposed that speakers of languages with different grammatical systems experience the world in different ways, according to the limitations of these linguistic frames of reference (Makihara 2010: 32–4; Silverstein 2000: 85–6). Whorf (1956 [1940]: 221) summarised the principle, observing that speakers of different languages were directed by the languages they speak 'toward different types of observations and different evaluations', thereby arriving at 'different views of the world'. In a collection of essays published posthumously, Sapir (1962: 68) described language as a 'guide to "social reality" [that] conditions all our thinking about social problems and processes'.

Such ideas once impacted greatly upon scholarly understandings of the relationship between language and identity, but have since generally fallen out of academic favour. The possibilities of translation, bi- and plurilingualism, and considerable social diversity among speakers of the same languages (especially those with large numbers of speakers) all tend to indicate that language does not in fact constrain the ways people think or identify (Kramsch 2004: 239). Ochs (1993: 288) has argued that since social identity is rarely grammaticalised or otherwise explicitly encoded in language; the relationship between the two is in fact 'a sociolinguistically distant one'. Rather than a direct association, therefore, the relationship of language to identity is viewed as being mediated through interlocutors' shared understanding of social conventions (Ochs 1993: 289). This conception frames the language–identity nexus in terms of speakers' respective positionality, a principle to which I return below (see Bucholtz and Hall 2004, 2005). The essence of Ochs's argument is that since both language and identity are fluid and in constant flux, a given linguistic variety or structure cannot straightforwardly be assigned to a given social identity (Ochs 1993: 297).

Nevertheless, Romaine (2000: 164) states that the 'relative discreteness of languages ... as markers of distinct ethnic identities' can have important effects on the way people think about themselves as group members, and about the groups to which they belong. Interactionist developments in sociolinguistic studies of bilingualism have increasingly addressed the ways in which linguistic resources can creatively and profitably be used to create social meaning, especially in relation to displays of ethnolinguistic identity (Heller 2007a, 2007b; Mendoza-Denton and Osborne 2010). In a similar vein, Romaine (2000: 163) remarks that the meaning of identity and ethnicity can change over time and across contexts, especially among minority communities under societal and political pressure, such as in contexts of language shift. The role and relevance that speakers attach to spoken varieties in the social life of bilingual communities is therefore often both contested and complex.

Fishman (2010: xxiii) has observed that linguistic identity draws on social circumstances and distinctions that influence and even recreate it. Edwards (2010a: 4) concurs with this view, stating that language shift itself must be understood as a 'symptom of social interaction', inseparable from its sociocultural context. Yet he argues that a shift in the language a community uses in the intimate settings of the home generally implies a correspondingly important shift of 'social and psychological significance' for that community (Edwards 2010a: 26). In large part, this reflects the enduring popular understanding of language as one of the most crucial components of group identity in contemporary society (Edwards 2010a; see also Williams 2008).

Williams (2010: 238) notes that ancestral languages are often regarded by minority groups in the modern world as a vital and necessary means of transmitting their cultures. Indeed, even majority, international languages such as French and English are feared by some to be under threat from migration patterns and resulting multilingual practices in the globalised economy (see Moïse 2007; Schmidt 2007), with important implications for political discourses (and sometimes, as a consequence, political decisions). A shared language can be a strong impetus for building associations of group identity, especially through institutions of education and the media; yet such associations, Makihara (2010: 42) argues, 'are socially constructed and change over time', depending on community members' linguistic awareness and attitudes. In this regard, Fishman (2010: xxix) has argued that ethnic identity and group consciousness are unevenly distributed throughout contemporary societies.

Rather than pre-existing social categories of which individuals may or may not be conscious, identities have been increasingly theorised from social constructivist perspectives to be both projected and shaped through language use, a principle referred to as 'emergence' (Ochs 1993; Schilling-Estes 2004; Bucholtz and Hall 2005). In this conception, identity is regarded of as a product of social intercourse, emerging through and arising within interaction (Schiffrin 1996: 169; Schilling-Estes 2004: 190). This principle of 'practice' is in turn inhibited by the concept of 'partialness', that an identity construction 'may be in part deliberate and intentional, in part habitual', and therefore below the level of consciousness (Bucholtz and Hall 2005: 606). In other words, an individual may in some cases be only partly aware of the identities he or she displays. On the other hand, García (2009: 82) notes that language often has 'a rhetorical function' to construct and display identities, tying in with Bucholtz and Hall's (2004: 380) point that identity is also expressed in language through 'performance', defined as a 'highly deliberate and self-aware social display' of identity.

In addition to these four concepts, Bucholtz and Hall (2004: 380–1) note that individuals' 'positionality' in identity constructions can vary from interaction to interaction, depending on the identity of one's interlocutor. Ochs (1993: 290) explains this principle in terms of individuals' linguistic use of speech and stance to construct their various identities. Such a conception views identity as 'inherently relational', and dependent on social interaction and the individual's position within this. Social constructivist approaches therefore view the communicative functions of language, and the various ways they form and inform identity in interaction, as key to understanding the fluid nature of identity from day to day, and across the lifespan (Ochs 1993: 298). Rather than a fixed, a priori category, a given identity may be viewed as contextually dependent and constructed through social interaction (Schiffrin 1996: 199). The relation of identity to language (in its communicative sense) is therefore viewed as complex and conditional.

2.1.2 The symbolic value of language

In addition to its communicative function, Edwards (2013: 19) states that language also acts as a conduit of tradition, culture and shared narratives. Apart from the instrumental sense in which language may be used to construct and perform identity, languages often also have a semiotic and symbolic function in the negotiation of group identities. In this regard, Makihara (2010: 43) has argued that language often serves as a significant symbolic source of identity (see Fishman 1991, 2001a, 2001b). Edwards (2010a) goes further than this, arguing that in situations of language shift, a community will not necessarily experience the associated cultural shift that might be expected to accompany language obsolescence. Rather, he suggests, 'the social and psychological cohesion of the group' may endure in the absence of a unique language, which may nevertheless still play a symbolic role in the maintenance of boundaries between groups (Edwards 2010a: 6).

Edwards (2009: 60) therefore sees a key distinction between language in its communicative sense and its symbolic significance for the negotiation of group identities. He argues that it is possible – and may often be desirable for individuals in contexts of language shift – for the latter to remain important to a community in the absence of the former. Jones (1998) has stated that the death of a language does not necessarily entail the death of the ethnicity with which it has traditionally been associated, while

Williams (2008: 88) notes that expressions of identity often continue long after an ethnic group's historical language declines, since no necessary correspondence exists between the reproduction of linguistic resources and that of ethnic identity (see Ó Riagáin 1997; Edwards 2009, 2010a).

Yet the relationship between language – in its instrumental, communicative sense – and ethnic identity lies at the core of Fishman's (1991) model for the maintenance of threatened languages or 'reversing language shift' (RLS; see section 1.2, above). He states that RLS efforts are often predicated on a 'sentimental' bond between speakers, and a 'stress on real and putative ethno-kinship, an aspiration toward consciousness and identity (re)formation' (1991: 383). Yet, crucially, in addition to Edwards's (2009, 2010a) observations, other researchers have identified obstacles to the feasibility of assigning a central and enduring position to language as a communicative medium in such contexts. Hoare (2000), for instance, has suggested that the relationship between ethnic identity and language is often one of association rather than actual use or competence (see also Eastman 1984; Jones 1998; Cole and Williams 2004). Similarly, May (2012: 134) avers that where language is considered crucial to identity, it is the 'diacritical significance' attached to it, rather than actual language use per se, that is often regarded as essential. Where there is an association of a given ethnic identity with a particular language, knowledge of that language is not always considered necessary for the expression of that identity. In certain contexts, the relationship between the two may nevertheless be more heavily accentuated than in others. Edwards (2013: 23) notes that while the connection between the communicative functions of language and its symbolic role is often taken as a benign and simplistic one by monolingual, majority language speakers, matters of language and identity are often more immediately foregrounded and problematic for minority language groups.

2.1.3 Essentialist perspectives on language and identity

The late Joshua Fishman's (1991) theory of RLS relies on a more straightforward and fundamental association between language and culture in minority language contexts than that hypothesised by the theorists cited immediately above, and, indeed, makes a strong distinction between the minority, 'Xish' language and culture, and majority 'Yish'. Although Fishman's (1991) model rests in large part on this type of ideological contrast, such sharp distinctions lack the nuance of much contemporary sociological and anthropological research on language shift (for example, Heller 2006, 2010). He states, for instance, that '[t]he premises that Xmen are not Ymen and that Xish culture ... is not Yish culture must not be skipped over, no more than the premises that Xish culture is worth maintaining' (Fishman 1991: 394). Fishman (2013: 473) later described this proposition in terms of developing a rationale for the maintenance of a community's 'own' language (as opposed to the less personal Yish language of wider communication), whether grounded in religious, ethnic or cultural distinctions. In certain respects, however, Fishman's models of language and ethnic identity sit uneasily with contemporary conceptions that problematise essentialist perspectives in social research (see Jaffe 2007a). Writers and researchers frequently distance themselves from positions of essentialism, which hold that members of a given identity category are 'both fundamentally similar to one another and fundamentally different to members of other groups' (Bucholtz and Hall 2004: 374).

Jaffe (2007a: 58) notes that, from an essentialist perspective, 'both "language" and "identity" and their iconic relationships are seen as fixed, ascribed/natural and unproblematic', in contrast with much modern scholarship on language and culture. Instead, Jaffe (2007a: 70) advocates approaches to language and identity 'that acknowledge the political and social character of all identity claims and that leave room for the multiple forms of language practice', without positing any direct and necessary relationship between the two. Elsewhere in the social sciences, and particularly within Feminist Studies, theorists have called into question the very concept of identity categories, viewing social life as too fluid and complex 'to make fixed categories anything but simplifying social fictions that produce inequalities in the process of producing differences' (McCall 2005: 1773).

Similarly, universalist theories of social life often reject identity categories as inadequate. Political philosopher Brian Barry (2001), for instance, argues that the accommodation of cultural and linguistic minorities within modern, liberal and multicultural societies has its intellectual basis in cultural essentialism, and overstates the importance of cultural identity. Conversely, it has been observed that much research on language revitalisation is conducted within contexts in which 'an essential relationship between language, culture and identity is posited as a given' by community members themselves (Jaffe 2007a: 74). In such cases, Bucholtz and Hall (2004: 376) argue, essentialist perspectives should not be altogether discounted as long as they have salience for the speakers whom linguists study. Bourdieu (1991: 221) comments that contested definitions of ethnic identity and the nature of its 'reality' can be understood 'only if one includes in reality the representation of reality'.

Drawing on this conception, Joseph (2010: 12) has argued that whilst identity categories may essentialise arbitrary differences between groups, they become meaningful, and socially 'real', when speakers make use of them as 'mental representations' of reality. Similarly, Jaffe (2007a: 57) advises against interpreting essentialist outlooks as entirely separable from meaningful representation; where an essentialist position is reflected in the language ideologies professed by researchers' informants, it may be interpreted as a significant and socially meaningful construction. Nevertheless, to appreciate the social reality of essentialist perspectives in various communities' conception of language and identity does not necessarily mean assuming such a perspective in one's own theoretical approach (Bucholtz and Hall 2004, 2005). Indeed, Dorian (2010: 89) cautions that the situated and contextual realities that actually link language and identity are in fact rarely as straightforward as essentialist conceptions would envisage.

2.1.4 Language and nationalism

One reason why essentialist perspectives positing a simplistic and unproblematic association between language and identity are commonly assumed is because of the perceived usefulness of language in the construction of national consciousness. A large sociological literature on nationalism addresses the conceived relevance and role of language to considerations of national identity in various ways. Benedict Anderson (1991: 6), for instance, notes that the concept of the nation as an ideologically constituted and 'imagined political community' relied heavily on conceptions of language in the nineteenth century, an approach that Pujolar (2007: 71) describes in terms of 'one language/one culture/one nation'. Heller (2007b: 4) states that the imagined centrality of language to national identity 'did not emerge fully-formed' at this time, having been particularly current in countries such as Spain in preceding centuries. Nationalism's enduring relevance to linguistic considerations can be traced to the emergence of the modern nation-state from the end of the eighteenth century (Nairn 1997).

At this time, language was regarded as vital to Romantic nationalist understandings in two key senses. Firstly, Anderson (1991: 76) argues, the importance of written language in the emergence of print capitalism at that time was key to raising national consciousness among literate classes. Whereas the pre-capitalist ruling classes had cohered chiefly around extra-linguistic notions of imagined community, (written) language and literacy were instrumental to the emergence and imagined solidarities of the industrial bourgeoisie in Western European cultures (Anderson 1991). On the other hand, Miroslav Hroch (1985: 150) argues that the peasantry, while initially rather averse to nationalist aspirations, were later presented as the 'natural repositories' of national languages and cultures. Secondly, Anderson (1991: 144) argues that the 'primordialness' of shared languages offered a continuous, almost ancestral connection to an imagined national heritage. Yet this conception of language, he argues, is not without problems, since many national languages are shared across multiple nations and states, while others are used by only a small proportion of inhabitants (Anderson 1991: 46). Anderson (1991: 133) thus regards nationalist conceptions of languages as emblematic of national belonging to be problematic.

In certain contexts – such as that of either Scottish (Nairn 1997; McCrone 2001) or English nationalism (Kumar 2003) – language is much less significant a factor than is true in others. Gellner (2006: 43) notes that nationalist movements not centred on language instead tend to allude to arguments of precedent, shared history and culture over linguistic criteria; as such, scholars of nationalism such as McCrone (1998, 2001) have argued that language cannot and does not define the nation. By contrast, Romantic nationalist philosophers such as Herder, von Humboldt and Fichte depicted language as absolutely central to national identity formation in Western Europe, especially Germany (Kramsch 2004; Edwards 2009). Herder (1960 [1772]: 100), for example, reasoned that every nation on earth 'speaks according to the way it thinks and thinks according to the way it speaks'. In terms prefiguring stronger formulations of linguistic relativity (Whorf 1956 [1940]; Sapir 1962), von Humboldt (1988 [1836]: 60) argued that 'there resides in every language a characteristic world-view'.

In the present day, May (2012: 135) has argued that linguistic nationalism of this kind, which conceives of the nation as a natural and linguistically determined entity, tends to be viewed as 'little more than sociological (and linguistic) nonsense' (see also Reicher and Hopkins 2001). More generally, Eric Hobsbawm (1992), Ernest Gellner (2006) and Anthony Smith (2010) critiqued nationalist conceptions of the natural centrality of nations to social life, and, in turn, of languages to nations. Hobsbawm (1992: 54) argues that national languages are in fact 'the opposite of what nationalist mythology supposes' – that is, the naturally occurring basis of national culture – instead constituting an explicit attempt to standardise a single idiom out of a multiplicity of speech forms.

Smith (2010: 11) includes language in a long list of 'objective' factors frequently invoked by nationalist philosophers in the definition of the nation. As emergent national identities coalesced around national (print) languages in the eighteenth century, Fishman (1991: 389) describes how writers such as John Stuart Mill linked traditional culture with incivility, promoting languages of wider communication on grounds of societal progress. Conceptions of ethnic group identity sat uneasily with nationalist aspirations of this kind; Fishman (1991: 393) argues that the concept of ethnicity has often been viewed as problematic as a consequence. By contrast, one reason why Edwards (2009: 205) has problematised Fishman's (1991, 2001b) own model (with its insistence on the close connection of ethnic identity and language use) is that the fluid, changing nature of group linguistic practices means there is no necessary connection between the maintenance of a traditional language and the continuation of a group's identity. Nationalistic rhetoric typically associates a language variety ideologically with a given national identity, with the result that the language in question 'comes to index particular ways of being in and belonging to' the nation in question (Bucholtz and Hall 2004: 385). In this way, Jaffe (2007a: 58) states, language can become an ideological tool for naturalising and legitimating political boundaries.

2.2 Language ideologies

A large sociological literature on ideology generally tends to address its importance in the exercise of social power. Theoretical and empirical work on ideology in political science similarly tends to address the production and reproduction of ideologies – as beliefs, myths and doctrines held by different social groups – and the manner in which they are contested by those groups in society (see Lukes 2005; Hearn 2008, 2012). Whilst sharing a focus on the manner in which perceptions and beliefs can influence behaviour, the use of the specific phrase 'language ideology' has a distinct history, having gained increasing currency in linguistic anthropology and the sociology of language, particularly since the 1990s (see Schieffelin et al. 1998).

In an early deployment of the term linguistic ideologies (more frequently language ideologies in subsequent works), anthropologist Michael Silverstein (1979: 193) defines them as the 'sets of beliefs about language articulated by users as a rationalization or justification of perceived language structure or use'. A wide variety of definitions have since been used to explicate the term 'language ideology', however. These extend from the wide-ranging 'beliefs or feelings about languages' (Kroskrity 2004: 512) to the more precise 'cultural system of ideas about social and linguistic relationships, together with their loading of moral and political interests' (Irvine 1989: 255). The usefulness of the concept in approaching questions of language use and identity is reflected in Makihara's (2010: 41) definition of language ideologies as speakers' 'cultural sensitivities . . . about language, its use, and its users'. As Heller (2007b: 14–5) notes, speakers' ideas about the language(s) they use are not neutral; the ways in which people make sense of the ways in which they draw upon their 'linguistic resources in the situations they find themselves in' are often, in fact, 'a matter of language ideology'. Indeed, the interrelationship of linguistic practice and language ideologies is a central concern in much linguistic anthropological research.

Building on this perspective, Cavanaugh (2013) argues that the language ideologies framework facilitates the analysis of how speakers view and use language (in both its communicative and symbolic functions). Crucially for the considerations of this monograph, Makihara (2010: 44–5) states that language ideologies have an important role in determining 'the direction of changes in languages and speech ways' by either motivating or militating against processes of language shift. Gal and Woolard (1995: 130) define language ideologies as 'cultural conceptions of the nature, form, and purpose of language'. Elaborating further, Boudreau and Dubois offer the following:

> Language ideologies are usually defined as a set of beliefs on language or a particular language shared by members of a community . . . . These beliefs come to be so well established that their origin is often forgotten by speakers, and are therefore socially reproduced and end up being 'naturalized', or perceived as natural or as common sense, thereby masking the social construction processes at work. Ideologies become political when they are embedded in the social principles on which a community organises itself institutionally. (Boudreau and Dubois 2007: 104)

It is the systematicity of language ideologies as cultural products, and their reproduction within social context, that is of greatest relevance here. Rumsey's (1990: 346) definition of language ideologies as 'shared bodies of common sense notions about the nature of language in the world' captures this dimension, but takes little account of variation in language ideological conceptions between and within groups. In this respect, Woolard and Schieffelin (1994: 58) have noted that the development and construction of language ideologies is 'a process involving struggle among multiple conceptualizations'. As such, language ideologies are often found to be a source of conflict in social life. The contestedness of language ideologies has been investigated at length in various contexts, including that of German in Hungary (Gal 1993), Corsican (Jaffe 1999, 2009), Arizona Tewa (Kroskrity 2000c), and Gaelic in the Highlands and Islands (Dorian 1981; McEwan-Fujita 2010a, 2010b).

King (2000: 168) draws an important distinction between language attitudes and language ideologies, explaining that whilst the former are usually expressed as a specific response to aspects of a particular language, the latter tend to be articulated as sets of beliefs concerning that language generally. Not only are beliefs of this kind often advanced by speakers as attempted rationalisations for their language practices but also, in turn, they are frequently 'embodied' and reflected in those very practices (Kroskrity 2004: 496). Language ideologies are therefore reflected in the linguistic choices speakers make and the languages they use in daily intercourse, as well as in the content of what they articulate.

The increasing prevalence of the language ideologies framework since the 1990s reflects its perceived usefulness as a toolkit to examine linguistic practices within wider sociocultural considerations (García 2009). Woolard (1998: 3) sees language ideologies as central to notions of both the person and the social group, and as the means by which the two are discursively linked through interaction. Just as sociocultural identities are conceived of as multiple, contested and contextual, language ideologies that enact ties to them tend to be viewed within a social constructivist framework. In formulating language ideologies and producing ties of language to identity categories, speakers attribute values to particular languages and constructions through the related processes of indexicality and iconisation, terms originally derived from Pierce's (1955) work on semiotics.

When certain linguistic practices become associated with a particular sociocultural group, we may speak of their 'indexing' aspects of that group's social life, while 'iconisation' is seen as the representation of language usages and varieties as 'pictorial guides to the nature of groups' (Kroskrity 2004: 507; see also Johnstone et al. 2006). By contrast, the tradition of aligning language, nation and state within European Romantic nationalism may be seen as example of overt iconisation. Conversely, the inchoate iconisation of Gaelic as a symbol of Scottish identity (see Macdonald 1997; Oliver 2002; McEwan-Fujita 2003) may be viewed as a somewhat more covert example. Whereas indexical processes may indirectly enact ties of language and identity through interaction and social practice, iconisation is seen as the ideological association of a language or feature as 'formally congruent' with the social group with which it is associated, irrespective of that group's actual language practices (Bucholtz and Hall 2004: 380). Language ideologies that iconise linguistic varieties are seen by Irvine and Gal (2000: 37) to transform the symbolic relationship between language and group identities, as if a given language variety depicts the social group's 'inherent nature or essence' (see also Bucholtz and Hall 2004: 380).

The relevance of the foregoing considerations is apparent in Valdés et al.'s (2008: 108) identification of the education system as an important site for 'the legitimization of particular ways of speaking', whilst devaluing others. Macleod (2010) argues that the marginal place occupied by Gaelic in Scottish education had a powerful effect on the orientation of language ideologies within the Gaelic-speaking community (see Chapter 3, below). Jaffe (2009) distinguishes between ideological production and reproduction in multilingual educational settings, noting that bilingual schools, as sites of language ideological production, act to ideologise pupils' language use by attributing different values to different languages. By contrast, she argues, ideological reproduction refers to how students interpret the language ideological content of the education they receive, which may differ substantially from the intended ideological goals of the bilingual classroom (Jaffe 2009: 395). These considerations bring us to the notion of language socialisation.

2.3 Language socialisation

A rapidly growing literature on socialisation generally is concerned chiefly with the acquisition by children and other novices of what Bourdieu (1990: 59) termed *habitus*, which he defines as the 'system of dispositions common to all products of the same conditionings', which produces sociocultural practice within communities. The theoretical bases of language socialisation, initially formulated in the 1980s (see Peters and

Boggs 1986; Schieffelin and Ochs 1986b; Ochs 1993), focus on both the specific role of language as the medium through which practices of this kind are produced in the wider sense, and socialisation to use language(s) per se (Schieffelin and Ochs 1986a: 163; Garrett and Baquedano-López 2002: 339; Kulick and Schieffelin 2004: 349). Duff (2010: 172) sums up the theoretical premise of the framework, defining language socialisation as an ongoing process of explicit mentoring by which individuals learn the appropriate uses of languages, as well as 'the worldviews, ideologies, values, and identities of community members'. The language socialisation framework therefore provides a useful conceptual link from issues of language and identity discussed in section 2.1 to the notions of language acquisition and attrition discussed in the following section (section 2.4, below).

An early focus within the paradigm pertained to the language socialisation of children by primary caregivers in the home–community context, as exemplified in Watson-Gegeo and Gegeo's (1986) research in the Solomon Islands, or Crago et al.'s (1993) study of difficulties maintaining the home as an intact domain for socialisation in Inuktitut in northern Quebec. The framework has since broadened, however, to take account of socialisation experiences over the life cycle (Bucholtz and Hall 2004; Garrett and Baquedano-López 2002). Furthermore, Garrett (2007: 233) stresses that the ongoing acquisition of 'communicative competence' (after Hymes 1972) proceeds not only through novices' interactions with older or more experienced persons but also generally through interactions with peers.

Therefore the home, school, college and workplace – any site of habitual interaction – can all be conceptualised as important potential contexts for language socialisation. The importance of these contexts as sites for language socialisation tends to be foregrounded in multilingual settings (Garrett 2007), since the use of one variety rather than another often has important consequences for socialisation experiences. Bayley and Schecter (2003) report that young people's experiences in bilingual and multicultural settings provide a rich research site for investigating issues of cultural and linguistic hybridity, since young multilinguals often define their identities in terms of newer, multilingual affiliations rather than more fixed, traditional categories. In minority language settings in particular this can have important consequences.

Researching Gaelic language socialisation in the Western Isles, McEwan-Fujita (2010b: 30) regards language shift to English there as a phenomenon that is 'perpetuated by linguistic socialization of children and adults'. The Gaelic-medium classroom, as a site for the socialisation of young people in Gaelic, may thus be either undermined or bolstered by language use in social spaces such as the home, playground, neighbourhood, or (subsequently) workplace or even the pub. Will's (2012) doctoral research on Lewis schoolchildren in primary GME documented obstacles to Gaelic socialisation through the school system, particularly where home socialisation in the language was weak (as was generally reported of the community she studied). Duff (2010: 173) states that as language learners' aptitudes increase through the continual process of socialisation, they gain insight into 'cultural knowledge about ideologies, identities or subjectivities' specific to the language community. As will be seen in the following sections, however, the capacity for formal language education to address such fundamental sociocultural considerations may be undermined by various factors.

The potential importance of the formal educational setting for the development of students' identities and ideologies and for their socialisation, and the relevance of these social factors in determining prospects for language acquisition and maintenance in bilingual immersion programmes, are discussed further in section 2.4, below.

2.4 Education and the role of immersion schooling

In recent decades, bilingual education has assumed an increasingly prominent position in language planning and revitalisation initiatives internationally (Ferguson 2006; Hornberger 2008). Colin Baker's research, for instance, has documented diverse contexts of bilingual education over the past thirty years (Baker and Griffith 1983; Baker and García 2007; Baker 1992, 2007, 2011). I draw attention in this section initially to research specifically on language acquisition and attrition in immersion education settings specifically (sections 2.4.1 to 2.4.2). Skutnabb-Kangas (1988, 2000) distinguishes four kinds of bilingual education: namely, mother-tongue maintenance education, immersion education, segregation and submersion education. The first two of these (both of which are embraced within GME) are described as examples of additive bilingual education that contribute toward the maintenance of students' linguistic abilities in both their first and second languages, while the latter two constitute forms of subtractive bilingual education, in that they tend to diminish students' abilities in a particular language, while promoting only those in another (Wright 2013). Gardner (1982: 28) has observed that additive and subtractive approaches also have important consequences in students' formation of identities and attitudes, a point to which I will return in the following chapter. Firstly, however, sections 2.4.1 to 2.4.2 provide a synthesis of relevant research from the fields of language acquisition and attrition.

2.4.1 Language acquisition and immersion education

Lambert and Tucker (1972: 225) first coined the expression 'immersion' education, describing students' experience of bilingual education in a pioneering French programme for Anglophone children in the city of St Lambert near Montreal as 'immersion in a "language bath"'. In the St Lambert context, English-speaking parents who were unhappy with existing provision for both English- and French-medium education campaigned for the establishment, in 1965, of a system of primary education that would 'lead to bilingualism by the end of elementary school' without diminished competence in the mother tongue (Lambert and Tucker 1972: 231). The model that was introduced in St Lambert was characterised by full immersion in French until second grade, when English-medium instruction was first introduced, and then gradually increased until the proportion of languages used for instruction was 50/50 by the sixth grade.

The scheme was generally considered a huge success and French immersion education expanded throughout the country as a consequence; in 2011 over 5% of Canadian elementary school pupils (some 300,000 children) were enrolled in French immersion programmes (Baker 2011: 240). Wright (2013: 611) explains that the perceived success of this bilingual immersion system led to its being replicated in diverse contexts internationally (see section 2.4.3, below). In Scotland, GME developed on the basis of this model via the experience of Welsh-medium education, and as a consequence, functions both to instruct a majority of children's second language acquisition, and to aid a minority of Gaelic-speaking students' first language development (Her Majesty's Inspectorate of Education 2011; see section 3.1, below). While the structure and aims of bilingual immersion programmes may vary considerably according to context, Swain and Johnson (1997) note that they tend characteristically to include the use of a second language (L2) as the principal medium of instruction by bilingual teachers, and a parallel curriculum to that used in dominant (L1) medium classes, with exposure to the L2 largely limited to the classroom.

Various models have been proposed to represent the processes by which individuals acquire a second language. Krashen's (1982) 'input model' conceived of acquisition as a subconscious process, which is guided by innate psycholinguistic mechanisms through exposure to comprehensible language input. Building on this, Long's (1985) interaction hypothesis posited that language acquisition from comprehensible input is most likely to occur through social interaction, in which context guides individuals' meaning-making. On the basis of research on French immersion education in Canada, Swain (1995) argued that the input hypothesis alone provides an insufficient explanation of the process, and that encouraging learners' linguistic output was necessary for stimulating productive skills; this has been termed the 'output hypothesis'.

Canale and Swain (1980) developed Hymes's (1972) notion of communicative competence in their theories of second language acquisition, arguing that language learners need to acquire not only linguistic competence – that is to say, knowledge of syntax, vocabulary and phonology – but also pragmatic competence to use language for conveying and interpreting meaning in real speech and day-to-day interaction. Building on this, researchers have added the goals of discourse competence, to engage in and manage conversation and extended writing, and sociolinguistic competence, to use language appropriately according to the domains, contexts and cultural understandings of the language community (Littlewood 2004; Butler 2013).

Ellis (2004) has observed that the speed of an individual's second language acquisition and eventual attainment can vary greatly, depending largely on social, cognitive and affective factors. Age is considered potentially to affect cognitive factors but not to be a factor in and of itself; Birdsong (2009) has observed that the influence of age in second language acquisition is still relatively unclear, with earlier formulations of the 'critical period hypothesis', which posited a relatively brief opportunity for optimal second language acquisition ending in adolescence, having subsequently been challenged. Whilst citing a wealth of evidence that tends to go against the hypothesis (see Flege 1999; Flege et al. 1999; Bialystok and Miller 1999; Hyltenstam and Abrahamsson 2000; Birdsong and Molis 2001; Mitchell et al. 2013), Birdsong (2004, 2009) nevertheless allows that age-related decline in language learning aptitude may nevertheless play some role in inhibiting second language acquisition.

Edwards (2013) argues that immersion classrooms constitute a unique context for examining the interplay of these social, cognitive and affective factors in second language acquisition, and Johnstone's (2001) review of bilingual immersion internationally suggests that immersion programmes are generally highly effective in producing students with bilingual competences. Johnstone (2001) nevertheless reports differences in attainment in productive and receptive skills as a frequent finding in research on immersion education. In Canada, for instance, studies by Harley and Swain (1984), Swain (1997), and Swain and Johnson (1997) found that French immersion students' listening and reading skills in French were equivalent to those of native speakers in many respects, but that their productive skills in speaking and writing lagged behind (L1) Francophone children. These studies each emphasised the potential for the target language in immersion education to become associated with school and to be seldom used beyond the classroom.

On the basis of various meta-analyses of the effectiveness of French immersion education in Canada, Edwards (2010b) notes that in spite of their greater command in the target language, immersion pupils generally appear not to seek out opportunities to use their second language to a greater extent than, for instance, students studying it as a subject. As Baker (2011: 265) phrases it, there is always a chance that '[p]otential does not necessarily lead to production' of the language in daily life. Studies by Potowski (2007) and Dressler (2012) both found low social use of target languages (Spanish and German) among students in bilingual programmes in the USA and Canada, respectively, with students expressing a marked preference for use of English with peers in both contexts.

Baker (1992: 31–2) distinguishes between instrumental and integrative motivations in learning language, with positive instrumental attitudes reflecting 'pragmatic, utilitarian motives', such as perceptions of socio-economic advantage to be gained by learning a language, while integrative motives concern 'attachment to, or identification with a language group and their cultural activities'. Issues of cultural identification often take on particular significance in bilingual programmes, which Baker (2011: 250) states can aid children in the 'establishment of a more secure identity'. Individual attitudes toward the language community and personal motivation to integrate with it have been observed, particularly in Canada, to play an important role in determining second language acquisition outcomes (Gardner and Lambert 1959, 1972), if not in promoting actual use of the target language. Integrative motivation of this kind has been described as reflecting the 'sincere and personal interest in the people and culture' associated with the target language (Gardner and Lambert 1972: 132). Yet Edwards (2013: 19) has observed that the development of competence in additional languages may in reality involve widely varying degrees of sociopsychological identification with the language communities in question.

On the basis of much of his early work with Lambert, which appeared to demonstrate the primacy of integrative motivational factors in second language acquisition, Gardner (1985) had initially argued that instrumental factors played a less significant role in learner motivation. Recently, however, he has modified this view, acknowledging that instrumental motivations are extremely (if not equally) important in many contexts (Gardner 2010; see also Kruideiner and Clement 1986).

An individual's orientations and motivations in second language acquisition may change substantially over time, and in response to ongoing research on integrative motivations, Dörnyei (2005) has advocated a reconceptualisation of language learners' social identifications with the target language in terms of the 'L2 Motivational Self

System', accounting for learners' idealised representations of themselves and their language learning aspirations. Ushioda and Dörnyei (2009: 1) state that motivations for L2 learning are consistently in the process of being 'reconceptualised and retheorised' in response to contemporary conceptions of personal and social identities (see section 2.1). Relatedly, Edwards (2013: 21) proposes that the deeper a learner delves into the target language and culture, the greater the impact on their identities is likely to be (see also Butler 2013). Nevertheless, he cautions against 'lumping together' the bilingualism of children who acquire fluency in Gaelic in the home setting with that of children who become bilingual through the education system in Edinburgh or Glasgow (Edwards 2013: 14). This point will be examined further in the next chapter.

2.4.2 Immersion education and language attrition

As with second language acquisition, issues of language attrition – the loss of linguistic skills and structures by an individual – are widely held to be inseparable from their wider social context (Andersen 1982; Edwards 2004; Schmid and de Bot 2004). Research on the phenomenon has demonstrated that attrition is affected by linguistic factors – such as influence from the dominant language, frequency and quality of input, loss of register differentiation and morphological complexity – as well as extra-linguistic, social factors like age, initial level of proficiency, length of time without input and attitudinal motivation for language maintenance (Bardovi-Harlig and Stringer 2010; Schmid 2011; Schmid et al. 2013). Crucially, speakers' opportunities and choice to use an attriting language play an important role in rates of maintenance and loss; whereas the former may be out of a speaker's control, Schmid and de Bot (2004: 221) observe that the latter tends not to be.

A threshold question in relation to the study of language attrition is whether the process involves the 'total loss' of linguistic structures from an individual's memory, or if the problem is essentially one of access and the 'restimulation' of knowledge that may be retained on some subconscious, psycho-linguistic level (Bardovi-Harlig and Stringer 2010: 2). The 'dormant language hypothesis', in particular, proposes that remnants of linguistic knowledge may be maintained at some subconscious level within the mind, even if they appear to be irretrievable. Related to this conception is the 'critical threshold hypothesis', which maintains that linguistic features that are learned best (rather than earliest) are least vulnerable to attrition and are thus maintained longest (Lambert 1989), while the 'interference' or 'interlanguage hypothesis' holds that attrition results directly from the influence of the dominant language (Köpke and Schmid 2004). Highly divergent, as well as less frequently occurring, features of the attriting language have similarly been shown to be vulnerable to loss.

Second language attrition studies have often focused on the school summer break as a common interruption period in the language development trajectories of immersion pupils (Cohen 1975; Clark and Jorden 1984; Russell 1999). Second language attrition has been found to develop faster for the productive skills of speaking and writing than for receptive skills, and vocabulary is generally lost faster than grammatical structures (Lambert 1989; Lambert and Freed 1982). Snow (1982) investigated rates of L2 retention and attrition among graduates of a seven-year Spanish immersion programme in a California elementary school by the time they started in high school, suggesting that the motivations of successful Spanish retainers were pivotal to their retention of productive abilities. A subsequent paper (Snow et al. 1988) concluded that the continued study of Spanish after primary school immersion courses had terminated had no immediate impact on vocabulary maintenance, with significant differences in language proficiencies observed not to develop until later in high school. Johnstone's (2001) comprehensive review of research on immersion education internationally found the extent of attrition after the completion of immersion programmes to be widely variable. As suggested by Snow et al. (1988) for Spanish immersion in the US, attitudes to the learning process and target language itself have often been found to be important for retention of the target language by French-immersion students in Canada (Lambert and Tucker 1972; Harley and Swain 1984; Harley 1994).

Studies by MacFarlane and Wesche (1995) and Nix-Victorian (2010) investigated the language use of former French-immersion students in Canada and Louisiana, both reporting low levels of French use in the present day. It is worth noting this decline in the use of a relatively prestigious target world language. By comparison, research on former immersion students' use of minority and Indigenous languages subsequent to leaving school appears relatively sparse in the international literature. Notable exceptions to this are to be found in the studies by Murtagh (2003), Woolard (2007) and Hodges (2009), however.

Murtagh's (2003, 2008) longitudinal study focused on post-school attrition of Irish, a minority language that nevertheless enjoys high formal status as the 'national' and first 'official' language in the Republic of Ireland (Ó Riagáin 1997, 2001). An important early finding in this regard was that use of Irish at home had an important impact on both pupil motivation and achievement in Irish (Harris and Murtagh 1999). Another factor found by Harris and Murtagh (1999) to influence rates of language retention was the density of an individual's social network (see Milroy 1987; Stoessel 2002). Importantly, Murtagh (2003, 2008) reported relatively high levels of retention among eleven graduates of Irish-medium programmes, a finding she related to the high levels of comprehensible input and output that are characteristic of bilingual immersion.

Yet Murtagh (2003, 2008) also suggested that sufficient time might not have elapsed between the two data collection times in her longitudinal study (20 months) to analyse rates of language attrition sufficiently among this group. Nevertheless, it is notable that only 45.5% of former Irish-medium students claimed to have 'native-speaker' abilities at Time 2 (while enrolled in undergraduate study), compared with 72.2% at Time 1 (whilst sitting the final year of the Irish Leaving Certificate). Significant limitations were also found in relation to former Irish students' language use after leaving school.

Hodges's (2009) investigation of Welsh language use among former Welsh-medium students in south Wales similarly found relatively low rates of Welsh language use in the present day, even among informants from Welsh-speaking homes. An important exception to this was found within the sphere of employment, with that formal domain constituting an important site for Welsh language use for several of her informants. As a qualitative case study of only eight informants, however, the generalisability of these findings to Welsh-medium students throughout Wales is clearly limited, though this was not an objective of the study.

Similarly, whilst Woolard's (2007) analysis of five graduates of a Catalan-medium high school may be limited in terms of generalisability, it offers a unique and seminal insight in relation to longer-term outcomes of minority language immersion education. Contrary to expectations that Woolard (2007: 641) had formulated on the basis of observations from a case study she conducted in 1987, a large proportion of the twelve informants she subsequently contacted twenty years later reported using Catalan extensively in the present day.

In 1987, L1 Castilian speakers in the Catalan-medium high school in which she conducted her study were reticent and even hostile to using Catalan, but the participants she was able to contact in 2007 all displayed considerable development in their Catalan abilities, due in large part to their engagement with and use of the language subsequent to leaving the school. The Catalan context represents a rather distinct example of language revitalisation, as Catalan is very widely used across most public domains in Catalonia. As such, the Catalan context presents a highly divergent environment from that of either Welsh or Irish, and constitutes one of only three of Fishman's (1991: 287) 'success stories' for reversing language shift internationally; the unusual status of Catalan in this respect brought increased opportunities (and in some cases obligations) for use of the language in the post-Franco period. Woolard's (2007) study nevertheless highlights the potential for unexpected changes in the development of the bilingual's engagement with different languages over the lifespan.

Potential rates of language attrition, and the longer-term outcomes of immersion programmes, currently appear relatively unclear, and their implications for the linguistic practices, language ideologies and sociocultural identities of participants are not easy to gauge on the basis of existing literature. Crucially, there is a notable shortage of investigations of attrition rates following a longer period of interruption after the completion of immersion education. In light of the research on bilingual immersion education in Canada discussed above, however, it would come as a surprise to find that the majority of adults who leave minority language immersion systems maintain the same degree of engagement with their classroom language years and decades after completing school.

2.4.3 Principles from overseas: Immersion revitalisation education in Europe, North America and Australasia

Language use in the context of minority language education often has important functions beyond that of communication (Hymes 1974; Fishman 1991; Edwards 2010a, 2010b; McCarty 2003, 2013; Weiyun He 2010). Friedman (2010: 193) notes that education is often viewed in such contexts as a primary vehicle for 'legitimating cultural identity', while Dorian (1987: 64) has discussed the value of language promotion efforts that are unlikely to succeed, noting greater community self-confidence, increased understanding of traditional knowledge and heritage, and economic development as potentially beneficial by-products of maintenance efforts.

If the school is regarded as an important site for identity and (language) ideology formation, however, the extent to which sociopsychological factors such as strong identities and supportive attitudes will impact upon actual language use is unclear. King (2000, 2001; King et al. 2008) has argued that in many contexts of language revitalisation, it is common for minority language speakers to hold positive attitudes to the revitalisation of their variety, yet simultaneously make little use of the endangered language in their daily lives (see also Dauenhauer and Dauenhauer 1998). Overtly expressed pro-revitalisation attitudes 'may only reveal one of several existing language ideologies' that influence linguistic behaviour (King 2000: 168–9; see section 2.2, above). Within contexts of language shift, the picture is often further complicated by sharp contrasts in linguistic ideologies and beliefs among learners on the one hand, and traditional speakers on the other (McEwan-Fujita 2010a, 2010b).

Bale (2010: 60) observes that researchers in diverse contexts have concluded that 'formal schooling cannot be the lone site' of language revitalisation for minority, heritage and Indigenous varieties, and prospects for the maintenance and revitalisation of minority languages through education alone often seem to be limited (Hinton and Ahlers 1999; McCarty 2003; see also Cochran 2008, Will 2012 and Landgraf 2013 in the Scottish Gaelic context). Kondo-Brown (2010: 24–8) has noted that much research on Indigenous minority language education has focused on immersion pupils' academic achievement, rather than language use. As discussed further below, the maintenance of bilingual abilities by former immersion pupils appears to be a crucial lacuna in research on minority and Indigenous language education internationally (although see Hodges 2009; Woolard 2007). I limit my discussion here to examples of 'immersion revitalisation' education (after García 2009: 128) in (Western) Europe, North America and Australasia. As will be demonstrated, research findings often support Fishman's hypotheses concerning the limited effectiveness of education in revitalising minoritised languages.

2.4.3.1 European perspectives: The Celtic world and Iberia

In Europe, McLeod (2007) has noted that developments in Wales and the Basque Country in particular, and Ireland and Brittany to some degree, have demonstrated the impact that bilingual education can have on boosting numbers of potential speakers of threatened languages (if not, perhaps, on creating day-to-day users). In Wales, Newcombe (2007: 5) has described education as having been '[a]rguably, the most important influence' in the revitalisation of Welsh during the twentieth century. The Welsh Assembly Government's (2010) strategy for Welsh, *Iaith Fyw* ('A Living Language'), identified supporting learners in Welsh-medium education to attain fluency as a key focus of language policy.

Some 63,000 primary school pupils (24% of the total) and 38,000 secondary students (20%) were enrolled in some form of Welsh-medium education in Wales in 2012–13 (Statistics for Wales 2013), whilst in the remainder of schools, Welsh is a compulsory subject up to the age of 16. In particular, the growth in the late twentieth century of Welsh-medium education in Anglicised parts of the country raised the hopes of language activists for a revival of Welsh in those areas (Williams 2003: 7; Coupland et al. 2005: 2). Edwards and Newcombe (2005: 303) for example, observe that almost two-thirds of primary school pupils who were reported as fluent in Welsh in the 2001 census came from English-speaking homes, although the results of Welsh language use surveys have demonstrated that such pupils' use of the language outside of school may be severely limited (Welsh Language Board 2008).

Disappointingly for Welsh language activists, the 2011 census recorded a 20,000 fall in the total number of Welsh speakers to 562,000, and 73.3% of the population were reported to have no Welsh language skills (Statistics for Wales 2014: 15). The census also revealed, however, that 40% of 5–15-year-olds in Wales could speak Welsh, the largest proportion of any age group (Statistics for Wales 2014: 15). A large proportion of this 5–15 age group might not be expected to progress to fluency in adulthood, however, since 40% of Welsh-medium primary pupils are currently reported to progress to English-medium secondary schools (Statistics for Wales 2013: 5). Studies by Edwards and Newcombe (2005: 300) and Coupland et al. (2005: 16) both suggested that interactional use of the language by Welsh-speaking teenagers declined over time, particularly where it is not the language of the home, a finding that Baker (1992) had reported over twenty years ago.

Conversely, Selleck (2013: 23) has argued that the education system in Wales promotes an unrealistic 'monolingual ideal' of Welsh use that fails to recognise Welsh-speaking students' bilingual repertoires, and the bilingual (or English-dominant) environments in which they live. The degree to which a more flexible approach here would facilitate students' acquisition of and socialisation in Welsh would appear limited, however, in light of what Baker (1992), Edwards and Newcombe (2005) and Coupland et al. (2005) report in respect of pupils' Welsh use, even within Welsh-medium schools where they are actively encouraged to use the language. Indeed, Thomas and Roberts (2011) have suggested that Welsh-medium pupils' reliance on English use is perpetuated by a widespread tendency to view the latter as the inclusive variety in social interaction. As noted above, Hodges's (2009) case study of Welsh-medium high-school graduates reported low social use of the language in the first five years after leaving high school.

Ó Riagáin (1997) has traced the twentieth-century decline and rise of Irish-medium education in the Republic of Ireland. From the 1920s onwards, the Irish government promoted Irish-medium education throughout the twenty-six counties of the Republic, and in the 1940s around 30% of schools were Irish-medium. Following government criticism and a popular backlash against the system in the 1960s, however, a grass-roots campaign to develop 'all-Irish' schools from the 1970s (initially outside the state system) led to the growth of the Irish-medium Gaelscoileanna in non-Irish-speaking areas. Meanwhile, all schools in the Gaeltacht (the legally designated majority Irish-speaking areas) were made entirely Irish-medium from 1922 onwards.

Studies by Mac Donnacha et al. (2005), Ó Giollagáin et al. (2007) and Ó hIfearnáin (2007, 2008) have each investigated the reality of language use in Gaeltacht communities, finding declining Irish use and abilities, especially among school-age children. In both the Republic and Northern Ireland, Irish-medium education as it currently exists developed from grass-roots parental initiatives to establish it (Coady and Ó Laoire 2002; Ó Baoill 2007). Some 35,710 primary and 9,663 secondary pupils were enrolled in Irish-medium schools in both jurisdictions in 2012–13 (Gaelscoileanna Teo 2013). Of these, 3,172 primary pupils and 773 secondary pupils were enrolled in Irish-medium education in the six counties of Northern Ireland, where, Ó Baoill (2007) argues, the system has been absolutely central to language revitalisation efforts since its establishment by six West Belfast families in the 1970s.

Fleming and Debski (2007) reported low levels of Irish use outside school by pupils in both Gaelscoileanna in English-speaking areas and Irish-medium schools in Gaeltacht areas. However, students in Gaelscoileanna were found to be more likely to speak Irish to friends within school, while Gaeltacht pupils reported greater use of the language outside of the school. Ó Riagáin (1997, 2001) has observed that Irish-medium schools have often had important consequences beyond the realm of education, impacting on use of the language, but particularly improving attitudes and optimism about the future of Irish. Coady and Ó Laoire (2002: 150) found that 66% of students attending Irish-medium schools outside the Gaeltacht came from English-speaking homes, and only 9% came from homes in which Irish was 'often' or 'always' spoken. They found that Irish-medium teachers in these schools had come to see revival of language use through Irish-medium schools as unrealistic, regarding their job as providing a decent education and fostering Irish-language proficiency (Coady and Ó Laoire 2002: 154).

Moriarty (2010) compared the language practices and attitudes of university students in the contexts of Basque and Irish. While not all the informants in the Irish context were educated in Irish-medium schools, high levels of attrition reported in this study have implications for post-school language use. Crucially, Irish competence and school medium of instruction were found to be the first and the second most influential predictors of L2 Irish retention. Ó Baoill (1999) addressed the types of Irish speakers that are produced through Irish-medium schools, questioning the assumption that Irish learners in Gaelscoileanna want to integrate in any serious way with Gaeltacht Irish speakers. Gaeltacht communities, he argued, often seem distant, remote and largely irrelevant for students in urban-based, Irish-medium schools, and Irish speakers in these areas are therefore unlikely to constitute a social and linguistic model for pupils' integrative orientations (Ó Baoill 1999).

Crucially, Ó Duibhir (2009, 2018) has examined the linguistic accuracy and motivations of Irish-medium students in Northern Ireland and the Republic, reporting positive attitudes and motivations in both contexts to derive in large part from the fact that pupils regard the language as an important part of Irish identity. Yet he notes that pupils in both polities seem to be 'less concerned about their oral language accuracy when conversing with peers', and that favourable attitudes do not seem to be sufficiently strong enough to motivate them to learn to speak Irish more accurately (Ó Duibhir 2009: 115), emphasising the limitations of the Irish immersion system in generating active and accurate users of the language outside the school setting.

Just under 20% of all 45,400 pupils in Irish-medium education were based in Gaeltacht areas in 2011–12, with the remainder based in Gaelscoileanna in areas where the language is less widely used in the community (Gaelscoileanna Teo 2013). In spite of this apparent distinction, Ó hIfearnáin (2007: 512) has stated that a dominant ideology among policymakers is that the Gaeltacht is Irish-speaking, when often this is not in fact true of community members' language use. Ó Muircheartaigh and Hickey (2008) found that entering Irish-medium education at any stage has implications for language learning outcomes, with late-immersion students lagging considerably behind early-immersion students in terms of Irish ability. Notably, Ó hAineiféin (2008) has advocated an increase in partial immersion programmes in order to improve relatively poor outcomes of compulsory Irish teaching (in non-Irish-medium education) and supplement the all-Irish Gaelscoileanna.

In Brittany, Breton-medium education is currently provided within three distinct systems, comprising bilingual classes in public schools (supported by the Div Yezh association), bilingual classes in private Catholic schools (Dihun), and independent, Diwan immersion schools (Ó hIfearnáin 2011, 2013b; Köhler 2009). The Breton language office's (Ofis ar Brezhoneg) *Brezhoneg 2015* language plan outlined the goal of increasing the number of students in the three systems to 25,000 by 2015, on the grounds that new speakers created through education might thereby replace the 10,000–15,000 elderly Breton speakers who die each year (Ó hIfearnáin 2013b: 123). As Ó hIfearnáin (2013b: 123) goes on to explain, however, the number of new speakers the education systems produce – or even if this is an explicit goal of the schools themselves – is unclear. There is an important difference, he notes, 'between children acquiring competence in the language and those same children necessarily becoming active speakers outside the classroom' (ibid.). In an earlier study Ó hIfearnáin (2011: 105) conducted interviews with two graduates of Diwan schools who were among the first cohorts to enter the system and are now in their thirties. These informants reported that they would use Breton with old schoolfriends, some of whom were acutely conscious of limitations in their language abilities, having 'never had the opportunity or inclination' to use the language within the Breton-speaking community.

Broudic's (2010: 34–8) research in Breton-medium schools demonstrated that pupils' language use is dominated by French outside the classroom, and that teachers struggle to encourage the use of Breton among peers in the schools. In spite of this, Ó hIfearnáin (2011, 2013b) found evidence that some school leavers do continue to make frequent use of their Breton, particularly those who received an immersion education through the independent Diwan schools. Elsewhere in France, research by Roquette (2005) and Alén Garabato and Boyer (2005) in Provence has suggested that graduates of the Calandretas, Occitan immersion primary schools, made limited use of the target language – and in some cases exhibited only limited mastery of it – in later life.

Across the border in Catalonia, the closely related Catalan language occupies quite a distinctive sociolinguistic space compared to other contexts discussed in this chapter, being spoken by over 80% of the population, and just under 50% as a first language (Woolard 2007). Additionally, the linguistic distance between Catalan and the other, 'majority' language used here (Castilian), is relatively minor compared to other most contexts discussed in this section (McPake et al. 2013: 19). Catalan is used as a medium of instruction in most schools at all levels, and as a consequence, knowledge of the language among young people is 'extremely high', though actual use of Catalan by this group is considered by Woolard (2007: 620), on the basis of several decades of fieldwork in Catalan schools, to be 'lagging considerably behind'. Yet in contrast with other Catalan-speaking regions in Spain, the language is in a comparatively stronger position (see Huguet and Llurda 2001). As noted above, Woolard's (2007) case study of twelve past Catalan-medium students found extensive use of the language even among first-language Castilian speakers, contrary to her expectations, though this may be limited in terms of generalisability.

In the Basque Autonomous Community (BAC), bilingual education began with the creation of the Basque-medium *ikastolak* in the 1960s (Cenoz 2001, 2009; Elorza and Muñoa 2008). Azurmendi and Martinez de Luna (2011: 327) comment that education 'is the sphere that is mostly responsible' for the language's revival in this region. In 2011, 32% of the population of the BAC were reported to be Basque speakers, with a further 17.4% of the population passive bilinguals (Eusko Jauriaritza 2013: 67). Basque-medium pupils account for 79% of all primary and 61% of all secondary school students in the BAC (compared to 25% of school students after the *ikastolak* first started; Cenoz 2001: 51). Nevertheless, Elorza and Muñoa (2008: 86) suggest that achievement and proficiency in Basque at school tend not to translate to informal use 'outside or even within the school itself'. Echeverria (2003) reports that Basque-medium students use the language within the classroom, but often switch to Spanish when the teacher leaves the room, and Azurmendi and Martinez de Luna (2011: 329) have suggested that 'the symbolic value of Euskara is greater than the pragmatic one' at present (see Elorza and Muñoa 2008; Zalbide and Cenoz 2008).

2.4.3.2 Indigenous language education in North America and Australasia

Indigenous minority language revitalisation efforts in the US and Canada (as elsewhere) often place a particular emphasis on wider goals of Indigenous cultural survival, self-determination and the (re)assertion of cultural identity (De Corne 2010; Henze and Davis 1999; McCarty 2003, 2013; McCarty et al. 2008). Internationally, one of the most celebrated contexts of revitalisation immersion education is that of Hawai'i, although McCarty's (2003: 152) identification of Hawai'ian immersion education as arguably 'the most dramatic language revitalisation success story to date' must be set against Wong's (1999: 94) assertion of the need to evaluate the degree to which increased official speaker numbers and new domains of use in the sphere of education alone can be regarded as progress. McCarty (2003: 154) concedes that (as has been seen elsewhere) use of the language 'is still largely restricted to the domain of schooling'.

Although accurate estimates of speaker numbers are problematic, McCarty (2013) explains that the Navajo language, with between 100,000 and 180,000 speakers in the US, constitutes the largest Indigenous American language north of Mexico (see McCarty et al. 2008). Although it does not enjoy official state support in the same way that Hawai'ian does, there is a widespread belief among the Navajo nation that community control of formal education can aid Indigenous identity maintenance (Manuelito 2005: 73–4). This has led to the growth of Navajo bilingual and immersion education programmes in the south-west US, though data from schools have tended, again, to show that school-based efforts need to be supported by family and community initiatives to influence young people's actual language practices (McCarty

2003: 157). In particular, McCarty (2013: 182) argues that community elders' support is needed to help young school leavers develop their language skills. For Californian Indigenous languages, no longer reproduced in the home or school, several tribes have turned to 'Master–apprentice' language-learning schemes, whereby older native speakers and younger tribe members are partnered and interact for up to 20 hours a week (Hinton and Ahlers 1999: 59).

Research on Indigenous languages in Canada has suggested that intergenerational transmission of First Nations languages is severely disrupted, and minority groups have increasingly turned to bilingual education to maintain their languages, cultures and identities (Dementi-Leonard and Gilmore 1999; Duff and Li 2009; De Corne 2010), though it is clear that formal (immersion) education opportunities vary considerably from one context to the next. Conversely, studies by Wright et al. (2000) and Usborne et al. (2009) have suggested that whilst Inuktitut in Nunavik (northern Quebec) remains a relatively vibrant and functional language in the private sphere, access only to dominant (French) language-medium or transitional education seems to promote patterns of subtractive bilingualism among Inuit children. Both studies therefore suggest that home use in the absence of additive bilingual provision in the classroom appears insufficient to safeguard language maintenance among children in certain contexts, providing a compelling counterpoint to the above examples of provision in the school outstripping language support in the home and community.

In Australia and Aotearoa/New Zealand, very different levels of provision have been made for minority Indigenous languages in the education systems, with scant provision in Australia often viewed as serving to proliferate rates of subtractive bilingualism (Baldauf 2005; De Courcy 2005; Nicholls 2005). In Aotearoa/New Zealand, the 2013 census recorded 125,352 people able to hold conversations in Māori, around 20% of the total Māori population (Statistics New Zealand 2013: 11). The 2001 Māori Language Survey suggested that, in fact, only 22,000 could be regarded as 'highly fluent'; conversely, only 58% of Māori adults could speak the language 'beyond a few words or phrases' (May 2012: 313).

In contrast to Indigenous language policies in Australia, however, the Māori language is an official language in Aotearoa/New Zealand, used as a medium of instruction in almost 300 schools (May 2005; Harrison and Papa 2005). Bilingual and immersion education has been used to bring the language back from a situation where it had declined from being the mother tongue of 96.5% of Māori schoolchildren in 1930 to 26% in 1960 (May and Hill 2005: 367; May 2012: 311). A distinction is made in Aotearoa/New Zealand between Māori-medium (immersion) and bilingual education, with four levels in operation: Level 1 (Māori-medium) is 81–100% through Māori; Level 2 is 51–80%; Level 3 is 31–50%; and Level 4 is 12–30% (May and Hill 2005: 378). By 2001, 25,580 Māori students (17%) were enrolled in Māori-medium education, of whom 87% were in primary school (May 2005: 368). A further 8,000 children were enrolled in bilingual education at this time, and May (2012: 314) reports that numbers in bilingual and Māori-medium programmes have 'held relatively constant' since then, as recently verified by the New Zealand Department of Education's (2018) education counts.

May and Hill (2005: 379) state that Māori-medium education typically recognises no distinction between L1 and L2 students – in spite of the fact that the majority of Māori-medium students acquire the language as an L2. Ironically, the widespread parental preference is for English-medium education at secondary level, based on the unfortunate assumption that 2–3 years of immersion education is sufficient for acquiring additive bilingualism in Māori, and a mistaken belief that the English medium is required for students' acquisition of English (May and Hill 2005: 396).

Whilst Māori-medium education receives a great deal of attention in the international literature, little research appears generally to have addressed the language practices of past students, as has been noted of the various other contexts discussed above. It is therefore possible to identify an apparent lacuna in the literature: namely, the long-term outcomes of immersion revitalisation education, and of second language immersion education generally, in relation to past students' language use. With a view to filling this apparent lacuna, the following chapter reviews the specific situation of GME in Scotland before introducing the research design of the study.

2.5 Concluding remarks on language, culture and immersion education

This chapter has demonstrated the relevance of several theoretical frameworks in linguistics, psychology and anthropology to the present monograph. Theoretical approaches to the relationship of language and identities (outlined in section 2.1) draw on a large and multidisciplinary literature, and research in socio- and applied linguistics, anthropology, psychology and sociology has consistently demonstrated that the nexus of language, culture and identity is profoundly complex. In addition to the ways in which language is used to convey, communicate and construct identity (section 2.1.1), it is also theorised to have an important and quite separate role as a symbol of group identity (sections 2.1.1 to 2.1.4). A language may therefore be regarded as important to a community or individual, irrespective of its continued use in social context.

Theoretical and applied work on language ideologies offers a valuable avenue for conceptualising the relationship between the communicative and symbolic functions of language, and for relating considerations in respect of identity to individuals' actual language use. Empirical work on language socialisation has demonstrated that the degrees to which children and other novices are exposed to and immersed in language throughout the lifespan can have important impacts on the ways they view, use and relate to particular languages (section 2.1.3). The relationship of these three issues, as examined through the qualitative and quantitative approaches adopted in later chapters of this book (4–6), will be of particular importance for investigating the principal research questions.

Whilst research findings in the fields of language acquisition (section 2.4.1) and attrition (2.4.2) seem to suggest that use of target languages by former bilingual and immersion students tends to decline after schooling is completed, there is an apparent dearth of research on longer-term outcomes. Similarly, whilst research on the role of bilingual and immersion education in Europe (section 2.4.3.1), as well as North America and Australasia (2.4.3.2), has often demonstrated limitations of education in terms of promoting bilingual language use among pupils outside of school, relatively few studies have addressed the period after this (although see Murtagh 2003; Woolard 2007; Hodges 2009). Internationally, therefore, the current investigation contributes to filling an apparent lacuna in the research literature. The following chapter will explicate how this research adds to scholarly understandings in the local context of Gaelic education in Scotland, and outlines the research design adopted to do so.

3

Exploring Outcomes of Gaelic-Medium Education: Research Design and Analysis

GME as it exists today developed as an indirect consequence of the Western Isles Bilingual Education Project (1975–81), the limitations of which led in 1982 to the establishment of Comhairle nan Sgoiltean Àraich (the Gaelic Pre-School Council) and, eventually, the opening of two primary GME classes in 1985. Yet the origins of the system's development can be traced a long way further back than this. This chapter will outline the immediate context and parameters of the study that informs this book, including the research methods and design adopted to establish validity and investigate the key social and linguistic questions identified in previous chapters. Section 3.1 provides a succinct overview of GME in Scotland, outlining the system's growth and identifying the expectations of parents and practitioners in its earliest years, and situating the present research within the wider experience of GME in Scotland. Section 3.2 summarises the overall design of the research, which makes use of both quantitative and qualitative methods. Semi-structured interviews and an online questionnaire are employed to examine language use and attitudes, and to facilitate data triangulation of research results.

In section 3.3 I outline and describe the pool of participants among whom the research is conducted, and describe various methods used to contact this group, and analyse quantitative and qualitative datasets. The method of transcription, qualitative analysis and the methodological framework adopted will be described and explained in relation to the data. Attention will additionally be drawn to the data collection process in the field and the reflexive approach I adopted in producing interactional data and interpreting conversational discourse through the 'ethnography of speaking' analysis. I will discuss how the dual focus on content and form thus contributes to the validity of the narrative analysis by delving below the surface semantics of speech acts to consider speakers' pragmatic meanings holistically.

3.1 GME: Past, present and prospects for revitalisation

This section introduces the context of GME in Scotland specifically, considering the history of provision for (and exclusion of) Gaelic in the Scottish education system, with particular reference to the growth of GME in the latter decades of the twentieth century (section 3.1.1), the expectations and experiences of parents and policymakers with regard to GME in the earliest years of its availability (section 3.1.2), and reviewing research on the system's limitations in respect of revitalising Gaelic (section 3.1.3).

3.1.1 The development of GME in Scotland 1872–1985

While Gaelic was used as a teaching medium to some extent by various voluntary organisations in the eighteenth and nineteenth centuries, the Education (Scotland) Act 1872 made no mention of – or provision for – the Gaelic language, despite its still being spoken by over a quarter of a million people in Scotland (MacKinnon 1977; Dunbar 2006).

Importantly, however, Paterson (2003: 45) has argued that policymakers were not 'systematically hostile' toward Gaelic at this time but rather were generally unenthusiastic, leaving potential provision for Gaelic at the discretion of individual school boards. O'Hanlon (2012: 38) locates this approach within a legislative tradition for Scottish education that she describes as being 'permissive rather than prescriptive'. The overtly antagonistic attitude to Gaelic that some writers have subsequently attributed to contemporary policymakers (see, for example, Mulholland 1981; Thompson 1985) may not therefore be an accurate portrayal of the background to the 1872 Act. Rather, a sense of 'benevolent neutrality' – to use a phrase employed by the Scottish Education Department itself at a later stage – might better reflect authorities' treatment of the language in education at this time (Dunn and Robertson 1989: 44; Withers 1984).

Nevertheless, a notable consequence of the 1872 Act was that the various charitable institutions that had previously provided Gaelic-medium instruction to Highland pupils were increasingly replaced with English-medium schools. In the years preceding the 1872 Act, organisations including the SSPCK, the General Assembly of the Church of Scotland, the Free Church and the Inverness Society for Gaelic Schools sponsored provision for GME (Durkacz 1983: 178). These organisations were increasingly disenfranchised as public education became established, and Dunbar (2006: 4) states that the development of a generally English-only system of education in the Highlands and Islands had 'a significant and highly negative impact' on the maintenance and transmission of Gaelic at that time, contributing substantially to its long-term demographic decline.

In spite of this impact, Gaelic continued to be taught as a subject and used as a teaching medium to a limited extent after 1872, and examinations in Gaelic were permitted after 1905 (Durkacz 1983: 178–9). These provisions, and official encouragement of transitional approaches to Gaelic use, were largely motivated by authorities' concern that Gaelic-speaking pupils acquire English proficiency, however. As a result of campaigning by An Comunn Gaidhealach (The Highland Association), the 1918

Education (Scotland) Act required education authorities to make adequate provision for the 'teaching of Gaelic in Gaelic-speaking areas', but failed to specify what 'teaching of Gaelic' meant or which specific areas were understood to be 'Gaelic-speaking' (McLeod 2003: 121). Such issues were again left at the discretion of education boards, and as a consequence, use of the language as a teaching medium remained rare until the 1960s (Macleod 1963; McLeod 2003; Dunbar 2006). In the 1930s, for instance, An Comunn Gaidhealach (1936: 9–10) reported that the use of Gaelic as a teaching medium at primary level was confined to humanities subjects, recommending increased provision for Gaelic both as a teaching medium in Gaelic-speaking areas, and as a subject in secondary schools across Scotland.

On this point the Scottish Office Education Department's 1950 primary curricular memorandum provided a flexible vision of Gaelic as teaching medium (Scottish Office Education Department 1950), while its 1951 annual report recommended a greater emphasis on its use for classroom instruction (Scottish Office Education Department 1951: 20–1). These documents contributed to greater official provision for Gaelic as a teaching medium in 1960, when the Inverness-shire Gaelic Education Scheme was introduced (Macleod 1963). This system enacted the teaching of Gaelic in Skye and the outer Isles of Harris, Uist and Barra (Her Majesty's Inspectorate of Education 1989: 2), and was later extended to mainland districts of the county, embracing schools in Inverness, Lochaber and Badenoch (MacLeod 2009: 229). The Scottish Office Education Department's 'Primary Memorandum' in 1965 advised that it was the duty of individual primary schools to develop Gaelic as a means of communication, recommending that schools should use Gaelic, when appropriate, 'as a means of instructing Gaelic-speaking pupils in other subjects' and, furthermore, that 'Gaelic should be treated as a living language' (Scottish Office Education Department 1965: 199–201).

In spite of these important developments, however, it has been described as a matter of shame that almost a century elapsed after the foundation of state education before the use of Gaelic as a teaching medium became commonplace in the language's heartland areas (Robasdan 2006: 88). The regionalisation of local authorities in 1975 established the Islands Council (Comhairle nan Eilean) as an all-purpose local authority with responsibility throughout the Western Isles (MacLeod 2004a: 199). The Comhairle established the Bilingual Education Project in the same year, with the stated aim of letting the Gaelic language 'flow across the curriculum' at the primary school level, and placing an emphasis on promoting oral skills in the language (Her Majesty's Inspectorate of Education 1989: 5). M. MacLeod (2004a, 2004b) and D. J. MacLeod (2009) have examined teachers' and pupils' experiences of the system, emphasising its importance for establishing links with the community and natural environment. The Project was designed both to contribute to validating pupils' lives in their local communities, as well as to produce speakers 'who were equally fluent' in English and Gaelic by P7 (MacLeod 2009: 230).

In hindsight, the Project has generally been regarded as highly successful in terms of the wider social aims it set out, but less effective in relation to this last, linguistic objective (Murray and MacLeod 1981; Murray and Morrison 1984). Dunn and Robertson (1989: 48) note that teachers involved in the project had 'no formal training' in the principles of bilingual education, and that it is likely in fact that some had little, if any, experience of Gaelic in their own schooling. Concerns were raised as to the system's efficacy in promoting bilingualism in a 1987 Scottish Office-funded assessment of the Bilingual Education Project (Mitchell et al. 1987; Mitchell 1992).

MacLeod (2009: 230) notes that numbers of school-age Gaelic speakers in the Western Isles continued to decline apace in spite of the Project, stating that the form of bilingual education 'simply wasn't robust enough' to counteract the various effects of language shift at the time. In a pamphlet published at the start of the 1980s, Mulholland (1981: 12) advocated a more immersive approach to learning Gaelic, requiring 'serious, intensive teaching and intensive use' of the language. GME as it exists today emerged in the 1980s from the grass-roots initiatives of parents who campaigned for its establishment (Comunn na Gàidhlig 1989: 6). Comhairle nan Sgoiltean Àraich (CNSA), the Gaelic Pre-School Council, was set up in 1982, and in its first seven years oversaw the growth of Gaelic-medium pre-school provision to 44 playgroups throughout Scotland, including 18 in the Scottish Lowlands and 1 in Cape Breton, Nova Scotia (Her Majesty's Inspectorate of Education 1989: 8).

CNSA in effect grew from a small-scale effort to co-ordinate previously scattered, voluntary provision of pre-school care through Gaelic to become a nationwide body, inspired principally by parents' concerns that only 738 children under 5 were reported to be able to speak Gaelic in the 1981 census, and their desire to replicate the Welsh-medium pre-school system for their own Gaelic-speaking children (Scammell 1985: 21). Under the organisation's co-ordination, parental demand for the continuation of Gaelic-medium provision into school years led to the foundation, in 1985, of Gaelic-medium units within two primary schools in Glasgow and Inverness (Comunn na Gàidhlig 1989: 6; Dunbar 2006: 4). Crucially at this stage, pressure from campaigners and local authorities prompted the Scottish Office to introduce the Grants for Gaelic Language Education (Scotland) Regulations 1986, entailing grant allocation specifically for Gaelic education (see Her Majesty's Government 1986; Comunn na Gàidhlig 1989). This crucial development became effectively the first national policy initiative to support Gaelic education.

Nevertheless, the Gaelic development agency Comunn na Gàidhlig's (1989: 6) progress report described developments in GME during the early 1980s as having proceeded in a 'piecemeal' fashion, so that classroom practice varied considerably in GME, an inconsistency that O'Hanlon et al. (2012) observed to endure well into the twenty-first century. In particular, Comunn na Gàidhlig's (1989: 12) report identified an emerging crisis in respect of the shortage of Gaelic language skills among teachers. The rapid growth of parental demand for GME was identified as a key factor in this disparity, and, as discussed below (section 3.1.3), demand for Gaelic-speaking teachers continues to be a major challenge in GME provision. In its first two decades of availability, primary GME provision grew from 24 students in the Glasgow and Inverness units in 1985/6 to over 2,000 by 2004/5 (MacKinnon 2005: 8, see Table 3.1). As may be seen, the growth of GME as it exists today is therefore a relatively recent phenomenon, though the system's rapid growth in its first thirteen years slowed dramatically from 1998/9 (Robertson 2001; McLeod 2003; MacLeod 2007).

Table 3.1 Growth of GME 1985–2005. Primary GME provision by area (MacKinnon 2005)

Academic year	Argyll and Bute	Western Isles	Highland Council	Other Scotland	Total
1985/6	n/a	n/a	12	12	24
1986/7	n/a	4	31	29	64
1987/8	4	19	44	44	111
1988/9	8	20	75	66	169
1989/90	14	51	127	94	286
1990/1	26	107	178	120	431
1991/2	36	189	234	155	614
1992/3	47	272	328	187	834
1993/4	57	365	425	233	1,080
1994/5	54	457	472	275	1,258
1995/6	61	555	528	312	1,456
1996/7	66	629	577	315	1,587
1997/8	73	605	633	365	1,676
1998/9	70	643	703	400	1,816
1999/2000	82	599	718	432	1,831
2000/1	100	589	704	469	1,862
2001/2	115	563	678	503	1,859
2002/3	127	542	707	552	1,928
2003/4	149	503	717	603	1,972
2004/5	152	491	730	635	2,008

3.1.2 Expectations and experiences of GME: 1980–90

Dunbar (2006: 4) notes that GME became 'one of the main foci' for revitalisation efforts in Scotland during the late twentieth century. I draw attention in this section to the hopes, expectations and experiences of policymakers, parents and teachers who were involved in the early years of GME in Scotland, particularly in relation to the system's perceived role in revitalising Gaelic. As noted above, the first GME units were each established in response to predominantly Gaelic-speaking parents' lobbying efforts to ensure their children would speak Gaelic into adulthood (Fraser 1989; Grant 1983; MacIlleChiar 1985).

On the day that GME started in Glasgow, the *Glasgow Herald* carried an article by future government minister Brian Wilson, who commented that pupils entering the Glasgow class, 'whose parents want them to grow up as Gaelic speakers', were expected subsequently to take the language forth into their adult lives, thereby 'ensuring that Gaelic lives into future generations as a mainland, as well as island language' (Wilson 1985: 14). A clear expectation of both policymakers and parents in 1985 was that GME pupils would become fluent Gaelic speakers with both the ability and the inclination to use the language in daily interaction, to pass it on to their own children in the future, and to be counted within demographic projections for the anticipated revitalisation of Gaelic in Scotland.

Later in the same year, the *Glasgow Herald* quoted Ford Spence, chairman of the Gaelic Language Promotion Trust, referring to the Glasgow GME unit as 'a dream come true' for language activists hoping to safeguard the future of Gaelic (Lowe 1985: 14). Reflecting the expectations of such activists when visiting the school, Spence is quoted as asking a young pupil: 'Do you promise to speak Gaelic when you grow up and take the language into the next generation?', to which the child dutifully replied 'Yes' (Lowe 1985: 14). A poster designed by Comunn na Gàidhlig in 1992 displayed the caption that Gaelic was 'Eroded by time ... but the tide is turning!'. Fraser's (1989: iv) PhD research was informed by language use questionnaires and interviews with parents and teachers, and the 133 families in her sample accounted for 91% of all children in GME when the survey was conducted (1989: 214). She notes that parents of the first cohorts of GME students often regarded the system as a means to support Gaelic language maintenance in the home and community, and as a way to encourage habitual use of the language among children (Fraser 1989). Yet by the end of the decade, the majority of parents enrolling children in GME units in urban settings were non-Gaelic speakers (see Fraser 1989: 1; Trabelsi 1998: 181–2).

Fraser (1989: 2) regards these parents' motivations for choosing GME as reflecting expectations for their children's future use of Gaelic, but also their engagement with Scottish national identity, a view also reflected in V. MacGregor's (2009) retrospective account of the foundation of the Edinburgh GME unit at Tollcross Primary School. Finlay MacLeod, a key figure in the crucial work of the CNSA in the 1980s, exemplified the significance of contemporary parents' and stakeholders' expectations when interviewed for Catriona Timms's thesis on language revitalisation, stating: 'We never imagined that our children in GME would grow up and want to be lawyers. We never imagined that they would choose not to use it with their children' (Timms 2012: 78).

Trabelsi (1998: 343) notes that some parents' expectations of GME as a major (and sometimes sole) focus of their children's Gaelic language socialisation were unduly optimistic, particularly in terms of advancing their children's use of Gaelic outside of the classroom. Almost since its inception, the urban GME unit was expected to function simultaneously as an aid to Gaelic language maintenance among a minority of children who were already bilingual, and as a means of teaching the language as a second language to the majority of other pupils (Fraser 1989: 152). A 1989 report on the growth of GME by Her Majesty's Inspectorate of Education (HMIE) notes that this complicated task was compounded by the 'complete lack of previous models to draw on' in Scotland, coupled with a lack of both teacher expertise and materials (Her Majesty's Inspectorate of Education 1989: 11). In addition to teachers' dedication, parental support for GME was also instrumental to the fledgling system's success in urban settings (Campbell 1983). If attitudes to the new system among parents in urban areas were often highly enthusiastic, many parents in the Western Isles expressed more uncertain feelings in the earliest years of GME, being hesitant to enrol children in a system that was regarded as highly experimental (Fraser 1989; Roberts 1991).

In contrast to Western Isles communities with GME units at this time, however, Fraser (1989: 169) noted of pupils in urban areas that 'the school is the only source of Gaelic input for the majority of children'. Describing the extremely limited opportunity that most pupils in these areas had to use Gaelic outside the classroom as 'the most striking feature' of her data (Fraser 1989: 230), she noted that non-Gaelic-speaking parents' motivations for GME choice tended to pertain to issues of cultural identity rather than encouraging Gaelic use as such (1989: 313–14). If, in the future, it were to transpire that the majority of parents choosing GME were satisfied with their children's educational progress within the system, regardless of their lack of Gaelic abilities, Fraser (1989: 266) predicted that this would have crucial implications for its future.

3.1.3 Limitations of GME in Gaelic language revitalisation

Johnstone (2001) has cautioned that there are clear limitations as to what can be expected of L2 immersion education, particularly in classes or units within schools wherein most pupils are taught exclusively through the majority L1, as is often the case with GME. MacCaluim (2007: 15) notes that the development of GME has 'tended to be viewed in a vacuum' by policymakers, without adequate attention at the home–community level. Building on the relatively early identification of problems by researchers in the 1980s and 1990s, research this century has emphasised enduring obstacles while also indicating fresh challenges to the system's further development. For instance, Stockdale et al.'s (2003) study of GME uptake in the Western Isles found that many Gaelic-speaking parents continued to lack confidence in the system, echoing findings from the system's early years (Roberts 1991). Conversely, Müller (2006: 136) found of GME pupil households in Skye, in which both parents spoke Gaelic, that pupils almost always used English with siblings. This section will discuss similar obstacles that have been identified in relation to GME as an instrument of language revitalisation in Scotland.

All three previous iterations of the National Gaelic Language Plan, developed by Bòrd na Gàidhlig (2007, 2012b, 2018) to direct national language policy, focus to a significant degree on the importance of developing GME as a means of maintaining and revitalising the language. Crucially, however, the Council of Europe's (2014: 35) Committee of Experts stated of Gaelic education, in its most recent report in respect of the European Charter for Regional or Minority Languages, that the position of the language 'remains fragile', especially with regard to the shortage of teachers, materials and buildings. The 2012–17 National Plan emphasised its aims for primary GME in terms of 'doubling the current annual intake to 800 by 2017', as well as targeting 'an expansion in the availability of Gaelic-medium subjects in secondary schools', and pledged to target resources to address ongoing staffing problems (Bòrd na Gàidhlig 2012b: 22–3).

Yet the obstacles these policies were designed to address are by no means new; a chronic shortage in staffing and the inability to train sufficient numbers of qualified Gaelic-medium teachers have been described as 'greatest single obstacle' to the survival of the system in the early years of this century (Dunbar 2006: 5; see also Nic a' Bhàird 2007; Pollock 2010). MacKinnon (2005: 30) states that teacher recruitment problems impeded the growth of GME in its first fifteen years, with the initial impetus having levelled off by the end of the 1990s (see Table 3.1, above). Highlighting the enduring scale of this issue, problems in respect of understaffing and a shortage of teaching materials were also highlighted in Landgraf's (2013) investigation of obstacles and strengths in GME.

The 1993 Gaelic 5–14 Curriculum guidelines stated that schools providing primary GME should ensure 'the development of all the language skills in both languages by the end of P7' (Scottish Office Education Department 1993: 6). This guidance allowed for considerable flexibility in teaching practice, and MacNeil (1994), O'Hanlon (2010) and O'Hanlon et al. (2012) each demonstrated a great deal of diversity in observed teaching practices in GME classrooms. In this regard, HMIE (2011: 6) recommended that national guidance be made available advising of best practice in the delivery of GME by teachers. Meanwhile, studies by MacLeod (2009) and Pollock (2010) suggested that the linguistic competences of teachers, particularly those who learn Gaelic as an L2, may have negative consequences for children's language development and for the transmission of idiomatically rich Gaelic in GME.

Four recent studies in particular have documented limitations in GME students' language acquisition and linguistic production. Landgraf (2013) and Macleod et al. (2014) observed systematic shortcomings in the Gaelic language abilities of current GME pupils, particularly among learners with no home background in Gaelic. Doctoral research by Will (2012) and Nance (2013) also identified the shortage of opportunities for primary pupils to use Gaelic outside of the classroom as a potential shortcoming in terms of developing pupils' competences.

In a short conference paper, MacMillan (2012) reported that former GME students enrolled on undergraduate Gaelic courses at Glasgow University consistently produced grammatical errors and atypical usages in their spoken and written Gaelic. Crucially in this regard, Stradling and MacNeil (2000: 23) suggested that home exposure to Gaelic tended to correlate with higher abilities in the language among primary GME pupils. Cochran (2008: 122), however, found that a slight majority of GME pupils in her study reported using little or no Gaelic in the home, concluding that even Gaelic-speaking parents' choice of GME for their children does not necessarily imply that they will use the minority language.

The crucial importance of language use outside the school to Gaelic language acquisition rates in GME is a recurring theme in research findings. For instance, O'Hanlon's PhD research (2012: 207) found primary and secondary GME pupils' use of Gaelic both within and outside of the classroom to be significantly lower than their Welsh-medium counterparts' use of Welsh. Landgraf (2013) suggested that whilst only a very small group of primary GME students in her survey could realistically be classed as fluent Gaelic speakers, all of these came from backgrounds in which the language is used at home. Even among students with this background, however, Will's (2012) research among GME pupils in the Western Isles found low levels of Gaelic language socialisation at home and in school. Identifying a 'communicative impasse' between primary GME pupils and adult speakers of the language in the Lewis community she studied, Will (2012: 222) argues that whereas GME is increasingly the principal site of Gaelic language socialisation for children in these areas, older traditional speakers tend to believe that the variety of Gaelic that they acquire is too different from their own to attempt conversation with them.

Cochran (2008: 74–5) noted that positive language attitudes 'co-existing with patterns of falling use' was a common theme in much research on young speakers of Gaelic. Indeed, Morrison's (2006a, 2006b) research in the Western Isles similarly found that whilst a large proportion of GME students viewed learning the language as something that was valuable for job opportunities and reasons of identity, their Gaelic use outside of school was weak. Therefore, whilst the impact of GME on students' language attitudes may be seen as a relatively positive development, this in itself appears insufficient to promote actual language maintenance. On this point, McLeod et al. (2010) suggest that GME is extremely unlikely to succeed in creating new generations of speakers unless it is accompanied by a range of targeted strategies at the community level. While GME may indeed have a role to play in realising the wider goals of Gaelic language revitalisation in Scotland, it seems clear from a wealth of evidence that the system will not succeed in this regard without a significant social stimulus within the home–community domain generally (see also MacCaluim 2007; MacLeod 2009).

The relative lack of continuity between primary and secondary levels – both in the past and today – is thought to present a further serious challenge to the success of GME in revitalising Gaelic (McLeod 2003; O'Hanlon 2012). In the few schools where it is available at secondary school at all currently, GME is not generally offered in subjects other than Gaelic, and where it is, options are usually restricted to subjects such as History, Geography or Religious Studies (Her Majesty's Inspectorate of Education 2011; Scottish Government 2011; Bòrd na Gàidhlig 2012a). Overwhelmingly, during the period in question for the present investigation, the first cohorts of pupils left primary GME without the opportunity to continue their bilingual education in subjects other than Gaelic itself (MacKinnon 2005).

Discontinuity in the provision of GME after primary school, in contrast to relatively well-developed secondary provision in contexts such as Wales and Ireland, therefore have crucial implications for the considerations of the present monograph. O'Hanlon (2012: 7) argues that the dearth of continuity in GME provision when the first primary GME cohorts were progressing in the 1990s was due partly to a lack of political will to provide secondary level GME. Crucially, this was demonstrated in a 1994 statement from Her Majesty's Inspectorate of Schools to the effect that 'the provision of Gaelic-medium secondary education in a number of subjects, determined by the vagaries of resource availability . . . is neither desirable nor feasible in the foreseeable future' (Scottish Office Education Department 1994: 3).

In terms of parental motivations, Johnstone (2001) noted that many parents who enrol their children in secondary GME have a strong sense of Gaelic's importance for heritage and identity even if they do not speak the language themselves, a finding also reported by Fraser (1989), V. MacGregor (2009) and O'Hanlon et al. (2010). Trabelsi (1998) and MacNeil and Stradling (2000: 9) both reported low levels of Gaelic use by secondary GME pupils, especially in contexts lacking the authoritative support of Gaelic-speaking teachers or parents, such as within English-medium classes, in the playground or outside of school. Both studies suggested that a more thorough engagement with Gaelic, built upon a strong identification in and with the language, would be required to bolster GME students' use of the language outside of the classroom.

Yet participants in Trabelsi's study often expressed ambivalent attitudes towards the relevance of Gaelic in Glasgow, their local area. Oliver (2002) found that the language often retained a degree of salience in the local and regional identity claims of Skye secondary pupils, as well as in the wider, national identity constructions of pupils in the Glasgow and Skye schools he researched. Oliver (2005, 2006, 2010) conceptualised these two levels of identification with Gaelic in terms of *Gemeinschaft* ('intimate community') and *Gesellschaft* ('impersonal society'), building on Fishman's (1991: 6) emphasis on the vital importance of the former to RLS initiatives.

By comparison, it is notable that pupils' identification with the label 'Gael' (/*Gàidheal*), or with the bounded, quasi-ethnic associations of that word, was much weaker in Oliver's (2002) study (see also Macdonald 1997). The symbolic significance attached to the language by former primary GME pupils in the identity constructions they made was a key finding of his investigation. Limited identification with the label 'Gael' among GME pupils, as reported in both Oliver (2002) and Cochran's (2008) research, has further implications for the applicability of Fishman's models of language and identity to Scotland. MacLeod (2009: 236) notes that lasting 'language loyalty' – the commitment to use and maintain a language like Gaelic through life – often relies on a belief 'that a language embodies, or symbolises, part of their personal or ethnic identity' (see also Dorian 1981).

Müller's (2006) study of secondary pupils in Skye and Lochalsh (including eighty-four GME students), Morrison's (2006a) research into the secondary pupils in the Western Isles and MacKenzie's (2013) study of former GME students' identities all reflected a strong sense of the language's symbolic importance in Scottish identity independently of its use as a communicative medium (see also Macdonald 1997; McEwan-Fujita 2003). Similarly, Oliver (2002: 168) emphasised generally low levels of Gaelic use by former primary GME students outside of the Gaelic classroom in both Skye and Glasgow, particularly with peers and friends. An 'iconic' association with Gaelic as a symbol of identity by pupils (see Irvine and Gal 2000; Bucholtz and Hall 2004; Edwards 2010a) may, therefore, be insufficient to promote the type of language loyalty to which MacLeod (2009) and Dorian (1981) refer.

Research findings in relation to the declining use of Gaelic by secondary pupils offer a riposte to HMIE's 1994 statement that the study of Gaelic as a subject at secondary level would be sufficient to bolster and 'extend' pupils' language abilities, and to develop their 'self-confidence as Gaelic speakers' (Scottish Office Education Department 1994: 3). Eleven years after the 1994 report, HMIE (2005: 36) stated that Gaelic-medium provision at secondary school was 'insufficient to maintain and develop fluency in a range of domains'. Building on a research literature dating from the first two decades of GME (Fraser 1989; Trabelsi 1998; Oliver 2002), however, a wealth of recent research on GME (Pollock 2010; O'Hanlon 2012; Will 2012; Landgraf 2013; MacKenzie 2013) has suggested the potential shortcomings the system may have in terms of former students' potential engagement with Gaelic after completing school. The continuing limitations of GME in changing the linguistic habits of students outside of the classroom, and, in turn, in revitalising Gaelic, have been widely documented in the literature.

3.1.4 Concluding remarks on GME as education system and research site

MacLeod (2009: 228) noted that in spite of a growing literature on GME, 'there has not been much critical analysis ... of its impact as yet'. Indeed, this seems true of bilingual and immersion education outcomes internationally; in Scotland, disparities between parents' and policymakers' expectations of GME and their experiences of the system were identified in the first decade of its availability (sections 3.1.1 to 3.1.2; Fraser 1989; Trabelsi 1998). Later research (discussed in section 3.1.3) demonstrated the complexity of GME pupils' identities in relation to Gaelic (Oliver 2002), as well as the limited impact this social dimension appeared to have on their actual use of the language (Morrison 2006a, 2006b; Müller 2006; Cochran 2008). Subsequent researchers highlighted enduring problems in the system in relation to creating functionally bilingual students who are likely to continue to use the language after school (Landgraf 2013; O'Hanlon 2010, 2012; Pollock 2010; Will 2012; Macleod et al. 2014). Nevertheless, the reality of past pupils' engagement with Gaelic in adulthood, several years after completing formal education, has not as yet been assessed in any detail.

The emphasis that policymakers continue to place on GME for the revitalisation of Gaelic in Scotland (see Bòrd na Gàidhlig 2012b, 2017, 2018) poses important questions about actual outcomes of the system among adults who received their education through it. In this connection, D. J. MacLeod stated ten years ago that:

> The oldest of the new generation of Gaelic speakers which has been created (in the main) by GME are now approaching 30 years of age . . . . The main evidence that the GME-led Gaelic revival has 'taken' will be that their children are raised as mother tongue Gaelic speakers. (MacLeod 2009: 242)

By and large, it is still too early to answer this particular question, though as I shall explain in the following chapters, participants' current patterns of Gaelic language use shed important light on the matter, and current prospects for the intergenerational transmission of Gaelic by past GME students may appear limited.

3.2 GME in its first decade: Sample design and analysis

This section firstly describes the methods and procedures adopted to define and contact the informant pool for the present research (section 3.2.1), and reflects on the response rates to the various approaches adopted to elicit the datasets. Section 3.2.2 outlines the quantitative methods used to analyse questionnaire responses, while section 3.2.3 explains the ways in which qualitative data were collected through semi-structured interviews, and provides an overview of the interview schedule I employed to structure interactions with interview participants. The discussion provided in this section frames the overall data corpus and sets up the following discussion of methods adopted to analyse the qualitative data, drawing in particular on frameworks employed in linguistic anthropology and sociolinguistics (section 3.3, below).

3.2.1 Defining the informant universe

As discussed in section 3.1, above, GME developed from two units in Glasgow and Inverness in 1985 and grew rapidly throughout the late 1980s and early 1990s. The system's growth during this period is shown in Table 3.2 (MacKinnon 2005). In a sense, this table delimits the maximum potential 'universe' of research participants for the present study, showing the total numbers of GME pupils in primary education during the first decade of the system's availability. As may be seen, the total number of individuals in this potential universe is relatively small, particularly those who started in GME during the 1980s (N=286). The initial 24 GME pupils who started in 1985/6 were joined by a further 40 in 1986, followed by another 48 in 1987, 57 in 1988 and 117 in 1989. Over the next five years, total numbers of pupils increased by 145, 183, 229, 246 and 178, respectively; as such, there exists a much larger pool of potential informants now in their early twenties than the pool of potential informants in their late twenties and thirties. It was nevertheless important to include in the survey as many informants at the upper end of this age range as possible, in order to capture the fullest spectrum of experiences across the first ten years of GME.

Potential participants' places of origin are diffuse in the universe delineated in Table 3.2. Alongside the three council areas of Argyll and Bute, Eileanan Siar (the Western Isles) and Highland, the 'Rest of Scotland' category includes GME pupils in the urban Central Belt, north-eastern Scotland, and peripheral Highland areas outside these three councils. In light of these considerations, a purposive sampling method was used to access potential participants. Qualitative research using criteria-based, purposive sampling aims to achieve representation of the informant pool by including a diverse range of individual experiences and characteristics within the dataset (Ritchie et al. 2003).

As a first step, a database of potential respondents was compiled from existing acquaintances of mine, and maintained as a spreadsheet whilst a 'snowball' method

Table 3.2 Primary pupils in GME 1985–95 (MacKinnon 2005)

Academic year/Area	85/86	86/87	87/88	88/89	89/90	90/91	91/92	92/93	93/94	94/95
Argyll and Bute	n/a	n/a	4	8	14	26	36	47	57	54
Comhairle nan Eilean Siar	n/a	4	19	20	51	107	189	272	365	457
Highland Council	12	31	44	75	127	178	234	328	425	472
Rest of Scotland	12	29	44	66	94	120	155	187	233	275
Total	24	64	111	169	286	431	614	834	1,080	1,258
Age: 31/6/2012	*31–2*	*30+*	*29+*	*28+*	*27+*	*26+*	*25+*	*24+*	*23+*	*22+*

was employed to gather additional names. An online questionnaire was designed to survey former Gaelic-medium students' reported language abilities, use and attitudes, which was piloted before a final draft was uploaded. Gaelic and English versions of the questionnaire were designed, and bilingual invitations to the corresponding web links were subsequently dispatched to potential respondents via email and social media, with participants offered the choice of completing the questionnaire in whichever language (Gaelic or English) they felt more comfortable with.

Potential questionnaire and interview participants were contacted systematically by various means and a catalogue of 210 individuals was eventually collated. I made use of both conventional and new media in order to access potential respondents, using direct messages via email and Facebook, targeted social media advertisements, and letters to editors of local newspapers, as well as a television and radio interview. Bilingual 'retweets' of a shortened participant invitation with links to the questionnaire and searchable hashtags #gaelic, #gàidhlig, #GME and #FMG [Foghlam Meadhan Gàidhlig, meaning Gaelic-medium education] were also forwarded to a wider audience on Twitter by several other user accounts. Letters posted to editors of five local newspapers in the areas where GME was first established each contained the same invitation to participate that I distributed elsewhere. Finally, an interview I arranged with a BBC journalist in May 2012 was subsequently broadcast on Radio nan Gàidheal's *Aithris na Maidne* ('The Morning Report'), as well as the evening news programme *An Là* ('The Day') on television channel BBC Alba (with a subsequent article on the BBC news website).

Through this multi-platform approach to accessing the informant pool, it is likely that dozens of other potential informants, in addition to the 210 I contacted personally, received information about the research and were provided with my contact details. Potential respondents were also requested to forward this invitation to any schoolmates (and other relevant contacts with whom they were in touch) via email, Facebook and other social media. In addition to the purposive 'snowball' method I employed, a further 117 invitations were distributed to former GME students by an acquaintance of mine who was involved in the organisation of GME during the early years of its availability, and who has been employed in the Gaelic education sector since then.

A total of 112 questionnaire responses were elicited, representing a response rate of 53.3% to the 210 invitations I distributed personally. This response rate would be smaller if the additional 117 invitations are factored into this total, though there may well have been some overlap between the two groups. If we assume that a total of 327 personalised invitations were received, the questionnaire response rate would be 34.3%. I also conducted and recorded 45 interviews with 46 participants, representing a response rate of 21.9% to the 210 invitations I sent, or 14.1% to the putative total of 327. Although all 46 interview participants were invited to complete the questionnaire, only 28 (60.9%) in fact did so; 25% of all 112 questionnaire participants were also interviewed, therefore. Thus the total sample size using both analyses was 130.

3.2.2 Questionnaire design and analysis

The online questionnaire contained thirty questions, spread over three overarching sections on social background, language use and ability, and language attitudes. The questionnaire design drew broadly on the Euromosaic (MacKinnon 1994) and Welsh language use surveys (Welsh Language Board 2008), and was also partly informed by Dorian's (1981) questionnaire on language attitudes as part of her research on East Sutherland Gaelic. In the first section of the online form, questions were asked about the date of birth, sex, occupation, current location and home town of participants, as well as their continuation with GME beyond primary school, and with the study of Gaelic generally. Additional questions in this section were asked on participants' further and higher education attendance, the proportions of languages that were used in their childhood homes and surrounding communities, and change in relation to Gaelic language practices and skills since leaving school. In addition to the social variables of age, sex and occupational class, therefore, data were elicited in the first portion of the questionnaire on the social geography and linguistic socialisation of informants during childhood, including their continuation with GME after primary school. These variables are examined in relation to language use, abilities and attitudes in Chapter 4.

The second section of the questionnaire asked participants to report their abilities in English as well as Gaelic, in order to facilitate a comparison of professed abilities in relation to reading, writing, speaking and understanding both languages. Respondents were next asked to quantify the overall frequency of their Gaelic language use at present, to identify which members of their immediate family were able to speak Gaelic, and to indicate the relative proportions of Gaelic and English that they currently use at work or university, at home, and in interactions with close family and friends. Lastly in this section, informants were asked to indicate what languages they use in the pursuit of leisure activities and when socialising, taking account also of their language practices in relation to internet and social media use. Respondents were next invited to indicate their principal national identities, and to respond to eighteen attitudinal statements using a five-level level Likert scale ('Strongly agree'/'Agree'/'Neither agree nor disagree'/'Disagree'/'Strongly disagree'). These eighteen propositions concerned the place of Gaelic in Scottish society, its relevance to personal and cultural identity, the Gaelic community, and the role of GME in revitalisation efforts generally. Finally, questionnaire respondents were invited at the end of the form to provide any comments they wished, providing a body of qualitative data to supplement the principal datasets.

In order to investigate and quantify the relationships between the different variables discussed in the preceding paragraphs, analysis using the correlational statistical test Spearman's rho was conducted on the dataset using appropriate software. In light of the self-selected, purposive sample analysed in this book, establishing causality in the relations of these variables to one another was not an objective. Additionally, the non-parametric ranks used on the questionnaire form to elicit responses to questions on social background, language use, abilities and attitudes made the dataset unsuitable for analysis using parametric correlational tests such as the Pearson product-moment correlation.

Spearman's rank order correlation co-efficient (referred to as 'Spearman's rho') was used to examine relationships between the ranked social and linguistic variables. This test calculates a value (ρ, or 'rho') to represent the correlation between two ranked sets of data, and is therefore used to investigate the relationships between different variables in the questionnaire dataset. Again, since self-selection bias was a clear factor in the elicitation of responses to the questionnaire, the results of this test are not discussed in relation to statistical significance. Rather, particularly noteworthy correlations in Chapter 4 are displayed in bold typeface within tables and discussed in light of what they may indicate.

3.2.3 Ethnographic interviews in the 'field'

Over the data collection period I travelled throughout Scotland, conducting face-to-face interviews that I arranged with informants beforehand. I personally met 22 interview participants at locations in the urban Lowlands, mainland Highlands, islands in the Inner and Outer Hebrides, and in England. Skype and telephone interviews were used for informants based farther afield (such as North America), however, or when informants themselves indicated a preference for this option; 24 interviews were recorded in this way. Digital recordings of the 45 interviews (with 46 participants) constitute a corpus of over twenty hours of speech, corresponding to some 24,000 lines of text and just under 240,000 words. This corpus was transcribed in full according to conventions that will be discussed below (sections 3.3.2 to 3.3.3). At each stage of the data collection process I was keenly aware of my own agency in interaction, as both interlocutor and research instrument, and the ways in which I might influence informants' responses in these capacities.

The location of our meeting was left to the discretion of the interviewee and arranged before we met. The 21 face-to-face interviews I conducted were generally conducted either in cafes or in participants' places of work during their lunch hour. In two instances, interviews were carried out in participants' homes. Generally speaking, most interviews lasted for approximately half an hour; the mean duration is 27 minutes 42 seconds. The language in which the interview was conducted was also directed principally by the preference of the informant before we met, although linguistic negotiation and code-switching often occurred. Some 25 speakers (54%) chose English as the medium of interaction for the interview, while 21 chose Gaelic (46%). It is noteworthy in this regard, however, that the 25 interviewees who chose English overwhelmingly used only English in the interview, whereas the 21 interviewees who chose Gaelic tended to alternate their language use (although to different degrees; see section 4.1, below). Verbal consent for the recording and analysis of the interview material was obtained from each informant at the start of every interview.

Of the 46 interviewees, 12 reported growing up in the mainland Highlands, 17 were raised in island communities (10 of whom came from the Western Isles), and another 17 came from communities in the urban Lowlands. A total of 31 interviewees were female (67%) and 15 male (33%). In the interview excerpts presented in the following two analytic chapters, informants are identified by a unique code signifying place of origin ('H' denoting Highlands, 'L' Lowlands and 'I' islands), gender ('M/F') and a number, reflecting the order in which interviews were collected. HM04 therefore corresponds to the fourth male informant from the mainland Highlands, IF05 the fifth female interviewed from the islands, and LM01 the first Lowland male.

Although I employed a broad interview schedule to facilitate and direct the semi-structured interviews, interviews did not necessarily develop in the exact order expected, nor did all participants provide equal amounts of detail when responding to my questions. Nevertheless, several possible topics were included in the schedule as a rough guide to direct the interview, while interaction was allowed to unfold and develop as naturally as possible. Interviewees were encouraged to elaborate on any aspects of their relationship to the Gaelic language that they felt strongly about, as well as being prompted in relation to matters in which they provided more guarded or circumspect responses. The degree to which the structure contained within the schedule was adhered to varied depending on the manner in which interaction unfolded in the interview, with certain informants needing more questions and prompting than others. I use the term 'semi-structured' to refer to the method by which the interviews were collected, an approach that provided a large amount of data for analysis, and I describe in the following section the principal methods that I adopted to this end.

3.3 Analytic methods

This section will briefly outline the research methods adopted to investigate the primary research questions identified in previous chapters. I firstly discuss the analytic approach taken toward qualitative data from the interview corpus, drawing on approaches taken to investigating language use, ideologies and identities. The method of transcription, qualitative analysis and the methodological frameworks adopted will be described and explained in relation to the data.

3.3.1 Research design: Mixed methods and data triangulation

The methodological foundations of the study outlined here are based on the notions of mixed methods and data triangulation in social research. Various scholars have emphasised the importance of multiple approaches in studies of language, culture and identity (Ricento 2006; Saville-Troike 2003) in order to obtain the most valid results possible. Data triangulation, or the empirical examination of one source of information against another to validate hypotheses, is commonly employed by ethnographers using multiple methods to focus in on a particular issue (Fetterman 1998: 93). Researchers adopting this approach may thus generate hypotheses from qualitative data through the continuous analysis of data rather than positing a priori theories (Glaser and Strauss 1967) whilst simultaneously cross-checking these against quantitative findings to minimise erroneous interpretations.

A mixed methodological approach has been strongly and consistently advocated by researchers in sociolinguistics and the sociology of language as a means of minimising margins of error, inasmuch as this is possible (see, for example, Baker 2006: 213; Canagarajah 2006: 154; Edwards 2010a: 66; Fishman 2010: xxx). Whilst, on the one hand, Pauwels (2004: 723) notes that questionnaires have been a prominent tool in linguistic research on language maintenance, Baker (1992: 19) cautions against an over-reliance on quantitative approaches, suggesting that respondents may tend in such surveys – whether consciously or unconsciously – to provide answers they perceive to be better or more desirable in the investigator's eyes, whilst answers and opinions elicited are often poorly contextualised, leaving findings open to misinterpretation (Baker 2006: 223–4). On the other hand, the limited generalisability and validity that in-depth but small-scale qualitative surveys may allow has similarly been critiqued by certain scholars (Hamel et al. 1993; Yin 2009).

As such, whilst employing a quantitative survey to ensure data triangulation, the semi-structured interview forms the principal method used to investigate the manner of informants' linguistic engagement with Gaelic, their language ideologies in relation to it, and the ways in which their ethnocultural identities may relate to these issues. Laihonen (2008: 670) notes that the study of language ideologies draws largely upon the interpretation in speech of either metalinguistic (language about language) or metapragmatic (language about language use) discourses. Much of the qualitative data analysed in Chapters 4 and 5 draw on metalinguistic and metapragmatic discourse of this kind, and this study makes particular use of Hymes's (1974) ethnography of speaking, discussed in greater detail below (section 3.3.2).

A fully ethnographic methodology was deemed impractical for the purposes of the present study, informants for which are dispersed widely throughout and beyond Scotland. As Forsey (2010: 566) notes, spending extended periods conducting participant observation with informants in developed, urban contexts is often impractical in the contemporary world (see also Fetterman 1998). Instead, semi-structured and ethnographically oriented interviews constitute the principal qualitative research tool utilised for generating insights into the complex issues of language use, ideologies and identities. These issues will be critical to understanding the role that Gaelic plays in informants' day-to-day lives and past socialisation experiences, and in turn, to prospects for the intergenerational transmission and long-term survival of the language.

3.3.2 Analysing language and culture in interaction: The ethnography of speaking

The present study employs a combination of content-based, thematic analysis (Silverman 2006) drawing on Glaser and Strauss's (1967) 'grounded theory', together with Hymes's (1974) ethnography of speaking to analyse the qualitative dataset. This approach is also known within linguistics, anthropology and the sociology of language as the 'ethnography of communication', in order to account for research conducted on non-spoken and sign languages in this area (Saville-Troike 2003). While Glaser and Strass's (1967) work was extremely influential in the development of the qualitative research methods within the social sciences, Hymes's (1974) ideas have had significant consequences in the orientation and development of interactional sociolinguistics and linguistic anthropology. Researchers using qualitative methodologies often characterise the research interview as distinct from naturally occurring conversation, though the constructivist understanding that both interviewers and interviewees construct meaning emphasises the centrality of social interaction to the interpretation of interview data (Gubrium and Holstein 2002: 14; Silverman 2006: 118). Under such a conception the researcher seeks an emic perspective on the culture in question, whilst acknowledging that their own positionality may influence this (Lazaraton 2003; Ewing 2006; Warren 2002).

A reflexive approach to analysing interactional data of this kind, taking account of the researcher's agency and influence, is therefore of considerable import to the analytic process (Canagarajah 2006; Ricento 2006; Talmy 2010). Rather than relying on 'decontextualized, stand-alone quotes of respondents' answers', it is argued that analyses should treat the research interview as a social practice in its own right, with data jointly produced by the informant and researcher (Talmy 2010: 136). Researchers employing methodologies informed by grounded theory pay attention to these concerns at the data collection and transcription stages, as well as during the coding and notation stages of the analysis proper (Charmaz 2002; Glaser and Strauss 1967; Lazaraton 2003). As I hope to demonstrate in this section, however, analytic principles that pay attention particularly to instrumentalities, or how language is used to deliver content, can also be profitably applied to more content-based analyses of discourse (Ewing 2006; Hymes 1974). These wider analytic principles – considering both the form and the content of spoken language – are integrated into the transcription and analysis presented in this book with particular reference to Hymes's influential (1974) 'ethnography of speaking' framework.

Duranti (1997: 8) has stated that ethnographers of language need 'the instruments to first hear and then listen carefully to what people are saying . . . [and then] to learn and understand what the participants in the interactions we study are up to, what counts as meaningful for them'. In this sense, it was necessary to adopt what Hammersley and Atkinson (2007: 230) describe as an ethnographic mentality: a 'particular mode of looking, listening and thinking' that avoids formulating hypotheses prematurely, and seeks instead to understand informants' perspectives on the issues in question (see also Warren 2002: 98). Cameron (2001: 54) describes the 'ethnography of speaking' as the application of ethnographic methods of this kind specifically to language use in its sociocultural context. The sociolinguist and anthropologist Dell Hymes developed his analytic model having advocated, over the course of his career, a much greater emphasis in those fields on performance and 'communicative competence', focusing specifically on interactional norms and rules of speaking.

Hymes (1974: 119) described bilingual education as 'a sociolinguistic subject par excellence', in so far as a central goal of education generally is to aid in the development of children's 'creative use of language as part of successful adaptation of themselves'. In order to investigate such considerations adequately, Hymes (1974: 4) argued that it is necessary to 'take as context a community, or network of persons, investigating its communicative activities as a whole'. A central premise in the ethnography of speaking is the conceptualisation of spoken interaction in terms of the speech situation, speech event and, at the most minute level of analysis, the speech act (Hymes 1974: 52).

A speech situation, firstly, can be understood as the type of interaction a particular setting represents; overwhelmingly, in my own dataset, the speech situation analysed is that of the semi-structured interview. Nevertheless, interviews conducted in person, via the telephone or online via Skype, each represent distinct kinds of speech situation. At the next level down, the speech event encompasses different kinds of interactive process: for example, questions, answers, stories or jokes. At the most fundamental level, the speech act – seen as 'distinct from the level of the sentence' – constitutes actions such as greeting, apologising or saying goodbye (Hymes 1974: 52). By focusing on these three levels of analysis, Saville-Troike (2003: 3) explains, Hymes emphasised that what constitutes a language 'cannot be separated from how and why it is used' in practice (see also Schiffrin 1996; Makoni and Pennycook 2007; García 2009).

A further central tenet of the ethnography of speaking holds that 'message form and message content . . . often cannot be separated in description and analysis' (Saville-Troike 2003: 120). Meaning is derived not only from the content of verbal and non-verbal production, but also from the paralinguistic content of speech in interaction. Analysis within the ethnography of speaking framework may pay particular attention to such (interrelated) phenomena as code-switching or the interrelationship of language and identity. In the context of my own interviews, code-switching may reflect a real lexical need (and lack of vocabulary) on the interviewee's part, but in other places it may be understood instead to signify processes of greater social significance. Language alternations of this kind may well in fact reflect particular ideological positions in interaction, as I discuss in greater detail in Chapter 5. Code-switching and linguistic mixing may also reflect the construction and negotiation of new, hybrid and dynamic identities (see Oliver 2002, 2006; Dunmore and Smith-Christmas 2015).

The use or disuse of a particular language variety by individuals with a (more or less) bilingual repertoire can be affected by the significance that language is ascribed as a marker of a desirable or stigmatised social identity. For instance, speakers in my own interview corpus sometimes make use of Scots forms in English-medium interviews, possibly to emphasise aspects of their (Lowland) Scottish identity. Similarly in interviews carried out mostly in Gaelic, speakers would often switch to English to emphasise their bilingual ability and identity, particularly when discussing aspects of the Gaelic community they view as undesirable (see section 5.1, below). In order to account for such diverse considerations, beyond the mere content of speech, Hymes (1974) introduced the mnemonic SPEAKING for the analysis of interaction within the ethnography of speaking. This abbreviation signifies a typology that lays out the contextual features to which analysts may choose to pay attention.

'S' refers to the 'setting' and 'scene' of an interaction. Hymes (1974: 55–6) distinguishes setting, which 'refers to the time and place of a speech act and, in general, to the physical circumstances', from scene, which constitutes the 'psychological setting' or 'cultural definition' of a physical scene. 'P' denotes the 'participants' in a particular speech situation: that is to say, the speaker/sender/addressor, as well as the hearer/receiver/audience/addressee. 'E' signifies the 'ends' of a particular speech event, defined by Hymes (1974: 56) as the '[c]onventionally recognized and expected outcomes' of such an event. Generally, my questions, prompts and suggestions were recognised by informants to require responses, and my own role in this regard will be important for the analysis of interviews. 'A' is the 'act' sequence, defined as the form and content or order of the event. 'K' denotes 'key'; the context-based clues that can be utilised in order to establish the 'tone, manner, or spirit' in which a speech act is intended (Hymes 1974: 57). Pauses, sighs, laughs, politeness cues and emphasis may all provide the key to a particular speech act. Hymes (1974: 58) clarifies that when the key is recognised to be 'in conflict with the overt content of an act, it often overrides the latter', as can be inferred from sarcasm, for example. Laughter may denote various manners of delivery, including nervousness and uncertainty, in addition to humour, and it will be crucial to take account of this in analysing data from interviews.

'I' refers to the 'instrumentalities', or 'channels and forms of speech' that participants make use of in producing speech acts (Hymes 1974: 60). Such considerations pertain to the linguistic resources, in terms of languages, varieties and dialects – as well as alternation between these resources and the use of code-switching – that participants may utilise in the speech situation. As well as Gaelic and English forms, it is notable that interviewees sometimes make use of Scots forms when conveying their ideas and beliefs about Gaelic in the qualitative dataset, and these were transcribed accordingly. 'N' signifies the 'norms' of interpretation of a particular speech act and event, including the social rules that govern the actions and reactions to a certain speech event in a particular community. Lastly, 'G' refers to the 'genre', or type of speech act or event. Such an event may, for example, constitute a poem, story or saying, either for entertainment or for illustration of a point of instruction (Hymes 1974: 61).

Attending to considerations such as these, which contextualise the content of speech produced in interactional settings such as the research interview, considerably enrich the qualitative analysis. Various transcription conventions have been used to reflect the criteria encapsulated in Hymes's SPEAKING mnemonic, especially keys to the tone or attitude of a particular speech act, and the use of sociolinguistic norms and instrumentalities by interviewees, which may further reveal information of social significance not apparent in the content of utterances alone.

3.3.3 Transcription: Approach and application

In general terms, the principal aim of transcription is to reflect in visual form the content of the primary data source: that is to say, the audial recording of interaction itself. Deborah Cameron (2001: 33) makes the crucial point that writing in its usual forms 'is not a direct representation of speech', but often an idealised model of language, which thereby influences speakers' perceptions of what a particular language – and language generally – ought to be. She argues that the written model of language can affect the ways in which qualitative researchers analyse our data, and has the potential to influence our interpretation. Whilst it may suffice – or even be preferable – in certain instances, to use standard written conventions and punctuation to represent speech, such as when analytic attention is focused purely at the content level of interpretation, Cameron (2001: 37) observes that the meaning of spoken data 'may lie in prosodic and paralinguistic features as much as in words'. As noted by Hymes (1974: 58), the context of an utterance and the manner in which it is articulated can be equally as important as the semantics of its content in interpreting qualitative data. All (spoken) language users make use of features such as pitch, stress, volume and voice quality to communicate their meaning and provide keys to its interpretation (Hymes 1974; Silverman 2006).

Eleanor Ochs (1979) noted some of the difficulties that researchers face in separating norms of written language when applying transcribed representations to real speech,

…and attempting to reflect non-verbal cues accurately that enrich our understanding of the pragmatic meaning of qualitative data. As an aid to researchers attempting to overcome this methodological obstacle, she set out a series of detailed tables describing transcription conventions to represent paralinguistic features to various degrees of complexity, ranging from the use of symbols in the body of the transcript to represent pragmatic cues, to sub- and superscript annotation to describe verbal as well as non-verbal signals (see also Cameron 2001; Poland 2002). For my own transcriptions, a number of conventions from Ochs's (1979) taxonomy were adopted. A key to transcriptions is reproduced below for clarity of comprehension:

[[words]]	Overlapping speech
=	Latched speech; no pause in dialogue
wor- word	Self-interruption
(.)	Perceivable pause (<1 s duration)
(2.4)	Perceivable pause (>1 s duration)
(word)	Uncertain transcription
(x)	Unintelligible
xxx	Personal/place name omitted
/werd/	Atypical usage or grammatical error
((word))	Analyst's comments
wo::	Elongation
<u>word</u>	Emphatic speech
word	Code-switch

English translations of Gaelic extracts are provided in italics directly underneath the speech event depicted. As already indicated, a number of more detailed transcription systems used in research traditions such as Conversation Analysis were avoided for the purposes of this project, and the detail provided in the above conventions was deemed sufficient. As Cameron (2001: 39) observes, 'there is never a point when your transcript becomes the definitive, "full and faithful" representation of your data'. As I hope to demonstrate in the following section, the various conventions adopted to transcribe interviews were chosen to render records suitable for analysis within an 'ethnography of speaking' methodology, which pays analytic attention to both the semantic content of interactional data, and the pragmatic context in which utterances are produced.

3.3.4 Coding and analysis procedure

As outlined above, close attention to both the content and form of transcripts is required to draw out the emerging themes in a corpus of semi-structured interviews, and it is the transliteration of raw qualitative data in transcript form into thematic, codable categories that forms the crux of the qualitative analysis. After performing an initial review of transcripts for general impressions of the dataset, salient and recurrent themes throughout the dataset were subsequently coded by the author, as I identified them through careful and repeated reading of the transcripts. At the conclusion of this complex coding process, four overarching, thematic codes emerged, encompassing the following four categories:

- Language use and ability in the present day;
- Gaelic language socialisation and acquisition at home and school;
- Ideologies of Gaelic language use;
- Ideologies relating to Gaelic revitalisation and sociocultural identities.

The first two of these overarching discursive themes are discussed in Chapter 4, pertaining to informants' varying degrees of engagement with Gaelic, in both the past and the present day, whilst the last two categories are analysed in Chapter 5, which examines the multiplicity and contested nature of language ideologies and attitudes among Gaelic-medium educated adults.

3.4 Concluding remarks

This chapter has presented the empirical and methodological underpinnings of the investigation, discussing the research context of GME in Scotland (section 3.1), listing the advantages of mixed methods and outlining fundamental concepts in interactional sociolinguistic research (3.2), as well as presenting the specific transcription conventions employed in collating and analysing the qualitative dataset with particular reference to Hymes's ethnography of speaking (3.3). In combination with one another, these methods have beneficial application in the following analysis of semi-structured interview data and the quantitative analysis of questionnaire responses in order to triangulate findings from the qualitative analysis.

4

Linguistic Practice, Gaelic Use and Language Socialisation: Findings from Qualitative and Quantitative Analyses

This chapter examines participants' day-to-day use of Gaelic, their past experiences of socialisation in the home, community and educational settings, and the relationship between these factors as demonstrated by qualitative and statistical analysis. I firstly assess the extent to which Gaelic is used at home, at work and socially, as well as the varying ways in which it is used with different interlocutors (section 4.1). This section employs qualitative techniques to examine participants' language use, and to distinguish the various different kinds of Gaelic users in the interview corpus, whether native speaker, semi- or 'new' speaker. As will be demonstrated, only a minority of interview and questionnaire participants reported currently using a substantial amount of Gaelic, presenting a clear challenge to contemporary policy to revitalise Gaelic through GME. To explore possible factors underlying limited use of Gaelic by this group, the following sections address social and attitudinal aspects of interviewees' Gaelic language socialisation in the home–community context (section 4.2), as well as in the formal educational setting (4.3). As will be seen, socialisation in Gaelic outside the classroom appears to be key factor motivating greater use of the language in adulthood.

Finally, in section 4.4 I consider from a statistical perspective the interaction and interrelationship of these linguistic and social factors in promoting or undermining participants' Gaelic language use at present. As I will demonstrate, accounts provided by interviewees in sections 4.2 and 4.3 and by questionnaire respondents in 4.4 contribute to our understanding of social correlates underlying patterns of present-day use discussed in section 4.1, and correlational statistical analysis is employed to quantify the strength and direction of these relationships. The qualitative ethnography of speaking is employed in tandem with statistical analysis of questionnaires to bring an element of triangulation to bear on the analysis.

4.1 Gaelic language practices: Discourses of (dis)use

I draw attention in the first part of this chapter to the varying degrees to which interview participants claim to use the Gaelic language in the present day. As I outline below, three discernible categories of use are apparent in interviewees' accounts (sections 4.1.1 to 4.1.3). I subsequently consider two particular categories of Gaelic use that are frequently reported within the interview corpus (sections 4.1.4 to 4.1.5).

4.1.1 'High' reported use of Gaelic and the role of Gaelic employment

I firstly consider the relatively few interviewees who report high use of Gaelic in their day-to-day lives (10 out of the 46 interviewees). Importantly, interviewees in this category were generally much more inclined to carry out the interview itself through Gaelic than interviewees in other categories, all ten speakers opting to do so. Interviewees in this group generally reported high levels of Gaelic language use at work, with some additionally reporting high social use, as in the following extract from an interview with a Gaelic professional who uses the language every day at work:

> HF03   Bidh mi a' cleachdadh [Gàidhlig] co-dhiù a h-uile latha em agus fiù 's Disathairne is Latha na Sàbaid- bidh mi ga cleachdadh gach latha obrach em co-dhiù (.) agus air an deireadh-sheachdain cuideachd
> *I use [Gaelic] at least every day em and even Saturday and Sunday- I use it every working day anyway (.) and at the weekend as well*
> [...]
> SD   Agus a bheil Gàidhlig aig do charaidean as fhaisge?
> *And do your closest friends speak Gaelic?*
> HF03   Aig cuid dhiubh- cuid mhath dhiubh [...] tha mi a' smaointinn-feadhainn a tha ag obair tro mheadhan na Gàidhlig, tha sinn nas buailtiche a bhith a' bruidhinn na Gàidhlig
> *Some of them- a good few of them [...] I think- those that work through the medium of Gaelic, we're more likely to speak Gaelic*

This extract is typical of the ten speakers classified in this first category of high use. Interviewees in this group frequently demonstrated the importance of their working through Gaelic on promoting frequent use of Gaelic. It should be noted, however, that none of the ten speakers in this category reported having children at present so it is not possible to consider rates of transmission by this group from interview accounts. Nevertheless, participation in Gaelic-medium employment or higher education clearly appears to accompany higher levels of day-to-day use of the language, and to increase the number of opportunities to speak the language that are available outside of those more formal contexts (see MacLeod 2008). The availability of work within the Gaelic labour market may therefore be a vital means of continued support for the language after formal schooling is completed. Yet it is likely that only a small proportion of children to have started in GME in its first decade would have gone on to find employment within that labour market (Campbell et al. 2008). It is likely, furthermore, that interviewees in this group were relatively easier to contact than those who had no continued involvement with Gaelic at all. In this sense, the number reflected here should not necessarily be considered as representative of all adults who started GME in the first decade of its availability in Scotland.

4.1.2 Intermediate to limited use: Family and peers?

A slightly larger group of participants reported Gaelic use that can be described as ranging from 'intermediate' to 'limited'; 12 of the 46 interviewees (26.1%) described language use that I have interpreted and categorised in this way. Whilst their reported use of Gaelic is not as frequent or wide-ranging as that of interviewees in the first group, a somewhat meaningful engagement with the language is described nevertheless. Varying degrees of Gaelic use with family members tend to be related by interviewees in this group, whether with parents, partners or siblings. Some interviewees described making limited use of the language with their children, as exemplified in the following extract:

SD	How often would you say that you use Gaelic?
LF01	Em: probably a few times a week, not daily em: and not weekly (.) so in between
SD	Yeah
LF01	So a few times a week cos I'll (.) um do my son's reading with him in Gaelic, and sort of very basic conversation- I wouldn't class that as sort of using Gaelic cos it's not a full conversation but it's still=
SD	=Yeah but it's speaking it isn't it?
LF01	Yeah

Limited use of Gaelic with children in this way clearly has implications for the intergenerational transmission of the language, and for the socialisation of children into certain patterns of language use. Nevertheless, Gaelic is regarded as something that interviewees may use with children, whether in support of GME or at pre-school age. As such, the above extract reflects the language's continued – if relatively limited – importance. Use of Gaelic with one or more parent, as related by the second informant above, is another context frequently mentioned by this group:

1. SD [W]ould you still speak Gaelic with your family- your parents?
2. LM08 Yeah yeah occasionally- not all the time but=
3. SD =Yeah=
4. LM08 =e:m (.) y:eah I try and speak it (.) as much as I can
   [. . .]
5. SD So you use it fairly regularly do you these days?
6. LM08 E:m y:eah well I'd speak it to family yeah [. . .] when I'm home but (.) not really when I'm (.) like- well my friends don't really speak it

7. SD Do you find you use much Gaelic in the course of your work with people- with people- or?
8. IM04 Well:: ((sighs)) not (1.1) not regularly but saying that um certainly a number of people here do speak Gaelic um [. . .] an:d I speak Gaelic outside of here

9.	SD	Mm hmm=
10.	IM04	=with- say with my parents (.) funnily enough not so much with my brother or sister even though they both have fluent Gaelic as well
11.	SD	Right okay
12.	IM04	That's a bit of a weird one

The two above interviewees – both from home backgrounds in which Gaelic was used extensively in childhood – express a degree of doubt when I ask (in lines 5 and 7) about their present use of Gaelic. Informant LM08 indicates this sense of uncertainty by elongating the initial sounds of 'em' and 'yeah' (lines 4 and 6), and IM04 produces a very drawn-out final /l/ in 'well' before pausing to sigh (line 8). Both go on to explain that their parents are generally the principal interlocutors with whom they speak Gaelic in the present day, and informant IM04 even states explicitly that while both his siblings are fluent Gaelic speakers, he does not use the language much when speaking to them. Limited use with peers of a similar age is also described here by informant LM08, whose friends are reported not to speak Gaelic. Use of the language with peers and friends of the same age group is clearly an important context for the considerations of this monograph. An even more crucial context in relation to the maintenance and reproduction to bilingualism relates to Gaelic-medium educated adults' use of Gaelic with partners or spouses, even when such communicative use is possible. For example, the following informant – who uses the language quite frequently at work – reports rather limited use of Gaelic with her husband at present:

1.	IF09	Tha Gàidhlig aig an duine agam- 's ann- thàinig esan à xxx ((Urban Lowland))
		My husband can speak Gaelic- he's from- he came from xxx
2.	SD	Seadh
		Yeah
3.	IF09	Gu xxx is rinn e ceum (.) sin far an do thachair mi ris, ach ged a tha an dithis againn fileanta chan eil sinn a' cleachdadh cus Gàidhlig a-staigh [. . .] ach: mar a thuirt mi bidh nuair a thig pàist'
		To xxx and he did a degree (.) that's where I met him, but although we're both fluent we don't use much Gaelic at home [. . .] but: as I said we will when a baby comes
4.	SD	Bidh (.) [[bidh sin math]
		Yes (.) [[that will be good]
5.	IF09	[[Tha mi dìreach-] tha e annasach (.) oir chan eil mo phàrantan a' cleachdadh Gàidhlig [[ri chèile]
		[[I'm just-] it's strange (.) because my parents don't use Gaelic together
6.	SD	[[Nach eil?]
		[[Don't they?]
7.	IF09	Ach 's e Gàidhlig a th' aca rinne fad na h-ùine- bidh daoine an-còmhnaidh ag ràdh **'that's <u>really</u> weird!'**
		But they speak Gaelic to us all the time- people always say **'that's <u>really</u> weird!'**

This particular extract highlights two important considerations. Firstly, the informant states that while her husband can speak Gaelic, the couple rarely do speak the language to each other at home (turn 3), a situation she relates to her parents' language practices, which mirror their own (turn 5). She switches to English in turn 7 to highlight just how strange a situation this is perceived to be by others. Secondly, the interviewee (who was pregnant when the interview was conducted) states her expectation in turn 3 that she and her husband will use more Gaelic with each other when the child arrives. This intention, whilst clearly a more important and pressing consideration for expecting parents than for individuals speaking theoretically, proved to be quite pervasive in the dataset as a whole and forms part of an ideology of language use, to which I will return in the next chapter.

This second group of interviewees, characterised by intermediate to limited Gaelic language use, therefore vary considerably in their language practices. Beyond the workplace, use of Gaelic with older generations (particularly parents) is often reported as one of the principal settings for language use by interviewees from backgrounds in which the language was used at home. Similarly, the idea that the language should be passed on to the next generation is frequently expressed by this cohort (see section 5.1.2, below, for further discussion). Yet use of Gaelic with peers in the same age group – whether friends, siblings or partners – is reported to be relatively weak. It remains to be seen how successfully the language may be transmitted to future generations by members of this group.

4.1.3 Low use of Gaelic

The final group I discuss here comprises former Gaelic-medium students who claim to use Gaelic only very rarely in the present day. A total of 24 of the 46 interviewees (52.2%) are classed in this group. Passing the language on to children (at present or in the future) is not felt to be a concern by interviewees in this category, in contrast to interviewees in the previous group, who often reflected at least on their wish to transmit Gaelic to the next generation, and of possibly changing their current language practices in order to do so. This general lack of interest in passing on the language is demonstrated by informant LF07 (raised in the Lowlands without Gaelic at home) below:

SD	Your partner doesn't speak Gaelic does he?
LF07	Nope nope
SD	Okay (.) do you speak Gaelic to the baby at the moment or?
LF07	Baby- no I don't I don't=
SD	=Uh huh=
LF07	=My wee brother- he's at the Gaelic [school] so that's the only member of the family that I would speak to now
SD	Right okay [. . .] how would you describe your sort of relationship with Gaelic these days?
LF07	Oh [. . .] not too much <u>now</u> (.) it'd be more like (.) hobby-like

As this interviewee has no familial connection to Gaelic or peers with whom to speak the language (apart from her younger brother, currently in GME), she describes her interest as 'hobby-like'. Yet even as a 'hobby', her engagement with Gaelic is very limited today; her partner does not speak it, and she appears to have little interest in passing the language on to her newborn child. It is apparent that in this case, GME as a context of language socialisation – without the support of Gaelic use at home – has had little impact on the participant's later language use (see section 4.4, below). Yet even where Gaelic language socialisation is reported in the childhood home, continued use of the language should not be assumed:

IF14   [M]y parents are both fluent Gaelic speakers and it was Gaelic that was predominantly spoken in the house [. . .] before I went to school and that- so it was kind of- and it was Gaelic kind of playgroup and nursery and that that I went to [as well so]

SD   [Mm hmm yeah] (.) **a bheil thu cofhurtail gu leòr cumail a' dol sa Bheurla?**
   are you comfortable enough continuing in English?

IF14   A's a' **Bheurla-** tha yeah please! ((laughs))
   In English- yes

SD   No problem that's fine!

IF14   It's- my Gaelic is em- I guess it's kind of like anything when you don't use it very often it kind of em (.) I guess these days the only time I really speak Gaelic is to my grandfather ((laughs)) [. . .] my fiancé doesn't speak Gaelic at all

SD   Does he not no?

IF14   Em: (.) but he's kind of quite keen to- well he under<u>stands</u> it

Having unexpectedly discovered that Gaelic was the language of this speaker's primary socialisation in childhood (her previous email interaction with me having been entirely through English), I switch to Gaelic to ask if she would nevertheless be comfortable conducting the interview in English. She is prompt to reply that she would indeed like to do so, explaining that her use of Gaelic is very limited today. Occasional use with family members is mentioned by some in this group, as in the first of the two extracts below, but a common theme throughout is the lack of Gaelic-speaking friends and peers, and consequently, of any real use of the language socially:

SD   [S]o have you spoken Gaelic much in the last month would you have said?

LM03   E:m a little (.) just as I say sorta sometimes on Skype to my parents

SD   Yeah on the phone to your parents

LM03   But that's about it [. . .] I think in all honesty if I had friends who spoke Gaelic I possibly would do to some extent, em: (.) but it's just a fact of em (.) in terms of back home I don't really have any friends who speak Gaelic e:m these days (.) so

SD   Yeah exactly

LM03   So it's a function of that- it's not something that I use

1. IF13 Are we gonna do it in English?
2. SD Uh **uill 's ann sa Ghàidhlig ma tha thu ag iarraidh?**
 well in Gaelic if you like?
3. IF13 Eh no- to be honest [[I've]
4. SD [[Okay] that's fine yeah
5. IF13 ((laughs)) barely spoken it in the last few years [[which you might want to]
6. SD [[That's absolut-]
7. IF13 include in your research
8. SD Yeah that's absolutely fine
9. IF13 I'm quite **lapach** *('rusty')* [. . .] I ca- I do speak in Gaelic but (1.1) I think I'm quite **lapach** because (.) I don't really have anybody that I speak it to regularly

As in the case of informant IF14, above, this speaker appears anxious in turns 1 and 3 to ensure that the interview will continue in English rather than Gaelic, and replies in English to my attempted code-switch to Gaelic. Ironically, in turn 9 she twice uses Gaelic to describe feeling *lapach* ('faltering', 'lame' – or in this context, approximating to 'rusty') when speaking the language, as she has relatively little contact with other Gaelic speakers today. Uncharacteristically of this group, one informant – who grew up with Gaelic at home in a Gaelic-speaking island community – chose to do the interview entirely in Gaelic. Nevertheless, she reports very low use of Gaelic socially or professionally, or even with her family in the present day. She attributes this pattern of weak use to her tendency to associate the language with her early childhood, and consequently, expresses a certain difficulty in expressing herself through the language as an adult:

SD Dè cho tric mar sin 's a bhios tu a' cleachdadh na Gàidhlig? Air a' fòn agus mar sin?
 So how often do you use Gaelic? On the phone and so on?
IF07 Cha bhi tric idir
 Not often at all
SD Nach bi?
 No?
IF07 Cha bhi tric idir [. . .] tha mi ceangal Gàidhlig gu mòr ri bhith beag- ri bhith òg [. . .] tha e duilich dhomh mi-fhìn a chur an abairt sa Ghàidhlig mar inbheach
 Not often at all [. . .] I really associate Gaelic with being small- with being young [. . .] it's difficult to express myself in Gaelic as an adult

Social use of Gaelic at present is therefore reported to be somewhat fragile across the qualitative dataset, and especially among participants whom I have grouped in the second and third categories discussed here. The relatively few interviewees in the first category (of 'high' use) are a possible exception to this pattern, and such individuals' participation in Gaelic-based employment or postgraduate study seems to encourage their social use of the language outside of these formal domains. Nevertheless, the discourses I have highlighted here as characteristic of the three categories reflect the state of Gaelic language use among the interview cohort as a whole; generally speaking, day-to-day use of Gaelic is limited to contexts such as work and speaking to parents or grandparents, with social interaction and the home environment seemingly dominated by English. Sections 4.1.4 to 4.1.5, below, discuss how certain discourses produced reveal distinctive ways in which the language is now used.

4.1.4 Language practice 1: Gaelic as a 'secret code'

Participants from each of the three categories speak of using Gaelic in such a way as to prevent others from understanding their conversations – a language practice that can be characterised as a 'secret code'. Although eighteen interviewees in total described using Gaelic in this fashion, I draw attention here to four excerpts that best encapsulate participants' descriptions of this particular language practice. In the first, the informant describes how the possibility of speaking privately without others understanding provides a motivation for him and his wife to use Gaelic together:

>   IM01   [A]irson daoine aig a bheil Gàidhlig, feumaidh [. . .] adhbhar eile a bhith ann (.) tha deagh adhbhar ann uaireannan eadar mi fhìn 's mo bhean-chan eil daoine eile a' tuigsinn na Gàidhlig **so** faodaidh tu
>   *For people who have Gaelic, there has to be [...] another reason [to use Gaelic] (.) my wife and I have a good reason sometimes- other people don't understand Gaelic* **so** *you can*
>   SD   **Yeah**
>   IM01   conaltradh a dhèanamh thall thairis no fiù 's ann an Alba agus tha-làn fhios agad nach bi- chan eil teans mòr gum bi daoine sam bith eile gad thuigsinn
>   *communicate abroad or even in Scotland and you know very well that they won't- there's not much chance that anyone else will understand you*

Although this particular interviewee reports generally low levels of Gaelic language use with his wife at home, the possibility of communicating privately through Gaelic provides a context in which the couple do use the language together in the present day. Similarly, while reporting generally higher levels of Gaelic use with her family, informant HF01 describes her family's use of Gaelic as a secret language while on holidays together:

>   HF01   Tha mi a' smaointinn gum bi sinn a' cleachdadh Gàidhlig cha mhòr fad na h-ùine nuair a tha sinn air saor-làithean ann an dòigh- airson 's gu bheil e math a bhith a' bruidhinn gun daoine a tha timcheall ort=
>   *I think we use Gaelic pretty much all the time when we're on holiday in a way- because it's good to be able to speak without people around you=*
>   SD   =Tha e math **yeah**!=
>   *=It is good*
>   HF01   =Agus tha fhios againn nach eil daoine eile a' tuigsinn!
>   *=And we know that other people don't understand!*

Some interviewees also refer to speaking Gaelic as a secret code outside of the family, such as meeting friends in a café. Informant IF14 even expresses some degree of shame when reflecting on the practice, noting that it 'sounds awful' in turn 1 and laughing in turn 3, partly out of embarrassment, partly out of sheer delight at being able to use the language in this way:

1. IF14 [I]t sounds awful but you know if you're sitting in a place like this and you're just talking you're having a private conversation=
2. SD =Yeah=
3. IF14 =and you want it to be private you would kind of- you know [[talk in Gaelic kind of] ((laughs))
4. SD [[Exactly yeah] ((laughs))

Few interviewees reported living with schoolfriends from GME classes at present, although the following two participants are an exception to this general pattern, describing the way in which they speak Gaelic to each other firstly as 'banter' in their shared flat (in turns 2–3), and then as a 'code' when outside (turns 4–8):

1. SD Do you ever use Gaelic together like in the flat?
2. IF03 Yeah as banter
3. IF04 Banter- yeah we do (.) that's (true)
   [. . .]
4. IF03 Yeah we use it for like code
5. SD Like a secret code yeah
6. IF03 ((laughing)) All the time (.) yep ((laughing)) all the time
7. IF04 ((laughs))
8. IF03 And you do feel like it's something that you have and no one else can hear what I'm saying (.) which is quite exciting

The fact that the use of Gaelic as a 'secret' language was referred to so frequently by interviewees across the three usage categories seems significant, and the ways in which metalinguistic comments on 'secret code' Gaelic are conveyed is quite telling. Much discussion of this topic was interspersed with laughter, and it is clear that interviewees in the cohort generally enjoy using Gaelic as a 'code' that others cannot understand. Ironically, many of the interviewees are more inclined to use Gaelic as a code to keep public conversations secret than they are to speak it to their peers when together in private; indeed, some report this to be the only way in which they continue to use the language today.

4.1.5 Language practice II: Code-switching and 'informal' Gaelic

Another linguistic practice reported frequently throughout the corpus is code-switching between English and Gaelic and 'informal' mixing of the languages. I was interested to see whether interviewees thought that this 'counted' as using Gaelic, or what their ideas about the phenomenon were in general. As in the last extract quoted above, flatmates IF03 and IF04 refer to quite specific instances in which they would switch to using Gaelic together, IF04 again mentioning 'speaking behind someone's back' or using the language in 'banter' (turn 10):

1. IF03 I mean there'd be phrases like **'a bheil thu ag iarraidh cupa ti?'** *(do you want a cup of tea?)* or something like that you know- that you'd just throw in in the middle of an English sen- in English chat- don't know I just kinda throw things in there
2. SD Yeah
3. IF04 Yeah (.) is that not code-switching?
4. IF03 'Where's my **bròganˀ** *(shoes)* 'I don't know'
5. SD Yeah exactly yeah
6. IF04 I just learnt that [[the other day]
7. IF03 [[What d'you call it?] What did you?=
8. IF04 =Code-switching
9. SD Code-switching
10. IF04 The way I unders- and correct me if I'm totally wrong- but like the way in conversation that you switch between languages [. . .] yeah we definitely do a lot of that but probably for (.) yeah kind of ((laughing)) speaking behind someone's back (.) or in banter rather than having general conversations [. . .] that's true that's what we do
11. SD Yeah so you do use Gaelic then- you know you=
12. IF04 =Yeah (.) in an informal way=
13. IF03 =Yeah in an informal way yes I suppose I do still speak Gaelic

Informant IF03 provides both examples of code-switching to Gaelic, offering constructed dialogues in turns 1 and 4 as illustrations of the practice. IF04 demonstrates some fairly detailed metalinguistic awareness of the phenomenon in turns 3 and 10, while it is clear in turn 7 that her friend has never heard of code-switching. She recognises that this does characterise their Gaelic language use, however, and both flatmates describe this as an 'informal way' of speaking Gaelic. The linguistic make-up of these kinds of interactions referred to by interviewees is clearly dominated by English, however, in contrast with the forms of language alternation demonstrated by Gaelic–English bilinguals in Skye and Harris, as documented and analysed by Smith-Christmas (2012, 2013, 2015). By contrast, many of my own interviewees describe using the occasional Gaelic word in conversation, as discussed below:

SD You still see some friends from school do you?
LF07 Uh huh yeah no (.) my best friends they're all- they had like Gaelic families you know so they're quite central to it
SD Right [[okay]
LF07 [[Yeah]
SD And would you speak Gaelic with them much?
LF07 Yeah like on occasion it [[just depends]
SD [[On occasion yeah]
LF07 It's like Galinglish we call it we'll just like (.) put in a wee Gaelic word now and then uh huh

In total, five other interviewees described this kind of bilingual interaction as 'Ganglish' and reported speaking in this way with old schoolfriends on the rare occasion of meeting up with them. Yet it again seems clear that this kind of interaction is qualitatively different from the patterns of code-switching displayed by bilinguals in Gaelic-speaking environments, or indeed, from what is generally reported of bilingual conversation elsewhere, such as that observed in bilingual communities in Africa, or among diasporic minority groups in Europe (see Gafaranga 2007, 2009). In the following extract, informant LM03 refers to language use that we may think of as being more representative of conversational code-switching generally:

LM03   Speaking to my parents is a bit mixed- sometimes we speak in Gaelic, sometimes in English (.) sometimes a strange mix of the two! ((laughs))
SD   Yeah
LM03   The only times I would tend to really have a conversation with them fully in Gaelic is when if there's other people either em (.) around me or when I'm on the phone or similarly in person if we're out somewhere we'll speak in Gaelic all the time
SD   Yeah
LM03   But if we're in the house it tends to be a bit of a mix of the two

While Gaelic generally functions as his family's out-of-home language when they are together, the interviewee reports mixing Gaelic and English within the home. As such, his description of the home language as 'a strange mix of the two' seems to recall a characteristic practice of native speakers generally. Thus while interviewees' depictions of code-switching and 'informal' Gaelic use of this kind tend generally to pertain to the occasional use of Gaelic words embedded in English conversation, the more commonly held conception of code-switching as a language practice *is* reported by some of my speakers. Such speakers constitute a minority in the informant cohort, however, and the kinds of code-switching most frequently referred to are distinct from the 'mixed-medium' interactions Gafaranga (2007, 2009) describes in his research, for example.

Interviewees throughout the corpus generally report low levels of Gaelic language use, especially in the informal 'home–community–neighbourhood' domains that are often regarded as crucial for intergenerational transmission and reversing language shift (see Fishman 1991, 2001a, 2001b). Gaelic employment may bolster such informal social use but prospects for intergenerational transmission by those employed in Gaelic are unclear, as none of the ten speakers described in section 4.1.1 have children at present. Two language practices commonly referred to by interviewees throughout the corpus – use of Gaelic as a secret code, and language mixing between Gaelic and English – reveal the fairly limited role that the language continues to play in the lives of most. If the general picture that emerges, then, is of relatively weak Gaelic language use and widely varying abilities among Gaelic-medium educated adults, we may turn our attention to the possible explanations underlying this pattern. As I hope to demonstrate in the following two sections of the present chapter, interviewees' descriptions of language socialisation – both in the home and at school – can contribute greatly to our understanding of this situation.

4.2 Gaelic language socialisation

In the following section I draw attention to interviewees' accounts and experiences of Gaelic language socialisation outside of the school system. Gaelic language socialisation of primary pupils in GME in the Western Isles has been thoroughly investigated in the last decade by Will (2012). Yet the picture of language socialisation she describes is likely to be somewhat different to the experiences of GME pupils who started primary school in the Western Isles over twenty years ago. Former students' accounts of childhood language socialisation can inform our picture of their current use patterns (as discussed above) and contribute to our understanding of the motives underlying them.

4.2.1 Gaelic language socialisation at home

Some 15 of the 46 interviewees (32.6%) reported growing up in homes in which both parents – or single parents without a partner – spoke Gaelic to them, while 20 (43.5%) grew up in homes in which neither parent did. In between these two categories, 11 (23.9%) participants reported growing up in homes where one parent spoke the language to them, of whom 7 had a Gaelic-speaking mother and 4 a Gaelic-speaking father.

Most of the interviewees with higher levels of Gaelic language use and ability reported socialisation in Gaelic by both parents at home, or by a single parent. A total of 15 interviewees reported Gaelic socialisation of this kind, 9 of whom were raised in Gaelic-speaking areas in Skye and the Western Isles. It should nevertheless be noted that 5 interviewees who described such socialisation experiences chose not to do the interview itself in Gaelic. As such, various linguistic trajectories can be identified among individuals in this category. In the following extract the participant describes using Gaelic most of the time at home and school in the Lowland city he grew up in:

> SD   Does your dad speak Gaelic as well or is it just your mum?
>
> LM03   No- no my dad does [. . .] when I was growing up that was the language we spoke in the house
>
> SD   Right okay yeah (.) so you spoke Gaelic before you started school?
>
> LM03   Yeah I spoke Gaelic before I spoke English actually [. . .] when I was kinda [in the] Gaelic-medium education system we used to speak in Gaelic pretty much all the time [. . .] for that part of my life I was probably speaking English less than I was Gaelic

Table 4.1 Interviewees' home linguistic backgrounds by current Gaelic use (N=46)

Level of Gaelic language use/ Home linguistic background	High	Intermediate	Low	Total
Both/single parents spoke Gaelic	5	5	5	15
Mixed: mother spoke Gaelic	1	3	3	7
Mixed: father spoke Gaelic	0	1	3	4
Neither parent spoke Gaelic	4	3	13	20
Total	10	12	24	46

LINGUISTIC PRACTICE, GAELIC USE AND LANGUAGE SOCIALISATION: FINDINGS 77

This informant therefore emphasises his language practices in childhood: Gaelic use in the home was bolstered by GME and vice versa, and as such, relatively high levels of Gaelic language exposure and socialisation during his early years can be inferred. Yet this contrasts with his present-day relationship to the language; the informant reported lacking confidence to speak the language today to anyone but his parents, and chose to do the interview in English. Others in this category expressed a slight degree of uncertainty over exactly which language could be considered their 'first' language, as both English and Gaelic were used at home:

IM04	[M]ost of my education's been bilingual
SD	Yeah
IM04	U:m (.) but I was- I was a fluent Gaelic- my first language is pro:bably Gaelic
SD	Mm hmm
IM04	I'm not actually sure about that but quite likely that it was [[um]]
SD	[[So probably] before you started school you'd have- you'd [[have (x) yeah]]
IM04	[[Yeah] most likely because my parents both speak Gaelic and I think they were trying to-trying to eh (.) make sure that we spoke Gaelic

Although this informant was raised in the Western Isles, the uncertainty he expresses – drawing out the first syllable of 'probably' – is a clue to his bilingual upbringing. Nevertheless, he states that his parents tried to ensure that he and his siblings spoke the language at home. Other interviewees from the Western Isles expressed no such uncertainty in identifying Gaelic as the first language of their childhood, however. Whilst using Gaelic only rarely today, the following participant reports having been socialised in the language through complete immersion in the language during early years in the home and community, as in the following excerpt:

SD	[An] robh Gàidhlig aig do theaghlach bho thùs?
	Did your family speak Gaelic originally?
IF07	O bha=
	Oh yes=
SD	=Glè mhath=
	=Very good=
IF07	=Bha bha- 's e (.) tha mo mhàthair 's m' athair (.) tha- (.) tha iad a' creidsinn gu mòr ann an Gàidhlig, tha iad beò gu mòr ann an Gàidhlig-cha robh Beurl' agam gus an robh mi::
	=Yeah yeah- it's (.) my mother and father (.) are- (.) they believe very strongly in Gaelic, they live very much through Gaelic- I didn't speak English until I::
SD	Nach robh?=
	Didn't you=?
IF07	=Chaidh mi dhan a' sgoil às aonais Beurla [. . .] mo mhàthair 's m' athair agus bha boireannach ag obair a's an taigh againn-**nanny**-Gàidhlig a bh' aicese [. . .] **pals** mo phàrantan, fear a' phuist, fear a bha tighinn timcheall leis na **vans** eh: na **pals** againn fhìn, a h-uile duine (.) cha robh Beurla timcheall

> *I went to school without English [...] my mother and father and there was a woman who worked in our house- a* **nanny**- *she spoke Gaelic [...] my parents'* **pals**, *the postman, the man who came around with the [grocery]* **vans** *eh: our own* **pals**, *everybody (.) English wasn't around*

Several of the 15 interviewees in this first category similarly describe having grown up in communities where English was seldom heard. While language socialisation experiences of this kind would probably be rare today (see Munro et al. 2010), several interviewees described such experiences when recalling their childhoods in the 1980s and early 1990s. Overall, therefore, relatively high levels of Gaelic language socialisation in childhood can be inferred from the accounts I have outlined here, which typify those of the 15 total speakers who were raised in such a setting. Gaelic socialisation in the home appears to have been a very important factor for these 15 speakers, though it is notable that not all who experienced such socialisation make frequent use of the language today.

4.2.2 Socialisation at home by one Gaelic-speaking parent

A total of 11 of the 46 interviewees reported growing up with one parent who spoke Gaelic and another who did not. Early bilingual socialisation in English and Gaelic, in contrast to some of the examples outlined in 4.2.1 of monolingual Gaelic socialisation, may not have encouraged home Gaelic use to the same degree. In some cases, interviewees reported that their parents could understand the language but not actually speak it, as exemplified in the following excerpt:

IM02	[M]y dad's (.) [I'd] probably say [a] native speaker but my mum's not from- she's from xxx ((Lowlands)) [...] she's sort of a learner and she can- she knows more than she'll speak (.) if you know what I mean
SD	Right okay
IM02	Eh and then my brothers and my sisters can all speak Gaelic eh [...]
SD	Did you speak it with your dad?
IM02	I kinda thought that I did but my mum- my mum's told me that I didn't really speak much at all before I went to school [...] and then I got into doing it all the time and cos you're that young you can pick it up straight away
SD	Yeah
IM02	I can't remember not being able to speak it if you know what I mean

For this particular informant, born and raised in a Western Isles community, active use of either Gaelic or English before starting in GME is reported to have been limited. He describes being unable to remember specifically when he acquired Gaelic, however, having used the language 'all the time' after that. While a certain degree of home socialisation in support of GME may be inferred, therefore, it is not clear that the informant was significantly socialised in the language by his father before school. Yet where IM02 expresses some degree of uncertainty on this point, claiming not to remember learning Gaelic in school, it is clear in the following informant's account that Gaelic language socialisation during his childhood in the urban Lowlands did not occur to any great degree:

> LM02   Well my mum's from- eh from xxx ((Western Isles)) and eh (.) and so they- my mum moved down eh (.) to xxx ((urban Lowlands)) with my dad before myself and my brother were born (2.1) so my mum speaks Gaelic em (.) I spose I was brought up with Gaelic [. . .] I do remember learning Gaelic at school rather than having a sort of a more developed em (.) position than others

Despite stating that he was 'brought up' with the language by his mother, therefore, the above informant remembers acquiring Gaelic mostly at school. I also interviewed the elder brother of the above informant, and asked him about his linguistic relationship with his mother today, and thereby gained additional information on language acquisition processes within this particular family:

> SD   Do you still speak it [i.e. Gaelic] with your mum?
> LM01   I can't speak it to my mum but I can speak it to somebody beside her
> SD   Yeah (.) okay
> LM01   For some reason I can't speak it to my mum
> SD   Right okay that's interesting
> LM01   She thinks it's because we all spoke English when we were babies

In the case of these two interviewees, then, Gaelic language socialisation did not occur to a significant degree in the family home. As a consequence, at least for the elder of the two siblings, English is the default code choice for interaction with his Gaelic-speaking mother, that linguistic relationship having been established from an early age. There are examples within this category of successful Gaelic language socialisation by one Gaelic-speaking parent, however, as described in the following extract:

> HF01   Bha Gàidhlig aig mo sheanair ach chaidh m' athair a thogail gun Ghàidhlig (.) cha robh Gàidhlig idir air taobh mo mhàthar agus ghluais mo theaghlach air ais a dh'Alba gus am b' urrainn dha m' athair Gàidhlig ionnsachadh aig Sabhal Mòr Ostaig
> *My grandfather spoke Gaelic but my father was raised without Gaelic (.) there was no Gaelic on my mother's side and my family moved back to Scotland so that my father could learn Gaelic at Sabhal Mòr Ostaig*
> SD   **Okay**
> HF01   Agus erm fhad 's /gu robh/ esan ag ionnsachadh na Gàidhlig bha e a' teagasg / mi-fhìn/ agus mo bhràthair
> *And erm while he was learning Gaelic he was teaching myself and my brother*

It is important to note in this excerpt that the father who successfully socialised his children in Gaelic was a learner who acquired the language in adulthood, a situation that was also described by several other informants. The importance of members of this generation in becoming 'new speakers' and passing the language on to their own children is an area in need of further research. A noteworthy finding in the present study, however, is that some of the most successful cases of Gaelic language socialisation by one parent, within a linguistically mixed home, stem directly from new speaker parents' commitment to recovering Gaelic as a heritage language.

4.2.3 No Gaelic at home

Interviewees in this category reported growing up in homes in which neither parent or other immediate caregiver spoke Gaelic. In some cases, at least one of the informant's parents could speak some Gaelic, but for whatever reason chose not to do so in the home. For example, in contrast to the above accounts of socialisation by parents who learned Gaelic themselves and then passed the language on to their children, interviewees' parents in both of the following extracts are described as having learned Gaelic (to varying degrees) but not using the language at home:

IF06	[M]y mum and dad like both moved to xxx- they're both English and they moved there like twenty- thirty years ago
SD	Right okay
IF06	Em and my dad (.) taught himself Gaelic and he's quite involved in all the cultural, music and Gaelicky stuff
SD	Oh brilliant
IF06	Em (.) but yeah it's definitely not- we don't like- we don't really speak it at home ((laughs))

As in-migrants to the island community she grew up in, this interviewee's parents made some effort to learn Gaelic but never spoke the language in the family home. The following informant's mother learned Gaelic as a heritage language, having not acquired it fully in childhood. Unlike the new speaker parent discussed above, however, she did not speak Gaelic to her children at home:

LM09	My mum- my mum <u>speaks</u> it but em (1.6) she- she went back to eh (.) school and did it when she was older
SD	Oh she did? Uh huh
LM09	But em my gran- like my grandparents are fae ((Western Isles)) [. . .] it was quite important (.) to my family
SD	Sure yeah (.) did your mum speak Gaelic to you before you started school do you think?
LM09	No ((laughs)) my mum's got <u>terrible</u> Gaelic
SD	Oh really? ((laughs))
LM09	She's got really bad Gaelic (.) she tries her best

Whilst the language was important enough to this informant's family to motivate his mother to start learning again Gaelic as an adult, his description of her language skills as 'terrible' may reflect her inability to attain the higher stages of competence in Gaelic necessary to pass the language on. The choice of parents with some Gaelic not to pass the language on was not limited to learners with limited proficiency in the language, however, and in some cases informants reported that their fluent parents declined to raise them in Gaelic.

I turn now to consider the relatively few, exceptional cases of adults who were not socialised in Gaelic at home, but who do use the language regularly today. Of these four 'new speaker' interviewees, two were raised in urban communities, while two grew up in rural Highland communities where the language was spoken to some extent. The latter two reported the use of Gaelic in the wider community to have had an important impact on their childhood socialisation in the language. All four could be described in the present day as 'new speakers', using Gaelic on a daily basis in their professional and social lives. The genesis of the 'new speaker' concept in minority language contexts is relatively recent; O'Rourke and Ramallo (2011, 2013) defined the new speaker as a person who chooses to use a language other than their language of primary socialisation in the course of their daily lives. Clarifying further, McLeod et al. (2014: 1) have defined new speakers of Gaelic as people who did not acquire Gaelic within the home in childhood, 'but have nevertheless acquired Gaelic to a significant degree of competence and are now making active use of the language in their lives'. It is this definition I adopt in respect of the four speakers I discuss here, with a key emphasis on 'active use' of Gaelic (see also Dunmore 2017, 2018). Informant HM01, below, is one of the former two participants raised in the city without Gaelic at home:

SD   Agus a bheil Gàidhlig aig do phàrantan mar sin?
           And can your parents speak Gaelic?
HM01 Eh cha /robh/
           Eh no they /couldn't/
SD   Nach robh?
           Couldn't they?
HM01 Tha- och- facal no dhà aig an dà chuid
           They- och- both can speak a word or two
SD   Hmm [. . .] so an robh Gàidhlig agad mus do thòisich thu ann am foghlam tro mheadhan na Gàidhlig?
           so *did you speak Gaelic before you started in Gaelic-medium education?*
HM01 Eh bho thùs? [. . .] Chan eil cuimhn' agam feumaidh mi aideachadh oir bha mi cho beag ach: cha bhithinn fileanta mura deach mi dhan (bhun-sgoil) mar eisimpleir
           Eh originally? [. . .] I don't remember I have to admit because I was so small but: I wouldn't be fluent if I hadn't gone to (primary school) for example

This speaker claims that he would not be fluent without doing Gaelic-medium at primary school, although he cannot remember exactly when he learned Gaelic. As one of the interviewees I categorised in the 'high use' group in the first section of this chapter (4.1), informant HM01speaks Gaelic with his Gaelic-medium-educated siblings and with his grandmother, as well as using it socially and professionally in the Lowland city where he is based. Notably, the other city-raised new speaker also had a Gaelic-speaking grandmother, though neither informant reported being socialised in Gaelic by grandparents in childhood. I should emphasise that only 4 of the 20 interview participants with no immediate family background in Gaelic continue to use it regularly at present. Furthermore, only 2 who continue to do so were raised in an urban context. By contrast, the following extract highlights the role that the Gaelic-speaking community played in the early lives of new speakers from more rural locales in the Highlands:

HF07   Is ann à Earra-Ghàidheal a tha mi ach thogadh mi ann an xxx ((Highland town))
        I'm from Argyll but I grew up in xxx ((Highland))
SD   Inntinneach aidh (.) so co ris a tha an dà sgìre coltach mar sin?
        Interesting yeah (.) so what are the two areas like then?
HF07   Tha an dà dhiubh anns a' Ghàidhealtachd (.) tha mi a' smaoineachadh gu bheil an cultar aca Gàidhealach- an dà [. . .] bha mi air mo chuairteachadh le Gàidhlig fad mo /h/-ùin'- mo- m' àrach
        Both of them are in the Highlands (.) I think their culture is Gaelic- both [. . .] I was surrounded by Gaelic throughout my/time/- my- my upbringing

The fact of having grown up in part of the mainland Highlands where Gaelic was used is therefore regarded by this interviewee as an important characteristic of her upbringing; indeed, she even describes having been 'surrounded' (*air mo chuairteachadh*) by Gaelic language and culture from an early age. Reported immersion in Gaelic from childhood is clearly an important aspect of her socialisation in the language, and I continued on this point, asking whether she spoke Gaelic before school:

SD   An canadh tu gu robh Gàidhlig agad mus do thòisich thu ann am foghlam tro mheadhan na Gàidhlig?
        Would you say you spoke Gaelic before you started in Gaelic-medium education?
HF07   Cha chanainn- chanainn (.) gu- thòisich mi cho òg- bha mi dìreach trì bliadhna a dh'aois, em (.) bha fios agam gu robh Gàidhlig ann, ach: [. . .] chan eil fhios 'am- bha mi òg, òg (.) chan eil cuimhne agam air beatha às aonais Gàidhlig
        No- I would say (.) that- I started so young I was just three years old, em (.) I knew Gaelic existed, but: [. . .] I don't know I was very young (.) I don't remember life without Gaelic

Again, as in the case of the previous interviewee, informant HF07 reports having imprecise memories of exactly when she first acquired Gaelic, having done so from a very young age in the rural community where she was raised. This would appear to be a very rare experience, reported by only 2 of the 46 interviewees. Given the changed nature of language socialisation within communities that appear at least in census returns to be 'Gaelic-speaking' (see Munro et al. 2010; Will 2012), it is likely that such experiences of socialisation will become even rarer in future. By comparison with the late 1980s when this informant was a young child, there are now even fewer communities – especially in the mainland Highlands, but also even in 'heartland' island locales – where children might have the opportunity to be immersed in Gaelic language and culture from an early age.

Across the categories discussed in section 4.2.1 therefore, at least three degrees of reported Gaelic language socialisation in the home domain are discernible. In homes where both parents, or a single parent without a partner, spoke Gaelic, high levels of socialisation in the language are typically reported. Participants' self-selection to volunteer for interviews may, of course, have a role in distorting this picture. Reported degrees of language socialisation are much more mixed among interviewees with just one Gaelic-speaking parent, and children of a new speaker, whether father or mother, report generally higher levels than those of parents who were native speakers in relationships with non-speakers. Low levels of language socialisation in the home and community are reported by interviewees in the last category, except in the cases of 2 of the 4 'new' speakers mentioned above, who grew up in communities that were at least somewhat Gaelic-speaking. These 4 continue to use the language frequently in the present day, in contrast to the 16 others in this category, who generally report doing so only rarely, reflecting the importance of socialisation in Gaelic at home for former GME students' language practices later in life.

4.3 GME and Gaelic socialisation

This section considers narrative accounts of language socialisation within GME, arranged into the following three categories: accounts concerning the acquisition of Gaelic at school (4.3.1); secondly, accounts relating to the role of GME in socialising students in Gaelic culture more generally (4.3.2); and lastly, narratives describing experiences of negative affect in the socialisation of former GME students at school (4.3.3).

4.3.1 Role of GME in Gaelic language socialisation

Interviewees attached varying degrees of significance to GME as a means by which they were socialised in the language, depending a great deal on whether or not they were also socialised in Gaelic at home. Conversely, clear distinctions in accounts of school socialisation are apparent, even between interviewees who were socialised in Gaelic by their two parents at home, as demonstrated in the following two accounts:

HF03 [T]ha mi a' smaointinn gum biodh e gu bhith gu math doirbh dha mo phàrantan a bhith em (.) a' toirt mo chuid Gàidhlig gu ìre (.) na=
I think it would have been quite hard for my parents to em (.) bring my Gaelic on to such a degree (.) the=

SD =Mura [[robh foghlam Gàidhlig agad]
If [[you hadn't had Gaelic-medium education]

HF03 [[mura robh foghlam tro mheadhan] na Gàidhlig ann agus mura robh comas ann a bhith (.) uh (.) gam oideachadh tro mheadhan na Gàidhlig 's a' faighinn Gàidhlig a's an sgoil [. . .] ach aig a' cheart àm tha mi smaointinn- foghlam tro mheadhan na Gàidhlig leis fhèin, nach biodh e air uiread de bhuaidh a thoirt orm- mura bithinn air a bhith ga fhaighinn aig an taigh cuideachd
[[if Gaelic-medium education hadn't] existed and if there hadn't been the chance to (.) uh (.) educate myself through Gaelic and get Gaelic in the school [. . .] but at the same time I think- Gaelic-medium education on its own, it wouldn't have had such an effect on me if I hadn't got it at home as well

In this first extract, therefore, informant, HF03, attributes an important role to GME in support of socialisation in Gaelic and intergenerational transmission of the language at home. The following informant, however, similarly socialised in Gaelic by both parents at home, is much less appreciative of the role of GME in her acquisition of Gaelic and her socialisation in the language:

IF07	Ag innse na fìrinn (.) chan eil mi smaoineachadh gun d'fhuair mi buannachd sam bith=
	To tell the truth (.) I don't think I got any benefit at all
SD	=Hmm
IF07	bho bhith am foghlam tro mheadhan na Gàidhlig
	from being in Gaelic-medium education
SD	Seadh
	Yeah
IF07	Ach: (.) nam bithinns' air mo thogail ann an taigh eile far nach robh na leabhraichean agus a' Ghàidhlig um ri fhaighinn- mar a bha san taigh againne, dh'fhaodadh mi /ag/ ràdh rud gu math eadar-dhealaicht'
	But: (.) if I'd been raised in another house where the books and the Gaelic weren't um available- as they were in our house, I would maybe say something different

Informant IF07 is consequently much more doubtful about the benefits of GME as a support for home socialisation, having enjoyed access to Gaelic books, language and literacy in the family home as well. The availability of these things in school is subsequently seen to be of significantly less importance. A highly proficient Gaelic speaker in both phonological and grammatical terms, she regards home socialisation in the language to have been much the more important for her learning Gaelic. A very different account is provided in the following narrative, in which informant IM01, a 'new speaker', reflects on his experience of Gaelic socialisation through GME:

IM01	[T]ha cuimhne agamsa mus do thòisich foghlam tro mheadhan na Gàidhlig ged-tà um (.) thàinig tidsear /a-staigh/ dhan an sgoil gach seachdain agus dh'ionnsaich sinn (x) òran 's mar sin 's chòrd e rium gu mòr (.) dh'ionnsaich mi e gu math luath chan eil fhios 'am carson, cha robh mi math air dad sam bith san sgoil ((laughing)) [. . .] sin mar a dh'ionnsaich mi Gàidhlig-'s e dìreach **immersion** a bh' ann
	I remember before I started Gaelic-medium education though um (.) a teacher came into school every week and we learned (x) a [Gaelic] song and so on and I enjoyed that a lot (.) I learned it quite quickly I don't know why, I wasn't good at anything in school ((laughing)) [. . .] that's how I learned Gaelic- it was just **immersion**

This speaker's earliest memory of Gaelic is therefore of learning songs with a visiting teacher before GME started in his area, something he states he enjoyed a great deal. When he started in GME after this, he learned Gaelic rapidly by being fully immersed in the language, something he states was very important to his socialisation in Gaelic – and especially to his exposure to the language. Other participants tended to draw a stark distinction between certain GME pupils' language use in the classroom and the playground:

> HF02 [T]ha cuimhn 'am- cha robh sinn a' bruidhinn Gàidhlig **you know** eadar na- na h-oileanaich- cha robh iad a' bruidhinn Gàidhlig ri chèile **you know** b' e dìreach Gàidhlig leis an tidsear agus fiù 's san latha an-diugh nuair a bha mi a' dol a-steach eh:: dhan eh sgoil Ghàidhlig xxx
>
> *I remember- we didn't speak Gaelic* **you know** *between the- the students- they didn't speak Gaelic to each other* **you know** *it was just Gaelic with the teacher and even these days when I was going into eh:: to eh xxx Gaelic School*
>
> SD Mm hmm
>
> HF02 Cha bhi iad a' bruidhinn Gàidhlig **like you know** ri chèile- **so** san sgoil em no sa **phlayground** em 's e dìreach an tidsear
>
> *They don't speak Gaelic* **like you know** *together-* **so** *in school em or in the* **playground** *em it's just the teacher*

This interviewee therefore draws a parallel between pupils' language use when she attended school and in the present day. Use of Gaelic by GME pupils, then as now, is reported to be restricted to interactions with the teacher alone (*'s e dìreach an tidsear*) and students are said not to use the language socially. The concept of GME units as sites of full immersion in the language, therefore, is not one that is frequently related across the corpus (see O'Hanlon 2010; O'Hanlon et al. 2012 on GME teachers' classroom language practices; and Nance 2013, 2015 on GME pupils' linguistic production). Instead a variety of language practices in the school are more commonly referred to by interviewees, with social use of Gaelic outside the classroom being only occasionally mentioned. Interviewees therefore expressed various opinions on the relevance of GME to their language socialisation experiences. For some, GME was viewed either as a support to home socialisation (though perhaps inadequate on its own) or as entirely irrelevant, while many depicted Gaelic use being largely restricted to the classroom. Experiences of Gaelic socialisation through GME are therefore somewhat mixed among former GME students, but very few report being socialised in the language through the education system alone.

4.3.2 GME: Socialisation in Gaelic culture?

Apart from the question of being socialised as bilingual speakers through GME, many interviewees raised the issue of becoming socialised into Gaelic culture through school. Various understandings of Gaelic culture are identifiable, with a number of interviewees conveying an understanding that pertains chiefly to traditional music and the arts, as in the following extract:

> HF06 Em (.) it was also like- it wasn't just the language it was just- it was very cultural cos- maybe this was just my school, but we'd do lots of Gaelic singing and music and (.) like all the you know all the stories that we listened to and told we were all Gaelic folklore-y type things

SD   So it's the culture as well as just being taught=
HF06   =Yeah it was the culture as well as just the language

As such, informant HF06 regards the exposure he received to Gaelic music, song and folklore as an important aspect of GME. A large number of interviewees referred to this cultural aspect of the system, many reflecting on their continued musical ability as the legacy of GME for which they were most grateful. A large proportion stated that while their linguistic ability in Gaelic may have declined since school, they continued to pursue an active interest in traditional music, which they attributed chiefly to the cultural components of GME.

LM05   [O]ne thing I guess- I don't think I've mentioned in our talk is probably my relationship with music
SD   Right
LM05   Em it grew (.) I was always interested in music but it probably grew quite a lot with the opportunities afforded during Gaelic-medium education [. . .] and that's continued and stuck with me
            [. . .]
SD   Yeah exactly, so there was a sort of a cultural component [[not just the language]
LM05   [[Yeah- I think yeah]
SD   Yeah
LM05   Yeah so to me that's probably one of the strongest kind of links yeah

As such, the above informant regards the cultural content of GME and his continued engagement with music as one of the strongest connections to the language he has in the present day. In the following excerpt, informant LF04 makes similar reference to feeling more 'connected' to Gaelic and Scottish culture from having been exposed to traditional song and dance through GME:

LF04   I really appreciate having been in Gaelic-medium I think I- I dunno (.) it kinda gives me a sort of connection to a whole sort of- even though my direct family haven't been (.) connected to- to Gaelic along with the Gaelic comes a whole lot of (.) other sort of (.) more (.) kind of cultural things [. . .] to do with singing and dancing and (.) all these different things to do with that sort of Scottish culture and things

In addition to continued engagement with traditional arts and music after school, broader conceptions of Gaelic culture pertaining to the region in which interviewees grew up are visible in certain interviewees' accounts of socialisation at school. I return to these considerations in greater depth in section 5.3 of the following chapter on Gaelic and identities. The 'connection' to Gaelic and Scottish culture that informant LF04 refers to in respect of having done GME, and in the absence of any family background in Gaelic, was mentioned quite frequently by interviewees of a similar profile. I return to these questions in greater detail in the following chapter, but it is important to note the wider conception of Gaelic culture that interviewees employ in narratives of this kind. If accounts of socialisation in the Gaelic language through

GME are somewhat mixed (section 4.3.1), many interviewees did create the impression that the socialisation into Gaelic culture they received through GME had a more lasting impact on their lives than the language itself.

4.3.3 Negative affect in school language socialisation

Finally, in this section I provide an analysis of certain interviewees' accounts of negative affect in GME. Such experiences may be expected to have a profound impact on the future relationships of interviewees to Gaelic and the ways in which they engage with the language after school. Importantly, experiences of negative affect in GME were described only by interview participants who reported making little use of Gaelic in the present day. Although it is clear that no causal relationship can necessarily be inferred here, negative experiences may contribute to our understanding of the motives underlying such interviewees' current usage patterns. The speaker in the following extract, raised with Gaelic at home in a Western Isles community, describes feelings of 'segregation' while in GME toward the end of primary school:

1. SD   What do you think was the- the main effect that it had on you- doing Gaelic at school?
2. IF14 I:: ((sighs)) (2.3) it was quite difficult in primary school we were very much kind of (.) segregated [. . .] I actually found it quite difficult (.) when we got to primary seven we did (.) two days a week we did the mainstream class (.) a:nd em (.) I still remember clear as anything there was a table at the very front of the room and that's where we had to sit [. . .] it was kind of like- it was the Gaelic table (.) that's what it was called
3. SD   Yeah
4. IF14 And little things like that they kind of like ((laughing)) they stick with you
5. SD   It's very stigmatising in a way [[isn't it? Uh huh]
6. IF14 [[It is yeah] absolutely but (.) I don't think it was done in any kind of tra- deliberately trying to make us different [. . .] it was to encourage us to speak Gaelic but we weren't- it wasn't being done and in the process of that happening you were separated from all the other- all your- your peers in the same year-group

This participant's feeling of being 'segregated' didn't develop until P7, at which point Gaelic-medium students were put into the same class as English-medium pupils, but were grouped together on the 'Gaelic table' at the front of the classroom. She understands in hindsight that this may have been to encourage Gaelic-medium students to continue using Gaelic, but at that age the feeling she describes of being 'separated', 'different' (turn 6) and 'segregated' (turn 2) militated against their doing so. In Hymes's (1974) terminology, 'keys' to the informant's stance and communication of negative affect are visible in turn 2, with elongation of 'I', sighing and a long pause (2.3 seconds) at the start of the speech act, followed by frequent, shorter pauses throughout the following utterance. Laughter in turn 4 when describing the stigmatising effects of the 'Gaelic table', and hesitation and self-interruptions at the end of turn

6 also provide the key to a sense of negative affect conveyed in these speech acts. This feeling was reported several times in interviews, and it is clear, therefore, that certain aspects of the GME experience continue to be a source of discomfort for some former students. In the following extract, two interviewees from the Inner Hebrides further describe the sense of stigmatisation that has already been alluded to:

IF03	I know what it was like growing up and being in school and being the Gaelic class it was <u>horrendous</u> because everyone was like 'oh yeah it's a dying language' and you'd be like 'no it's not- it's absolutely <u>not</u> a dying language' and then they'd go 'well how many people speak it?' About 2- 250 ((laughs)) max (.) other people took [[exception to it]
IF04	[[We got called] Gaelic aliens in school! ((laughs))
SD	Did you really? Yeah?
IF03	((laughing)) [[Yeah!]
IF04	[[Yeah!] ((laughing)) 'Don't play with them- they're Gaelic aliens' ((laughs)) but they're our friends now
IF03	They still think it's a dying language

The first informant, IF03, describes the experience of defending Gaelic as not being 'a dying language' when goaded by English-medium pupils at school as 'horrendous'. The use of 'Gaelic alien' as a term of abuse by the latter group – even in the partly Gaelic-speaking community where these speakers grew up – resonates with the feelings of stigmatisation and separation that have been described by previous interviewees. Although the second participant, IF04, mentions now being on friendly terms with these former English-medium students, IF03 interjects that their opinions on Gaelic and its supposed obsolescence have not changed. The most striking sense of alienation, however, is related by a native speaker from the Western Isles, who reports on her own feelings of embarrassment and 'shame' in GME:

SD	[A]m biodh sibh a' cleachdadh na Gàidhlig a's a- a's a' **playground**?
	Did you (pl.) use Gaelic in the- in the **playground**?
IF07	Uill bhiodh- cha robh Beurla againn! [. . .] Tha e **insular** is tha thu an uair sin faireachdainn car **embarrassed** a dhol a-mach sa **phlayground** agus gu bheil thu (.) chan eil fhios 'am a bheil e ceart um (.) sin a (x) gu bheil thu- mar gu bheil thu ann an clas: **a sort of- sort of special needs** ann an dòigh air choreigin
	Well yes- we couldn't speak English! [. . .] It's **insular** *and then you feel a bit* **embarrassed** *to go out to the* **playground** *and that you are (.) I don't know if it's right um (.) that (x) you- as if you are in* **a sort of- sort of special needs** *class in some way*
SD	Seadh
	Yeah
IF07	Mar gu bheil thu seòrs' de **remedial**- agus fhios agad fhèin nach e **remedial** a tha thu ach nuair a tha thu a' nochdadh às aonais comas a th' aig a' mhòr-chuid dhen a' chlann sa **phlayground** tha thu faireachdainn **remedial** [. . .] chan eil fhios 'am dè a' Ghàidhlig a th' air **sh:ame** ach tha rudeigin mar sin na lùib dhòmhs'

> *As if you are sort of* **remedial**- *and you know yourself that you're not a* **remedial** *but when you turn up without an ability that most children in the playground have you feel* **remedial** *[. . .] I don't know the Gaelic for* **sha:me** *but there's something like that connected to it for me*

Negative affect is communicated by this speaker as she reports feeling as if the Gaelic-medium unit she attended was a 'remedial' or 'special needs' class when surrounded by English-speaking pupils in the playground; it is notable that she uses English terms to communicate this sense. Her use of the English words 'insular', 'embarrassed' and 'shame' to emphasise her experience of negative affect is also very salient in this excerpt, and may constitute instances of adopting an 'other' voice when relating difficult experiences and potentially controversial views (see Dunmore and Smith-Christmas 2015). The impact of these kinds of experience on later language practices is a crucial consideration for the analysis, and I return to some of these issues in the following chapter in relation to Gaelic use and identities.

4.3.4 Gaelic language socialisation experiences: Some conclusions

Levels of socialisation in Gaelic reported by former GME students in interviews, both at home and in school, therefore vary to a considerable degree, depending a great deal on parents' use of the language during childhood. Without this input, the school is rarely described as having been an important site for Gaelic language socialisation, although some participants express a strong sense of connection to Gaelic culture through GME. Socialisation in Gaelic at home was mostly reported by speakers who make greater use of Gaelic today, while the four new speakers whose accounts I describe above may be considered notable exceptions. Even in instances where significant home socialisation in Gaelic is reported, however, high levels of use in the present day do not necessarily result, and it seems that experiences of negative affect in relation to Gaelic at school may play a key role in this dynamic; further research will be needed to address this question adequately. The following section takes a quantitative and statistical view of issues of Gaelic use, ability and socialisation already discussed in light of interviewees' narratives.

4.4 Language use, GME and Gaelic socialisation: Statistical analysis

This section outlines relevant results from the quantitative analysis of online survey responses, in order to facilitate triangulation with the qualitative data discussed above. As described in section 3.2, the online questionnaire on which the quantitative analysis is based contained thirty questions, spread over three overarching sections on social background, language use and ability, and language attitudes. The survey thus included questions on the age, occupation, current location and home town of participants, as well as their continuation with GME beyond primary school, and with the study of Gaelic generally. A total of 112 participants completed the online survey; although all 46 interview participants were invited to complete the questionnaire, only 28 in fact did so, representing 25% of total responses. In order to ensure that these responses were not significantly out of proportion to the other 75%, they were later disaggregated from the full dataset and analysed separately, and no such distorting effect was identified.

4.4.1 Social background variables

Of the 112 questionnaire respondents, 73 were female (65.2%) and 39 were male (34.8%), reflective of the self-selected nature of respondents in the dataset. Some 49 of the questionnaires were returned via the Gaelic version of the survey (43.8%), while 63 were completed in English (56.2%). In terms of age group, individuals in the 24–32 age bracket were initially targeted in email invitations so as to ensure coverage of respondents who started in GME between 1985 and 1992, the first eight years of the system's availability in Scotland. This age restriction was later relaxed in order to elicit as large a sample as possible, and the average age of all questionnaire respondents, as of 30 June 2012 (the midpoint of data collection) was 25. University or college attendance among questionnaire respondents was very high, at 93.8%; by comparison, the 2011 census showed that 36% of Scots report holding a level 3/4 qualification (equivalent to college diploma or university degree; National Records of Scotland 2013b).

Measurement of social class was based on reported profession, based on the National Statistics Socio-economic Classification (Table 4.2). It is notable that over 30% of questionnaire participants reported currently being in education or training. By way of comparison with data displayed in Table 4.2, the 2011 census demonstrated that 5% of Scottish adults reported being unemployed, and 4% being in education or training (National Records of Scotland 2013b). These percentages are clearly out of proportion to the figures displayed in Table 4.2. Of course, age is also an issue in this respect, and it is likely that many of the 30.4% of respondents currently in education or training will progress to occupations in the first two categories after graduating. As can be seen in Table 4.2, the traditional and modern professional class categories account for a majority of all participants (56.2%), again reflecting possible self-report bias in the sample.

The current location of questionnaire respondents varied considerably; a majority (54.5%) of informants report currently living in the urban Lowlands of Scotland, whether Glasgow (36.6%), Edinburgh (11.6%) or in and around the north-eastern cities of Dundee and Aberdeen (6.3%). Some 39.2% report living in the Highlands

Table 4.2 Occupational class

Class assessment	N	%
1. Traditional professional	24	21.4
2. Modern professional	39	34.8
3. Routine manual/service	13	11.6
4. In education/training	34	30.4
5. Not in education, employment or training/Unemployed	2	1.8
Total	112	100

LINGUISTIC PRACTICE, GAELIC USE AND LANGUAGE SOCIALISATION: FINDINGS

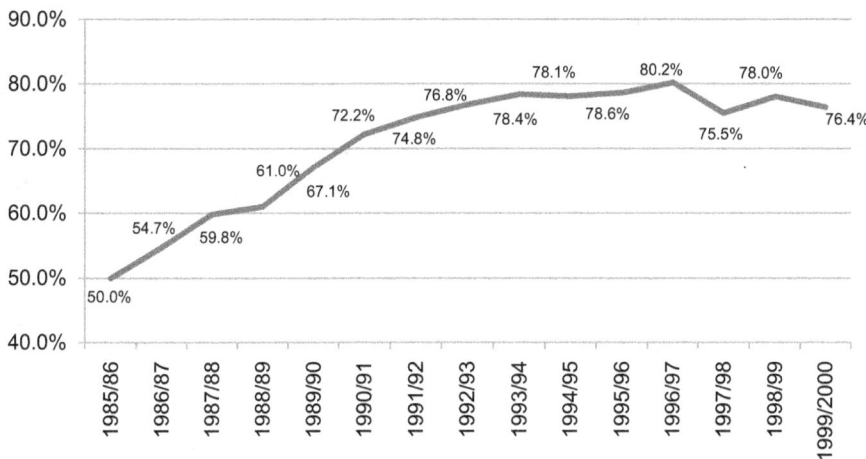

Figure 4.1 Percentage of GME students in Highlands and Islands, 1985–2000 (data from MacKinnon 2005)

and Islands region (comprising the three council areas of Highland, Comhairle nan Eilean Siar and Argyll and Bute) although almost a third of these live in or around the city of Inverness, while 6.3% are now based outside of Scotland. By contrast, informants' places of origin varied to a far lesser degree; 84% of participants report having grown up in the Highlands and Islands, while only 16.1% report growing up in Glasgow, Edinburgh and Aberdeen.

The corresponding out-migration patterns that may be interpreted from these proportions – that is, from more densely concentrated Gaelic-speaking rural areas to urban locations – are thus relatively clear. Whilst clearly unrepresentative of the overall Scottish population, of which only 6.6% were living in the Highlands and Islands in 2011 (National Records of Scotland 2013a), they correspond broadly to the numbers of GME students in these areas between 1985 and 2000. All 112 respondents would have started in GME during this fifteen-year period, at which time the majority of GME students lived in the Highlands and Islands (for present purposes, the three council areas of Highland, Comhairle nan Eilean Siar and Argyll and Bute; see MacKinnon 2005):

Tables 4.3 and 4.4 display informants' reported continuation with the study of Gaelic after completing GME at primary school. As can be seen from Table 4.3, continuation with Gaelic-medium instruction in subjects other than Gaelic is greatly reduced at secondary level compared to primary school, reflective of limited secondary provision at this time. Less than a third of respondents (32.1%) studied two or more subjects through Gaelic at secondary school. A further quarter (24.1%) studied one subject, but the largest group (42.0%) studied only Gaelic itself.

By contrast, levels of continuation with Gaelic as a subject are relatively high, with only 2 informants reporting that they ceased to study Gaelic at the end of primary school (category 9 in Table 4.4). A total of 55 further respondents (49.1%) reported continuing Gaelic study until some point in high school (categories 5–8),

Table 4.3 Continuation with GME at secondary school

GM subjects at secondary	N	%
None	2	1.8
Gaelic only	47	42.0
1 other subject	27	24.1
2 other subjects	17	15.2
3 other subjects	9	8.0
4 other subjects	6	5.4
> 4 other subjects	4	3.5
Total	112	100

Table 4.4 Continuation with Gaelic study

Level of study	N	%
1. Postgraduate degree	2	1.8
2. Undergraduate degree	36	32.1
3. Some university (HE)	10	8.9
4. Some college (FE)	7	6.3
5. Advanced Higher	5	4.5
6. Higher Grade	29	25.9
7. Standard Grade	14	12.5
8. Some high school	7	6.3
9. Primary school	2	1.8
Total	112	100

while the same number again continued to study Gaelic at college or university level (categories 1–4). Of the latter group, 38 went on to gain an undergraduate qualification in Gaelic, amounting to just over a third (33.9%) of all questionnaire respondents (categories 1–2). This proportion is likely to be far higher than that among all former Gaelic-medium students, although data on this issue are not currently available.

Lastly, in the portion of the questionnaire dealing with participants' social backgrounds, respondents were asked about languages that were used in the home and community in which they grew up. Responses to these questions are shown in Table 4.5.

As may be seen from the Table 4.5, 36 respondents reported growing up in homes where Gaelic was used to at least an equal degree as English (32.1%), while 42 report greater use of English than Gaelic (37.5%) and 29 report English only (25.9%). These proportions are comparable to the figures reported for Gaelic socialisation in Table 4.1 in section 4.2.1, above. It is conceivable that the largest category here – that of respondents who report 'more English than Gaelic' – is also the broadest in terms of language practice, ranging from the odd word or phrase in Gaelic while completing homework, to quite substantial use of the language in conversation. It is unfortunately impossible

Table 4.5 Reported socialisation in Gaelic

Languages	Used at home N (%)	Used in community N (%)
Only English	29 (25.9)	40 (35.7)
More English than Gaelic	42 (37.5)	45 (40.2)
Equal amounts English and Gaelic	12 (10.7)	11 (9.8)
More Gaelic than English	24 (21.4)	16 (14.3)
Other languages	5 (4.5)	0 (0)
Total	112 (100)	112 (100)

to know from these data, but if we consider some of the more limited kinds of Gaelic language use that were most frequently described by interview participants in section 4.1 of this chapter, it seems likely that some respondents included more limited Gaelic language practices within the 'more English than Gaelic' category.

This was again the largest category reported for languages used in the wider community that respondents were raised in, with 45 reporting 'more English than Gaelic' and 40 'only English'. In spite of the reported preponderance of English use within the homes and communities in which questionnaire participants were raised, however, relatively high levels of ability in Gaelic were reported at the end of primary school GME by the majority of respondents, as shown in Table 4.6. Almost two-thirds (64.3%) reported having about the same level of fluency in Gaelic and English at the end of primary school, while over a quarter (26.8%) reported being more fluent in English, and only 8.9% reported being more fluent in Gaelic.

Finally in the social background section, respondents were asked to select from a list of options reflecting changed language practices since leaving school, and were invited to select all options that corresponded to their own experience (with the choice of leaving any option blank, to reflect language practices that may not have changed substantially):

The most frequently reported changes in linguistic practice since leaving school are therefore reading less Gaelic (reported by 68 respondents), writing less Gaelic (62), speaking less Gaelic (61) and using more Gaelic media (55). It is likely that this last finding reflects the greater availability and output of Gaelic television since the establishment of BBC Alba in 2008. For speaking, reading and writing, by contrast, the proportions of respondents who report greater use of Gaelic are consistently and considerably lower than those reporting lower use.

Table 4.6 Language ability after school

Language of greater ability by end of P7	N	%
Gaelic	10	8.9
English	30	26.8
About the same in both	72	64.3
Total	112	100

Table 4.7 Change in Gaelic language practices since leaving school

Language practice	Speak more Gaelic	Read more Gaelic	Write more Gaelic	Use more Gaelic media
N (%)	41 (36.6)	26 (23.2)	33 (29.5)	55 (49.1)
Language practice	Speak less Gaelic	Read less Gaelic	Write less Gaelic	Use fewer Gaelic media
N (%)	61 (54.5)	68 (60.7)	62 (55.5)	38 (33.9)
Total N (%)	102 (91.1)	94 (83.9)	95 (84.8)	93 (83.0)

4.4.2 Reported abilities in Gaelic

In the second portion of the questionnaire, high abilities in Gaelic were reported by a clear majority of participants. A total of 78 respondents claimed that they were 'fluent' Gaelic speakers (69.6%), while a further 15 stated that they could 'speak a fair amount of Gaelic' (13.4%), 13 reported that they could speak 'some' Gaelic (11.6%) and 6 claimed to be able to 'speak a small amount of Gaelic' (5.4%). No single participant selected the final statement 'I can hardly speak Gaelic at all' to reflect their abilities in the present day.

In part, the very high levels of Gaelic fluency reported by questionnaire respondents may again reflect self-selection bias in the survey, since speakers who feel less confident and fluent in their Gaelic may well have been less inclined to answer the questionnaire in the first place. Additionally, completion of a high school Higher Grade qualification in Gaelic for 'Fileantaich/Fluent speakers' by many

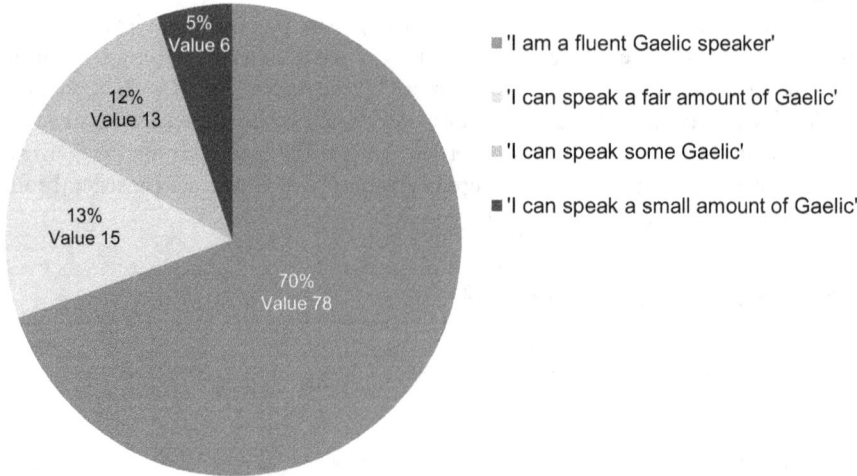

Figure 4.2 Reported Gaelic language abilities (N)

questionnaire respondents may have contributed to the high proportion reporting fluency. Participants were next asked to locate their language competences in both Gaelic and English on a scale of 0 to 10; the results are displayed in Tables 4.8 and 4.9.

As can be seen from a comparison of these two tables, generally very high levels of oracy and literacy were reported in both languages, yet the mean scores for competence in speaking, reading, writing and understanding Gaelic are consistently lower than for English, with differences of 1.8, 2.1, 2.4 and 1.2 in mean scores for each language skill. The possible relationship between professed Gaelic language abilities

Table 4.8 Competence in Gaelic

Ability scale	Speaking Gaelic N (%)	Reading Gaelic N (%)	Writing Gaelic N (%)	Understanding Gaelic N (%)
L 0	0 (0.0)	0 (0)	1 (0.9)	0 (0.0)
1	2 (1.8)	1 (0.9)	2 (1.8)	1 (0.9)
2	0 (0.0)	1 (0.9)	4 (3.6)	1 (0.9)
3	2 (1.8)	3 (2.7)	7 (6.3)	1 (0.9)
4	7 (6.3)	4 (3.6)	7 (6.3)	4 (3.6)
5	7 (6.3)	9 (8.0)	8 (7.1)	3 (2.7)
6	7 (6.3)	4 (3.6)	10 (8.9)	4 (3.6)
7	9 (8.0)	7 (6.3)	13 (11.6)	7 (6.3)
8	14 (12.5)	20 (17.9)	19 (17.0)	12 (10.7)
▼ 9	29 (25.9)	24 (21.4)	15 (13.4)	25 (22.3)
H 10	35 (31.3)	39 (34.8)	26 (23.2)	54 (48.2)
Total	112 (100)	112 (100)	112 (100)	112 (100)
Mean	8.0	7.7	7.1	8.7

Table 4.9 Competence in English

Ability scale	Speaking English N (%)	Reading English N (%)	Writing English N (%)	Understanding English N (%)
L 0	0 (0.0)	0 (0.0)	0 (0.0)	0 (0.0)
1	0 (0.0)	0 (0.0)	0 (0.0)	0 (0.0)
2	0 (0.0)	0 (0.0)	0 (0.0)	0 (0.0)
3	0 (0.0)	0 (0.0)	0 (0.0)	0 (0.0)
4	0 (0.0)	0 (0.0)	0 (0.0)	0 (0.0)
5	0 (0.0)	0 (0.0)	0 (0.0)	0 (0.0)
6	0 (0.0)	0 (0.0)	1 (0.9)	0 (0.0)
7	0 (0.0)	1 (0.9)	5 (4.5)	0 (0.0)
8	3 (2.7)	5 (4.5)	9 (8.0)	0 (0.0)
▼ 9	16 (14.3)	8 (7.1)	18 (16.1)	14 (12.5)
H 10	93 (83.0)	98 (87.5)	79 (70.5)	98 (87.5)
Total	112 (100)	112 (100)	112 (100)	112 (100)
Mean	9.8	9.8	9.5	9.9

Table 4.10 Frequency of Gaelic use

Frequency	N	%
Daily	53	47.3
Weekly	19	17.0
Monthly	17	15.2
< Monthly	17	15.2
Never	6	5.4

and actual usage practices is explored same from a statistical viewpoint in greater detail in section 4.4.4, below.

4.4.3 Overall Gaelic language use

In the third portion of the questionnaire, respondents were asked to indicate how frequently they spoke Gaelic at present, with options ranging from 'at least once a day' to 'never'. The results are shown in Table 4.10.

Almost half of all respondents indicated that they currently hold at least one conversation a day in Gaelic, the largest category overall (47.3%). Proportions of respondents claiming to speak Gaelic at least once a week (17.0%), once a month (15.2%) or less than once a month (15.2%) were very similar, with only 5.4% indicating that they 'never' spoke Gaelic at present. Over a third of respondents (35.8%) reported using Gaelic less frequently than once a month, therefore, while the category of informants who answered that they spoke Gaelic at least once daily may be extremely broad. In order to gain a more detailed picture of Gaelic language use, respondents were then asked to identify which language they would normally use in a range of settings and with various interlocutors. The results are shown in Figures 4.3–4.19, with Figures 4.3–4.4 showing reported Gaelic use at work and at home, Figures 4.5–4.9 detailing reported Gaelic language use with family members, Figures 4.10–4.14 showing reported use with friends, and 4.15–4.19 reported Gaelic language use in leisure activities. In each instance, participants were asked to indicate 'What language would you normally use in the following situations?', on a five-point scale of 'Only English' to 'Only Gaelic', with a further option of 'Not applicable'.

As can be seen from Figure 4.3, 46 respondents indicated that they normally used only English at work or university, representing a proportion of 41.1%. At the same time, 41.9% claimed to use at least equal Gaelic and English, with 10 individuals claiming equal use, 30 claiming to use mostly Gaelic and a further 7 claiming only Gaelic. This is likely to be unrepresentative of GME-leavers generally, particularly given the small size of the Gaelic labour market in Scotland (see Macleod 2008; Campbell et al. 2008). Yet, crucially, when we compare reported language use in the more formal domain of work and study to that of the home (Figure 4.4), we see substantially lower levels of Gaelic use in that setting:

A total of 82 participants claimed to use only or mostly English in the home, amounting to 73.2% of total responses. By contrast, just 25.9% claimed to use at

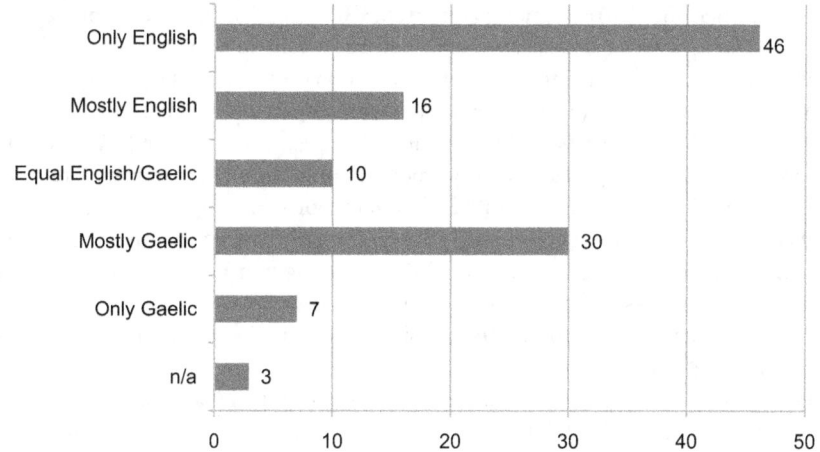

Figure 4.3 Language use at work or university (N)

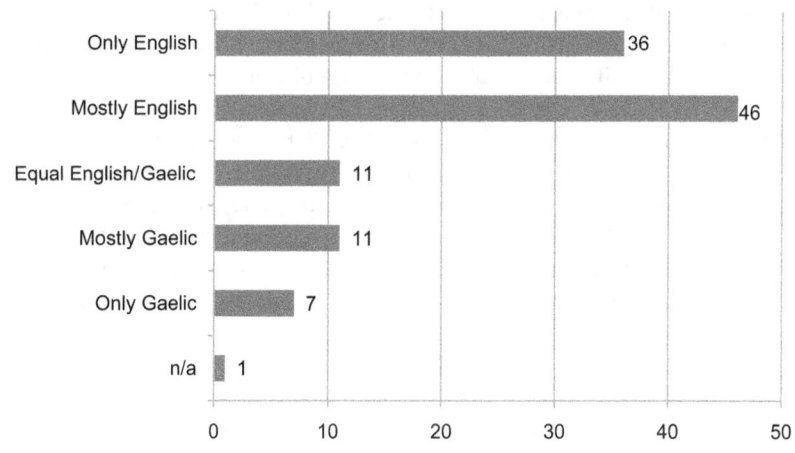

Figure 4.4 Language use at home (N)

least equal Gaelic at home, with 11 informants indicating equal English and Gaelic use (9.8%), 11 reporting mostly Gaelic (9.8%) and 7 reporting only Gaelic (6.3%). Informal use of Gaelic within the home setting therefore appears at first glance to be rather weak; it is noteworthy in this connection that over half of participants (57.2%) reported living with either a partner, a spouse or other family members at present (N=64).

4.4.4 Family Gaelic use, socialisation and intergenerational transmission

As can be seen in Table 4.11, the family members who were most often reported by respondents to be able to speak Gaelic were siblings (60.7%), followed by mothers

(41.1%), fathers (35.7%) and grandparents (26.8%). A total of 28 respondents reported that both their parents could speak Gaelic, and 58 participants had at least one Gaelic-speaking parent (51.8%, compared to 56.5% of interviewees; see Table 4.1).

Whilst 64 respondents (57.1%) reported having a spouse or partner (see Figure 4.7, below), only 12 of these reported that their partner can speak Gaelic (=18.8%). The low proportion reporting Gaelic ability among their children may be partly reflective of the age profile of respondents; only 23 in total reported having children (see Figure 4.8, below). Higher rates of ability in Gaelic reported for siblings compared to parents may reflect parental choice of GME for children among non-Gaelic-speaking parents. To investigate this issue further, Spearman's rank order correlations were calculated for reported Gaelic use to socialisation, ability, continuation in GME and the social variables of age, sex and class.

As suggested in sections 4.1 to 4.3, the interrelationship of Gaelic use and socialisation appears key to understanding the patterns of present-day Gaelic use by former GME students. As can be seen in Table 4.12, the social variables of age, sex and class do not correlate substantially with Gaelic language use. Relatively stronger correlations are, however, shown between Gaelic socialisation and both overall frequency of Gaelic use (=.344), and high home use (=.452). High levels of Gaelic socialisation therefore appear to correlate somewhat with higher levels of present-day use of the language in the home, as well as with general higher frequency of Gaelic use. Crucially, however, continuation with GME correlates strongly with general frequency of Gaelic use (=.690), use of the language at work (=.630) and, to a lesser extent, in the home (=.438). Higher levels of professed speaking ability also correlate with the same usage variables at −.664, −.582 and −.427, respectively (negative correlations here reflecting the lower values that corresponded to higher reported abilities in Gaelic on the survey). Thus, while Gaelic socialisation correlates only weakly with present Gaelic use, stronger correlations are shown for use and 'GME continuation' beyond primary

Table 4.11 Reported Gaelic ability among family members

	Mother	Father	Spouse/ partner	Son/ daughter	Grandparent	Brother/ sister	Other
N	46	40	12	9	30	68	15
%	41.1%	35.7%	10.7%	8.0%	26.8%	60.7%	13.4%

Table 4.12 Reported Gaelic use, socialisation and ability. Spearman's rho correlations

Gaelic use	Age	Sex	Class	Gaelic socialisation	GME continuation	Gaelic speaking ability
Overall frequency	−.076	−.008	.209	.344	.690	−.664
Work use	−.038	−.016	.224	.107	.630	−.582
Home use	.035	−.014	.078	.452	.438	−.427

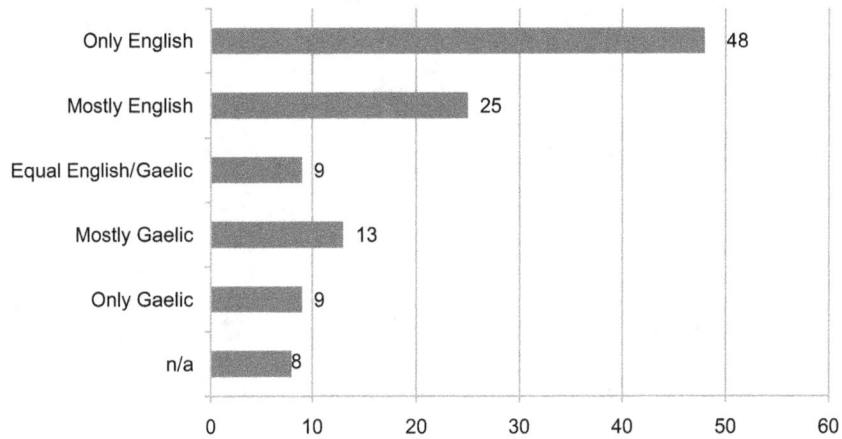

Figure 4.5 Language use with mother (N)

school, highlighting the importance of this factor for continued Gaelic use in later life. Yet as will be demonstrated in due course, socialisation correlates strongly with other crucial variables examined in the quantitative survey (see Table 4.13, below).

We may first examine participants' Gaelic use with key interlocutors. Since only 41.1% of respondents answered that their mother could speak Gaelic (see Table 4.11, above), figures for Gaelic use with a mother (Figure 4.5) show that 48 participants (42.9%) report using only English with their mother, while a further 25 (22.3%) claim to use 'mostly English', amounting to almost two-thirds of all respondents (65.2%).

By comparison, 35.7% of participants answered that their father could speak Gaelic (N=40; see Table 4.11). In light of this limited proportion, the figures for the full dataset again show reduced Gaelic use, with 52 using 'only English' (46.4%), 23 'mostly English' (20.5%), and only 29 informants (25.0%) speaking at least 'equal' Gaelic with fathers:

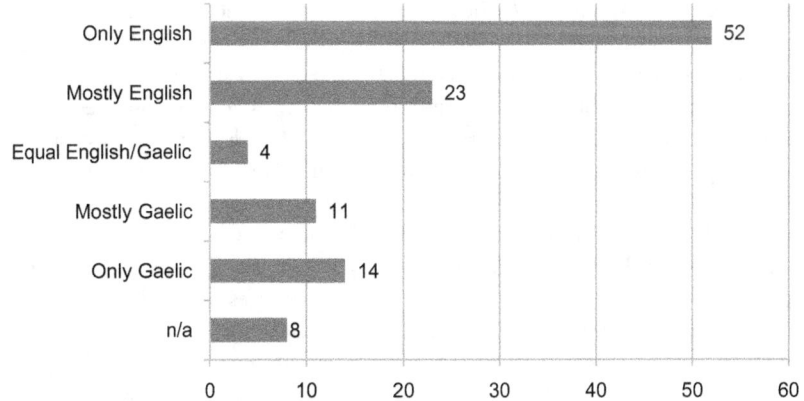

Figure 4.6 Language use with father (N)

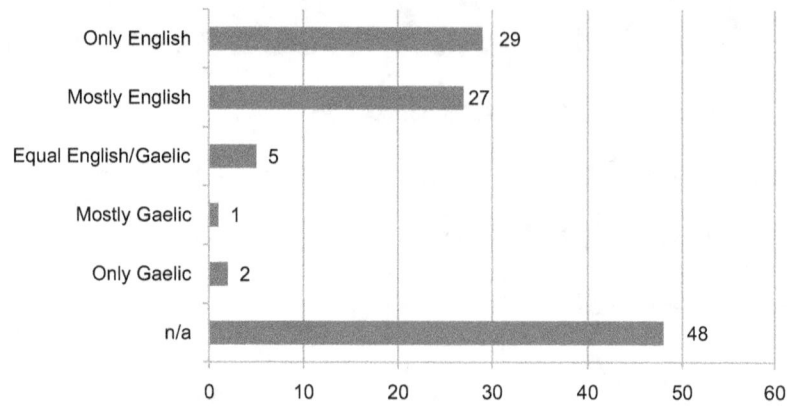

Figure 4.7 Language use with partner/spouse (N)

Yet while Gaelic language use with a parent who cannot speak Gaelic is realistically not a matter of choice for a participant, he or she may be thought to have more choice over their selection of a partner or spouse and the languages they speak to them (although, of course, many other factors may be more influential in an individual's choice of partner). Crucially in this connection, however, English language use predominates to an even greater extent with partners or spouses, as displayed in Figure 4.7:

Therefore, while 64 respondents (57.1%) reported that they were currently in a relationship, only 8 of these reported at least equal Gaelic use with their partner or spouse, amounting to just 12.5% of those in a relationship. As shown in Table 4.11, above, a total of 12 (10.7%) claimed to have a partner who could speak Gaelic, meaning that 4 of these respondents use mostly or only English with their Gaelic-speaking partner. Similarly, and perhaps even more crucially for potential intergenerational transmission rates, while just 23 of the 112 participants (20.5%) responded that they had a son or daughter (Figure 4.8), only 9 of these reported having a child who could speak Gaelic (Table 4.11, above). Of these 9, 5 (55.5%) reported speaking at least equal Gaelic and English to their children, with the remaining 4 speaking mostly English. The fact that only 11 of the 23 respondents with children (47.8%) reported using any Gaelic with them is especially notable, however, particularly in light of the high overall Gaelic usage and ability that was reported (see Figures 4.2 and 4.3, above).

Furthermore, 4 respondents who reported speaking Gaelic to their children did not claim to do so with their partners. Therefore, whilst a large majority of questionnaire participants (79.5%) reported not having children at present, intergenerational transmission of Gaelic among the 20.5% who did so appears from the above data to be weak. This finding may therefore suggest that prospects for the intergenerational transmission of Gaelic to future generations by GME-leavers are currently limited, though more research would be needed to verify this suggestion.

As was true of language use with partners/spouses (see Figure 4.7, above), low use of Gaelic was also reported for interactions with siblings, as shown in Figure 4.9. Significantly, siblings were the family members most frequently reported to be able to speak Gaelic in Table 4.11 (above), and it is notable that only 17 of the 68 (25.0%) that

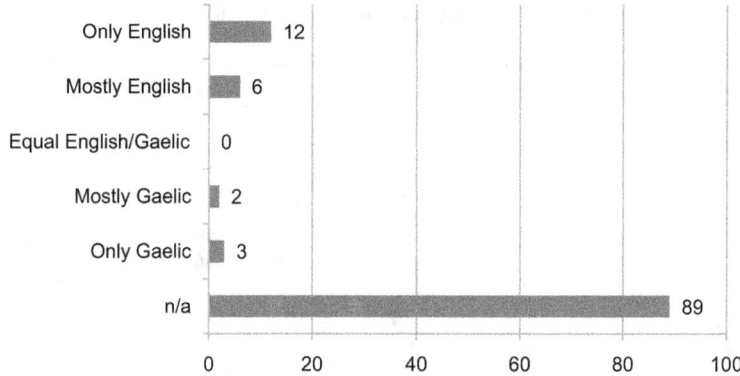

Figure 4.8 Language use with son/daughter (N)

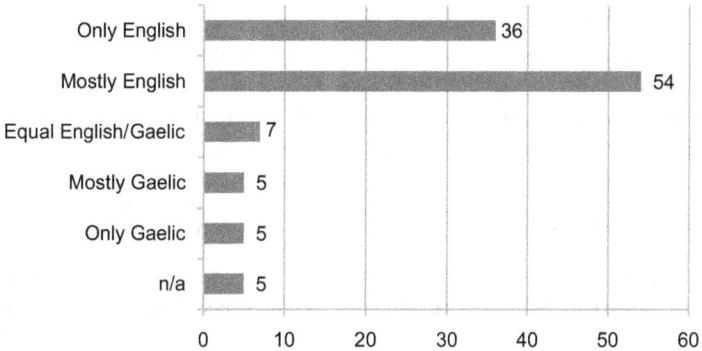

Figure 4.9 Language use with brother/sister (N)

reported having siblings who could speak it actually claim to use at least equal Gaelic with them; crucially, only 5 of these respondents report using only Gaelic with them (7.4%). Again, therefore, low levels of Gaelic use with peers in the same age group are clear from Figure 4.9. These findings have clear implications for the maintenance of Gaelic by siblings in GME who were not socialised in Gaelic by parents at home and, potentially, for the limited prospects for intergenerational transmission of the language by this group. To bring this issue more clearly into relief, Table 4.13 displays statistical correlations between family language use and social and linguistic variables.

Once again, age, sex and occupational class are observed not to correlate clearly with language use in Table 4.13 (compare Table 4.12, above). Yet significantly, high levels of Gaelic socialisation correlate consistently with high reported Gaelic use with mothers (=.511), fathers (=.502), grandparents (=.514) and, again, particularly strongly with Gaelic use with children (=.669). These correlations highlight the importance of language socialisation to participants' continued use of Gaelic (see sections 4.2 to 4.3, above), as well as, crucially, to their potential – and actual – ability to pass the language on. Importantly, however, relatively strong correlations are also observed between present Gaelic use with a son or daughter and continuation with

Table 4.13 Family Gaelic use – linguistic and social variables. Spearman's rho correlations

Gaelic use/ family member	Age	Sex	Class	Gaelic socialisation	GME continuation
Mother	−.161	.035	.161	**.511**	.362
Father	−.099	.015	.302	**.502**	.154
Partner/spouse	−.108	−.117	−.010	.161	.416
Son/daughter	−.145	.323	−.196	**.669**	**.645**
Grandmother/-father	.161	−.035	.052	**.514**	.465
Brother/sister	.110	−.121	−.010	.238	.203
Other family	−.053	−.055	−.007	.319	**.521**

Gaelic study (=.645), reflecting the vital importance of both variables for intergenerational transmission of the language. Whilst overall levels of family Gaelic use are low in comparison with English (see Figures 4.5–4.9), statistical analysis thus demonstrates the vital importance of both socialisation in Gaelic and continuation with GME beyond primary school, both of which correlate with high levels of continued Gaelic use with key interlocutors such as partners and children.

4.4.5 Social use of Gaelic: Conversation, technology and (social) media

Next in the online survey, participants were asked to identify the languages they use socially, firstly with all friends (Figure 4.10) and then specifically with friends who can speak Gaelic (Figure 4.11). As can be seen in Figure 4.10, use of Gaelic with all friends in participants' social networks is low in comparison with English, while a slightly different picture is apparent for conversation with Gaelic-speaking friends specifically.

While we therefore see greater levels of Gaelic use in conversation with friends who are able to speak Gaelic, with whom 40.2% of respondents report using at least

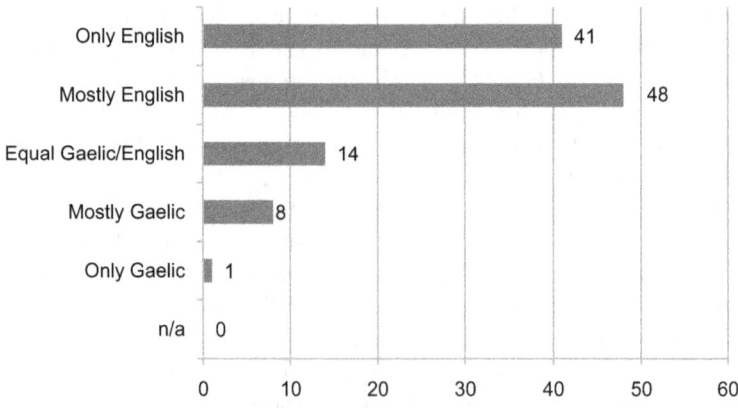

Figure 4.10 Conversation with all friends (N)

LINGUISTIC PRACTICE, GAELIC USE AND LANGUAGE SOCIALISATION: FINDINGS 103

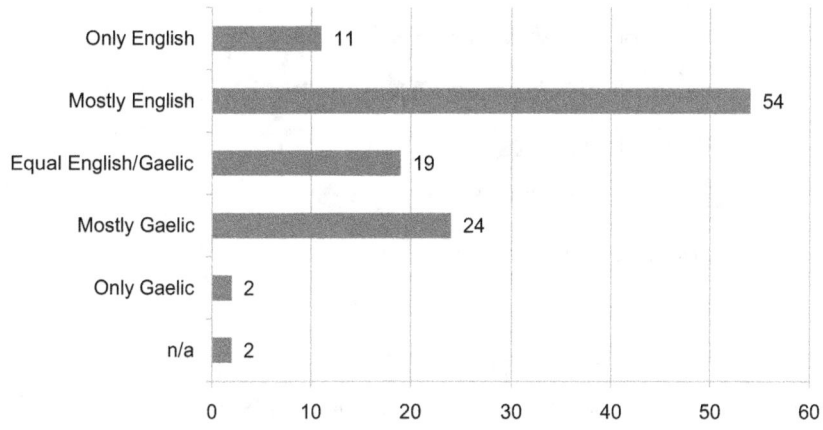

Figure 4.11 Conversation with Gaelic-speaking friends (N)

'equal' Gaelic (N=45; Figure 4.11) – compared to 20.5% with 'all' friends (N=23; Figure 4.10) – English use nevertheless predominates in both graphs. In conversation with friends who can speak Gaelic (Figure 4.11), although just 11 participants report using only English (9.8%), 54 use mostly English (48.2%). Crucially, just 2 (1.8%) report using 'only' Gaelic with such friends, the same number as indicate they have no friends who can speak it ('n/a'). This finding is particularly important from a language planning perspective, as it is clear that peer use of the language, even with friends who speak Gaelic, is notably low. When we compare face-to-face conversation with friends who can speak Gaelic (Figure 4.11) with communication via other means – such as phone, text or social media (Figures 4.12, 4.13 and 4.14) – even lower levels of Gaelic use are notable.

In Figure 4.12, 36 respondents claim to use at least equal amounts of Gaelic in phone conversations with Gaelic-speaking friends (32.1%). The corresponding

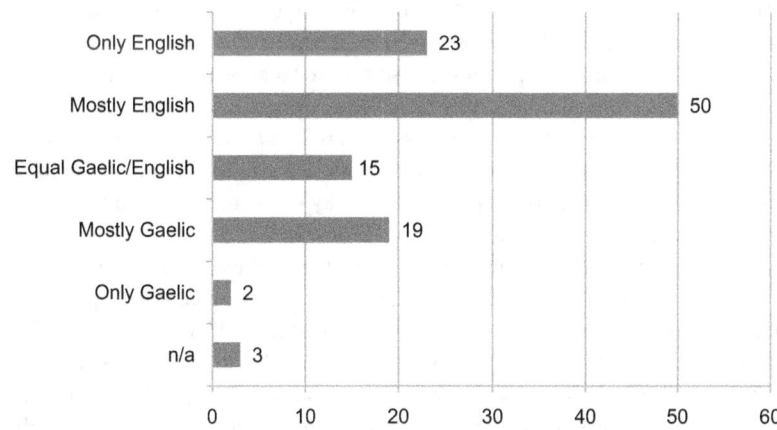

Figure 4.12 Communicating with Gaelic-speaking friends – phone (N)

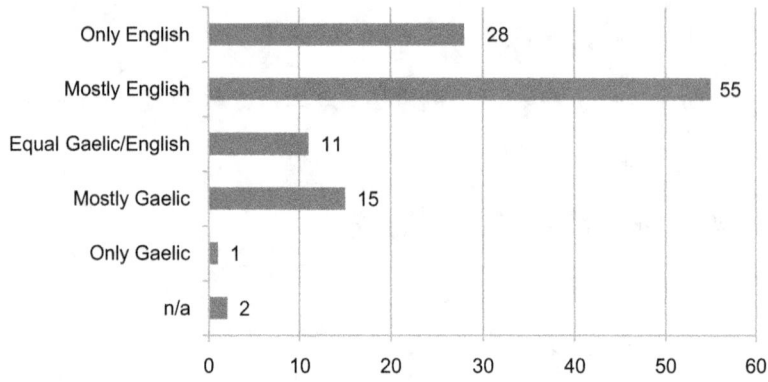

Figure 4.13 Communicating with Gaelic-speaking friends – SMS/text (N)

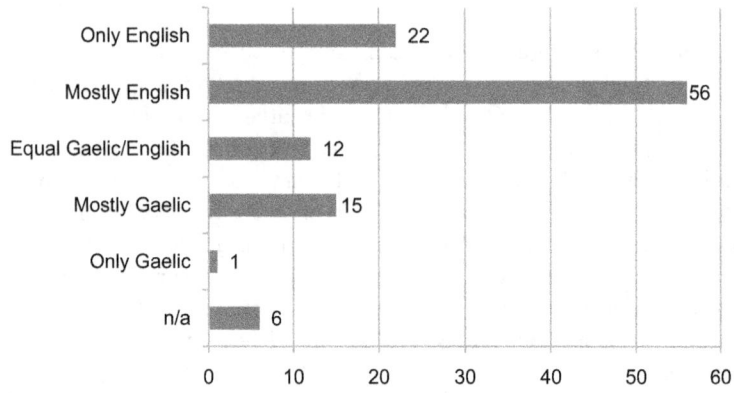

Figure 4.14 Communicating with Gaelic-speaking friends – social media (N)

percentages are just 24.1% for SMS/text message (Figure 4.13) and 25% for exchanges on social media (Figure 4.14). Since a greater proportion of social interaction now takes place via smartphones and social media apps than ever before, the low levels of Gaelic use reported here may have very important implications. Next on the language use survey, respondents were asked to reflect on the languages they used in their leisure time generally. Use of Gaelic across five areas of language use in leisure activity is displayed in Figures 4.15–4.19. As may be seen, use of English predominates to an even greater degree across these leisure activities:

A total of 25 respondents report making at least 'equal' use of Gaelic when listening to music and radio during leisure time (22.3%) and 16 using at least 'equal' amounts of Gaelic when watching television (14.3%), compared to 13 when reading (11.6%), 7 when using social media (6.3%) and 9 whilst using other internet sites (8.0%). Low engagement with Gaelic television compared to radio and music is notable in these data, as, again, is low use of Gaelic within the electronic domains of social media and the internet (see Crystal 2000). Table 4.14 displays correlations (calculated using

LINGUISTIC PRACTICE, GAELIC USE AND LANGUAGE SOCIALISATION: FINDINGS 105

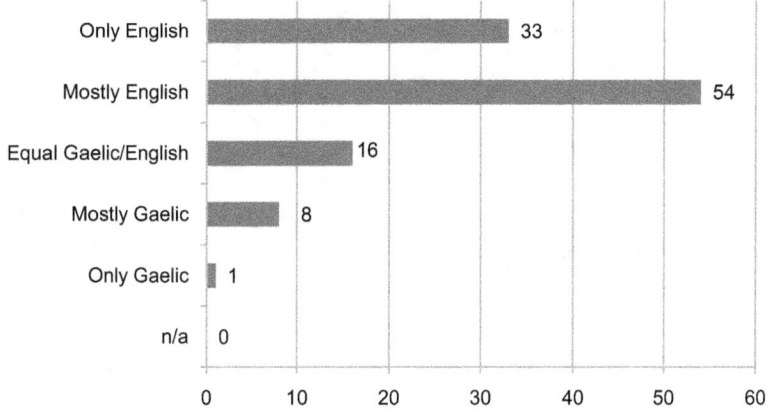

Figure 4.15 Listening to music/radio (N)

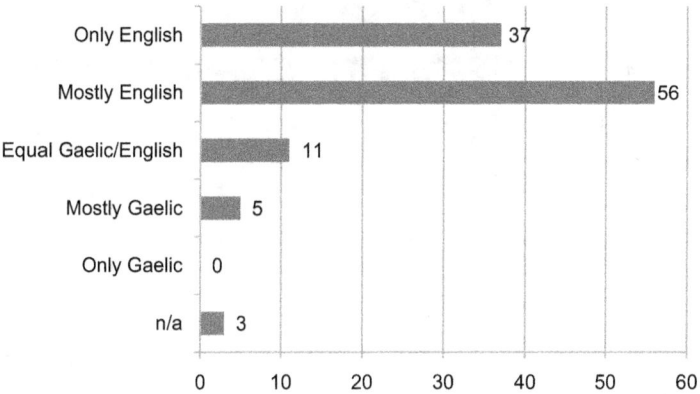

Figure 4.16 Watching television (N)

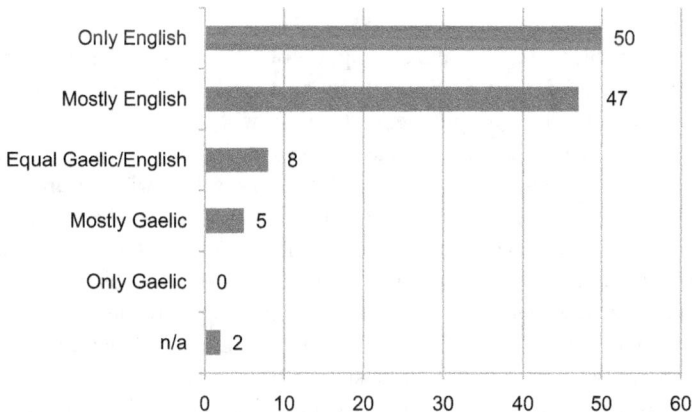

Figure 4.17 Reading books (N)

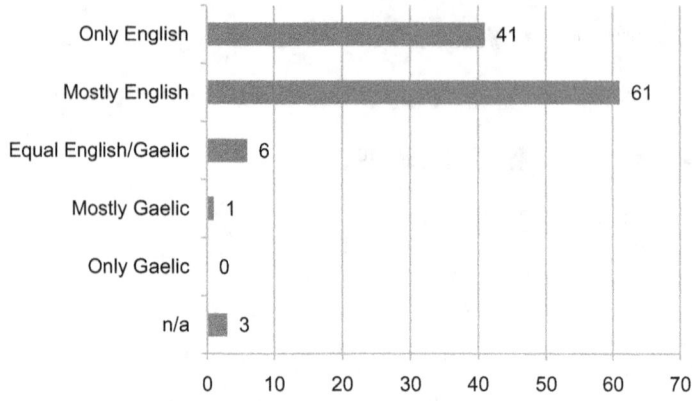

Figure 4.18 Using social media (N)

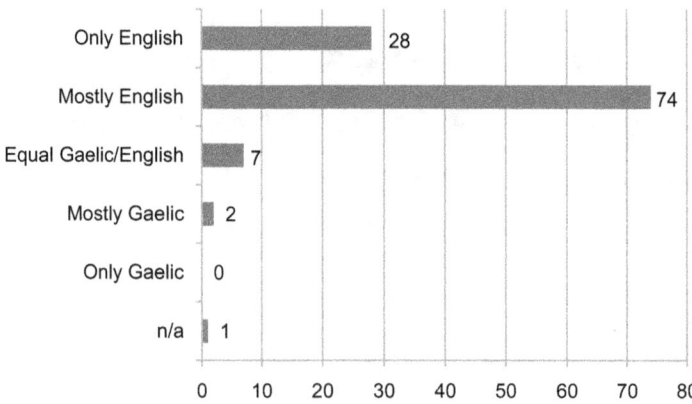

Figure 4.19 Using other internet (N)

Spearman's rho) between language use in these settings, as well as with friends, and social and linguistic variables discussed previously:

Whilst social variables of sex, age and class appear once again not to correlate with Gaelic use, notable correlations are displayed between GME continuation (see Table 4.4, above) and use of Gaelic with all friends (=.570), with Gaelic-speaking friends specifically (=.567), Gaelic use on the phone with Gaelic-speaking friends (=.630) and on social media with Gaelic-speaking friends (=.512), as well as with leisure time use of Gaelic radio or music (=.533) and on social media generally (=.512). This again suggests the crucial importance of continuation with Gaelic-medium study for former pupils' ongoing access to Gaelic-speaking social networks. By comparison, reported levels of Gaelic socialisation seem to bear little relationship to the use of Gaelic in these contexts, in contrast to Table 4.13 (above). GME continuation beyond primary school is clearly, therefore, a key variable in bolstering social use of Gaelic after completion of school, correlating particularly strongly with the use of Gaelic with friends and in leisure time.

Table 4.14 Social (/-media) use, social and linguistic variables. Spearman's rho correlations

Social use	Age	Sex	Class	Socialisation	GME continuation
All friends	−.054	−.109	.139	.285	**.570**
Gaelic-speaking friends	.025	−.034	−.001	.170	**.567**
– Phone	.050	−.069	.013	.214	**.630**
– SMS/text	.037	.001	−.081	.180	.485
– Social media	.051	.025	.025	.177	**.512**
Radio/music	.028	.000	−.017	.192	**.533**
TV	.019	−.084	.016	.188	.436
Books	.048	−.051	.020	.215	.495
Social media	.051	.025	.025	.177	**.512**
Internet	.039	−.009	.016	.265	.477

4.5 Concluding remarks and data triangulation

The results of the sociolinguistic questionnaire described above correspond closely to the qualitative results reported in sections 4.1 to 4.3 of this chapter, lending support to the conclusion that low levels of Gaelic use prevail among former GME students – particularly in their interactions with peers, friends and partners. There is clearly a consistent relationship between higher levels of Gaelic ability and use in the present day, as there is between high levels of Gaelic use and past socialisation in the language, and continuation with GME beyond primary school. Triangulation of the qualitative and quantitative datasets thus produces a clear picture of limited ongoing Gaelic use among the majority of 130 Gaelic-medium educated adults who participated in the study, particularly in respect of the key domains of home and community, which, as noted in Chapters 2 and 3, have frequently been theorised to be crucial to language maintenance. Indeed, the statistical analysis outlined in section 4.4 further confirms this view, emphasising the importance of past pupils' Gaelic socialisation in the home domain to their continued use of the language.

5

Underlying Language Use: Gaelic Language Ideologies and Attitudes

This chapter considers the role that participants' ideological and attitudinal stances may play in determining their current language practices. Language practices among former GME students – both the overall extent and the nature of interviewees' Gaelic use – were analysed in Chapter 4, and demonstrated to be rather limited among the majority of participants. Reported socialisation experiences were subsequently discussed in light of what these contributed to the picture of present Gaelic language use emerging from interviewee accounts, questionnaire responses and statistical correlation. This chapter presents an analysis of interviewees' language ideologies with a view to understanding how interviewees' linguistic ideologies may also influence their language practices. Ideologies will be examined in respect of (appropriate) Gaelic use and the wider Gaelic community (5.1), and the perceived relevance of Gaelic for cultural identities (5.2).

The analysis of ideologies, as presented in this chapter, thus contributes to our understanding of the attitudinal stances that may underlie participants' Gaelic language use, and demonstrates how ideological factors can both rationalise and reinforce present language practices. Ideologies of regret and 'guilt' with regard to current Gaelic (dis)use, perceptions of linguistic 'snobbery' in the Gaelic community, and opportunity and choice in Gaelic use each appear to convey rationalisations for participants' current linguistic practices. Similarly, a generally weak social identity in the language (section 5.2) clearly plays a role in rationalising and explaining interviewees' current language practices. Section 5.3 quantitatively analyses questionnaire respondents' reactions to eighteen attitudinal statements concerning Gaelic, its relevance to speakers' sociocultural identities, the Gaelic community and GME. As I demonstrate, language attitudes (examined here as responses to particular attitudinal propositions) pattern closely with language ideologies identified in qualitative interview analysis. Taken together, the analyses of attitudes and ideologies strongly indicate speaker rationales underlying the linguistic practices of adults who received a Gaelic-medium education.

5.1 Ideologies of Gaelic I: Language use

The first section of analysis presented in this chapter deals specifically with ideologies of Gaelic language use. Five discursive themes are discernible in the dataset with regard to Gaelic use, and I address each of these in turn. Firstly, section 5.1.1 considers interviewees' ideologies of regret and 'guilt' with regard to their current Gaelic use, while the following section analyses ideologies regarding the intergenerational transmission of Gaelic (section 5.1.2). The remaining three sections concern perceptions of linguistic 'snobbery' in Gaelic use (section 5.1.3), and ideologies concerning language loss (section 5.1.4) and of opportunity and choice to use Gaelic (section 5.1.5). I argue that these five discursive themes of Gaelic use can contribute in various ways to our understanding of the language use patterns that were presented in Chapter 4 of this book; crucially, the language ideologies conveyed by interviewees in this connection have a clear role in rationalising and explaining their current language practices.

5.1.1 Discourses of regret/'guilt'

The first category of ideas discussed consists of interviewees' beliefs concerning how the language is used or ought to be used, particularly the view that they should use Gaelic differently. This can be conceived of as an ideology of regret or guilt expressed by many interviewees when considering their engagement with the language in the present day. When stating a desire to use Gaelic differently, some participants therefore describe 'missing' the language in their daily lives:

> LF03   I do miss it actually- the (.)
> SD   Yeah?=
> LF03   =the Gaelic input
> SD   Uh huh
> LF03   For (.) every- well maybe not everyday use but for at least sort of for regular (.) regular use [. . .] it's the kind of thing that I don't want to lose [. . .] But ((sighs)) do you know- I would like to do something and (.) e:m if there was events sort of locally that I could (.) that I you know- maybe I'm just not looking hard enough really

A certain sense of regret at not using the language frequently in the present day is communicated by informant LF03 in the above account, although she admits the possibility that there may be opportunities to speak it more, for which she simply has not looked hard enough. In any case, she states that 'everyday use' as such is not something to which she would necessarily aspire. This mild and rather vague sense of regret has therefore not been sufficient to motivate the speaker actually to seek such opportunities. A lack of motivation is similarly referred to in the following extract:

> LF04   I suppose it's a bit of a sad story really [. . .] I had in my head that at some point it might be nice to have something where you can meet up with other people that did but uh it's just a lack of eh (1.1) lack of- not quite enough motivation to actually organise something like that

As such, the speaker's reflection here on the 'sad story' of her current disuse of Gaelic contrasts somewhat with her lack of 'motivation' to pursue the idea of seeking out other Gaelic speakers. This relatively mild expression of regret is notable in that it fails to provide sufficient incentive for speakers actually to change their current language practices. A stronger form of the discourse is visible in the following participant's reference to feeling a potent sense of 'guilt' at her disuse of Gaelic:

> SD   [N]ot using it you know- not having the opportunity to speak it- you become rusty and [. . .] it's not so easy to do
>
> IF05   No it isn't it's really, really hard (.) and I- but the thing is then I feel really guilty
>
> SD   Hmm
>
> IF05   I feel <u>really</u> guilty that I- my Gaelic isn't good and then I feel really <u>guilty</u> when I go home and I can't speak to my next-door neighbour and I answer in English [. . .] I'm sorry for sounding so negative, I'm really not as negative as I sound (.) I just- the guilt factor's massive for me

At the start of this excerpt, my reflection on my own experience of language attrition, after spending time away from the Gaelic community and living outside of Scotland, prompts speaker IF05 to comment on her own feelings of guilt at this situation. She refers three times to feeling 'really guilty' at her inability to speak Gaelic well, highlighting problems she faces trying to speak the language to her neighbour when returning home to the Western Isles. In contrast to the vague expression of this feeling described above, therefore, the palpable sense of negative affect in this extract may in fact militate against this speaker's greater use of Gaelic. She apologises for being overly 'negative' in this connection, and her claim that the 'guilt factor's massive' clearly reflects the strong feeling to which she refers here. In the following account, by contrast, a native Gaelic speaker absolutely rejects the ideology of guilt, along with the idea that speakers should use Gaelic more:

> IF07   [C]ha chleachdainn-sa barrachd Gàidhlig nam biodh (x) ann- can an-dràsta- nam biodh cuideigin **shìos** an staidhre 's nan robh cothrom agamsa cofaidh a / dh'òrdachadh/ ann an Gàidhlig
>
> > *I wouldn't use more Gaelic if there were (x)- say just now- if there was someone downstairs and if I had the opportunity to order a coffee in Gaelic*
>
> SD   Hmm
>
> IF07   Chan eil sin a' ciallachadh càil dhomh
>
> > *That doesn't mean a thing to me*
>
> SD   Chan eil
>
> > *No*
>
> IF07   Ma tha mi a' siubhal a dh'àiteigin agus 's urrainn dhomh na soidhnichean a leughadh ann am Beurla no ann an Gàidhlig (.) chan eil sin a' ciallachadh càil sam bith [. . .] chan eil fhios 'am dè a' Ghàidhlig a th' air **tokenism**, ach ma tha thu faicinn nan soidhnichean ann am Beurla 's ann an Gàidhlig tha mi smaoinich' '**oh come on!**'
>
> > *If I go somewhere and I can read the signs in English or in Gaelic (.) that doesn't mean a thing [. . .] I don't know what the Gaelic is for* **tokenism**, *but if you see the signs in English and Gaelic I just think* '**oh come on!**'

UNDERLYING LANGUAGE USE: IDEOLOGIES AND ATTITUDES 111

The opportunity to use more Gaelic in the Lowland city where this speaker now lives – for example, when ordering a coffee in the local café in which we meet – is likened to the 'tokenism' she sees in bilingual signage, and she states unequivocally that such banal use of Gaelic has no meaning for her (*'chan eil sin a' ciallachadh càil dhomh'*). The feeling that one should use Gaelic more often for its own sake is thus rejected by this speaker, and by several other interviewees in the corpus. Awareness of an ideology that speakers should use Gaelic in any situation in which the opportunity exists is demonstrated frequently across the dataset, and whilst some interviewees express that belief in its stronger or weaker forms, others appear to reject it out of hand. Yet even in cases where the ideology is conveyed in the strongest terms, it seems not to contribute to speakers' actual intentions to use more Gaelic. In some cases, feelings of regret or guilt seem instead to militate against increased Gaelic use, while other speakers react against this ideology, arguing that 'tokenistic' use of the language for its own sake is meaningless. In its various forms, therefore, this first set of ideologies seems not to encourage greater use of the language.

5.1.2 Intergenerational transmission and Gaelic use

A second set of beliefs concerning Gaelic use concerns intergenerational transmission, and speakers' anticipation that their desire to pass the language on to children may increase their use of Gaelic in future. Many participants voice the belief that speakers of Gaelic have a responsibility to pass on the language on to their children, as expressed in the following extract, for example:

> SD   Would you be keen in theory to pass the language on to your kids in future?
> IM02   Yeah definitely [. . .] I still think that if you've got the- if you've got it then you sort of have a duty to pass it on like

While not using Gaelic regularly today, informant IM02 states that he would nevertheless try to pass the language on to children in the future, asserting that he feels 'a duty' to do so. The following informant similarly reports wanting to raise her children with Gaelic in the future, whilst reflecting on her current use of Gaelic:

> SD   [W]ould you be keen that your children would speak Gaelic, or?
> LF03   Yeah no- I would definitely like to and I would- I (.) I hope (.) I mean I'm not sure (.) I suppose now because I do feel a bit (.) rustier ((laughing)) [. . .] I would probably want to um (.) definitely brush up on it – you know – to make sure that I wasn't (1.0) em that I was- that if I was doing that that I was doing it properly

The speaker reflects that she would definitely want to 'brush up on' her Gaelic language skills in order to pass the language on to her children, having at first hesitated when thinking about her current abilities. Doing so would obviously be easier for some participants than others, depending to a large degree on home linguistic background, having a Gaelic-speaking partner, wider family connections and so on. Yet even for speakers in relationships with partners who can speak Gaelic, use of Gaelic at home may be weak at present. In such instances, discussions or even decisions on future use of Gaelic are often reported, as in the following excerpt:

IM01   Tha sinn aig an àm nar beatha far a bheil sinn smaoineachadh air 's dòcha teaghlach a thòiseachadh agus **you know** bhruidhinn sinn mu dheidhinn- 'uill am bu chòir 's dòcha dhuinn a bhith a' bruidhinn Gàidhlig?' **You know** oidhirp a dhèanamh- feuchainn ri 's dòcha tionndadh gu Gàidhlig cho tric 's a ghabhas airson 's gum bi seòrsa
We're at the time of our lives where we're thinking about perhaps starting a family and **you know** *we spoke about it- 'well should we maybe speak Gaelic?'* **You know** *make an effort, try to maybe switch to Gaelic as often as possible so that there will be a sort of*

SD   Seadh=
       Yeah=

IM01   =suidheachadh Gàidhlig aig an taigh ach 's e misneachd a th' ann- tha e glè cheart
       =*Gaelic context at home but it's a confidence thing- it's true*

The matter of intergenerational transmission has thus recently been a point of discussion for this interviewee, who reflects on having spoken to his wife about switching to Gaelic at home to create a Gaelic environment before starting a family. Yet he raises the point that confidence ('*misneachd*') is a major consideration here, a lack of which is seen partly to explain why the couple do not currently use Gaelic together at home. As the following speaker states, however, introducing such a home language policy after a couple has become accustomed to using another language together may not be so straightforward:

IF12   [M]a dh'fhàsas tu faisg (.) le cuideigin ann/s/ an aon chànan (.)
       If you grow close (.) to someone in one language (.)

SD   Hmm

IF12   **You know** tha- mar gum biodh em (.) **you know bond in a language** mar gum biodh [. . .] seach gu bheil leanabh beag againn tha sinn feuchainn ri barrachd Gàidhlig a bhruidhinn (.) ach a-rithist nuair a thòisich sinn ri chèile 's e Beurla a bh' againn agus tha mi smaoineachadh g' eil e tòrr nas nàdarra dhuinn a bhith bruidhinn Beurla
You know there's a- as it were em (.) **you know bond in a language** *as it were [. . .] because we have a little child we're trying to speak more Gaelic (.) but again when we started going out together we spoke English and I think it's much more natural for us to speak English*

As this speaker observes, therefore, after a 'bond in a language' has been cemented, it may in fact be somewhat difficult to make the kind of switch to which the previous speaker (IM01) referred (see also De Houwer 2007). Speaking with the benefit of experience, informant IF12 describes how it remains 'much more natural' (*tòrr nas nàdarra*) for her and her husband to use English together, even as they try to raise and socialise their young child in Gaelic. Across the interview corpus, therefore, participants often report the belief that they should at least try to pass the language on, even if they themselves use the language only rarely today. The overall ideology maintains that this is the duty of adults with Gaelic, and many interviewees report their desire and intention to do so. Nevertheless, it seems unlikely that the pervasiveness of this belief will translate in most cases to substantially greater use of the language in future. The few interviewees who are currently raising children rarely report successfully implementing such a change in home language practices, though it is a relatively widespread belief among interviewees; twelve interviewees voice the belief that such a shift in language use will inevitably follow the experience of having a child. It appears from the above participants' accounts, however, that this anticipated change in language practices should not be assumed.

5.1.3 'Judgement' and 'snobbery' in the Gaelic community

The third set of beliefs concerning Gaelic language use that I consider here concerns interviewees' perceptions of judgemental attitudes and linguistic 'snobbery' within the Gaelic community. Participants generally attribute behaviour of this kind to some 'other' kind of speaker, whether a native speaker or learner, that they believe exhibits such snobbery. Informant IF03, for example, described judgemental behaviour of this kind as being possibly 'a generation thing':

IF04	I would rather people just used it in any way
SD	Yeah=
IF04	=And not feel pressurised to
SD	Yeah (.) or monitored or scrutinised?
IF03	Maybe there's a generation thing [. . .] we're in this sort of world with Gaelic and it's a bit controversial but you know it's very much like 'oh she speaks terribly' or 'listen to her'=
IF04	=Oh there's a huge snobbery in it [. . .] I think you just hit the nail on the head when you were saying that it's wrong and what you said earlier about there being a snobbery and it being=
SD	=Yeah
IF04	judgemental- it's like that is <u>very</u> true in Gaelic which is something that actually really, <u>really</u> frustrates me about Gaelic

IF03 offers constructed dialogues as examples of the denigrating comments of speakers that she objects to, comments that her flatmate (IF04) then characterises as being 'judgemental' and reflecting 'snobbery'. The latter states at the start of the extract that she would rather see people use the language 'in any way', without feeling pressured to do so correctly. This sentiment is similarly expressed in the following account, in which informant IM01 is particularly disdainful of such judgemental stances:

IM01	Mura h-eil thu air a bhith gu Sabhal Mòr Ostaig cha bhi fios agad no tuigse agad gu dearbh dè seòrsa daoine a tha a' frithealadh an /t/-àite sin agus an seòrsa (.) dè

> am facal airson **judgement**? [. . .] fhios 'ad **the judgement look**-'chleachdadh an tuiseal **instead of this** tuiseal **and blah blah blah'** you know na Gàidhlig **police**- you know na **grammar police** [. . .] **you know 'it's not aspirated'** rudan eile- **you know actually** tha mise caran coma uaireannan
>> *Unless you've been to* [Gaelic college] *Sabhal Mòr Ostaig you won't know or indeed understand what sort of people attend that place and the sort of (.) what's the word for judgement?[. . .] you know* judgement look- *'used the* case *instead of this* case *and blah blah blah' you know the Gaelic* police- you know *the* grammar police [. . .] you know 'it's not aspirated' *other things*- you know actually *sometimes I'm a bit indifferent*

This speaker switches with striking frequency to English in the above extract, mixing languages even at the morpho-syntactic level, as in the phrase 'na Gàidhlig **police** . . . na **grammar police**' to emphasise his objection to such judgemental practices. At the same time, his use of language mixing here may again have a role in adopting an 'other' voice when relating potentially controversial views (see Dunmore and Smith-Christmas 2015). We see the use of the speech device 'blah blah blah' to scorn the attitudes of individuals who are perceived to engage in unwelcome corrections of others' Gaelic language use. His example of Sabhal Mòr Ostaig, the Gaelic college on the Isle of Skye (a key site for the instruction and socialisation of many learners), as an environment where judgements of this kind occur, reflects his impression of the scale of the problem. Indeed, the detrimental effects of this kind of judgement are even reported to have been observed in the GME classroom:

> LF08   Somebody was doing an interview
> SD   Mm hmm
> LF08   e:m for the radio or something (.) and em (.) and it was very (.) Glasgow Gaelic if you like
> SD   Oh right uh huh
> LF08   And when we were listening to it on the radio the (.) who eh- the kid that was getting interviewed (.) kinda got knocked afterwards by the teacher saying 'oh that was very Glasgow Gaelic' and I think that really sort of knocked their confidence

The damage to speakers' confidence that comments of this kind can inflict is frequently referred to by interview participants, and these kinds of ideas and perceptions of the Gaelic community are described by speakers who reported widely varying Gaelic language use, ability and socialisation. The issue is described as an even more fundamental issue in the following excerpt:

> IF09   Em tha beàrn mòr an-dràsta eadar (.) **you know** na seann Ghàidheil aig an robh a' Ghàidhlig o thùs agus Gàidhlig an là an-diugh [. . .] tha: tòrr nach eil deònach a bhith a' bruidhinn ris an luchd-ionnsachaidh [. . .] em (.) **you know** tha gu leòr eile ann ag ràdh 'och, dè am feum ann a bhith a' bruidhinn na Gàidhlig?' neo 'dè a' Ghàidhlig (neònach) a th' agad?' Em **so** tha **tensions** an-sin tha mi a' smaoineachadh

> Em there's a big divide at the moment between (.) **you know** the old Gaels who are native speakers and present-day Gaelic [. . .] there's: lots who aren't willing to speak to learners [. . .] em (.) **you know** there's lots of others who say 'och, what use is there in speaking Gaelic?' or 'what (strange) Gaelic you speak! Em **so** there are **tensions** there I think

Rather than merely relating a perception of linguistic snobbery, speaker IF09 describes the phenomenon as a major divide (*beàrn*:'fissure', 'gap') between some traditional speakers whom she refers to as '*na seann Ghàidheil*' (literally, 'old Gaels') and the modern community of speakers. The constructed dialogues that she attributes to native speakers of this kind are not only judgemental but negative generally, questioning the value of speaking Gaelic at all. Whilst not all interviewees refer to such a fundamental divide in the Gaelic world, ideas concerning perceived linguistic snobbery and judgementalism are described frequently throughout the corpus. Whether such beliefs about Gaelic speakers generally are accurate or not, issues of ideology that are at play here clearly impact on the confidence of less experienced speakers actually to use the language. In this way, the ideology of snobbery and judgement in the Gaelic community is replicated, and with it perceptions of negative affect with regard to using the language are spread.

5.1.4 Disuse, loss and 'having' Gaelic

Two competing ideologies of language use in relation to the attrition of Gaelic language skills were reported by interviewees in interviews. Firstly, a large proportion of participants reported feeling that their abilities in Gaelic had declined because of their limited use of the language in past years, while a smaller number stated that using the language frequently had prevented such attrition. By contrast, other interviewees reported feeling that 'having' Gaelic, without necessarily speaking or using it in their day-to-day lives, was valuable to them in and of itself. Firstly, therefore, the following two extracts exemplify the belief of various speakers that attrition of Gaelic language skills arises because of disuse:

IF13	I think I'm quite **lapach** (*rusty*) because (.) I don't really have anybody that I speak it [*i.e.* Gaelic] to regularly
SD	Uh huh
IF13	Like you know if you're not using it it does kind of like (.) it's probably- it would be fine if I started speaking- speaking it right now but I wouldn't feel very confident [[kind of thing]
SD	[[Yeah that's the thing-] just a question of confidence I suppose
IF13	I think (.) I probably- I probably sh:ould go along to stuff ((laughs)) [. . .] I know if I don't use it then (.) I'll lose it kind of thing

The above participant thus reports feeling less fluent in the language than they used to be, a situation she blames on having limited opportunities to use the language; she claims in turn 1 that she is '*lapach*' or rusty in the language because of a lack of

Gaelic-speaking peers and interlocutors with whom she could use it. It is notable here that the speaker expresses a sense of culpability in the decline of her language abilities, recalling the first ideology described in section 5.1.1, above. She states in turn 5 that she 'probably should go along' to Gaelic events, placing particular emphasis on and elongating the initial consonant of 'should' – and laughing. The idea that using the language prevents attrition, or even helps to improve one's language skills, is advanced in the following excerpt:

> SD   A bheil thu a' creidsinn g' eil (.) cleachdadh làitheil air neo um (.) cunbhalach na Gàidhlig cudromach dhutsa?
> *Do you think that (.) daily or (.) regular use of Gaelic is important to you?*
> LM06   Em:: (.) tha ((laughs))
> *yes*
> SD   ((laughs))
> LM06   Tha (1.9) Siud an dòigh as fheàrr a bhith fàs nas fheàrr=
> *Yes (1.9) That's the best way to get better*
> SD   =Uh huh
> LM06   a bhith cleachdadh=
> *to use=*
> SD   =Ann a bhith ga cleachdadh?=
> *=Through using it?=*
> LM06   =cleachdadh làitheil (.) em (.) is toil leam gun urrainn dhomh sin a dhèanamh
> *=daily use (.) em (.) I like that I can do that*

Informant LM06 therefore considers the opportunity that he has to use Gaelic regularly as the best way to improve his own abilities in the language. Yet in contrast to the above extracts, which exemplify speakers' belief that disuse leads to language decline, various interviewees expressed a rather different view, that possessing abilities in the language and 'having' Gaelic without necessarily speaking it have value in and of themselves:

> IF13   You know I really should speak it a wee bit more (.) em: [. . .] I think it's really nice to <u>have</u> Gaelic and I think it <u>has</u> helped me- obviously I did it at uni which was good and if I'd wanted I probably could've gone on and got a job

> LF01   Um I think that if you learn to speak it even if you don't have the opportunity to use it every day that (.) it's still there
> SD   It's still there- and you can access it again?
> LF01   I mean personally after I left school I'd say there was about (.) two or three years when I didn't speak any Gaelic [. . .] even if there's not the opportunity to use it regularly, it's still a good thing

Although she has not pursued job opportunities that speaking Gaelic may have afforded after studying it at university, and therefore feels that she 'should speak it a wee bit more', informant IF13 nevertheless regards Gaelic as something that is 'nice to have'. Likewise, the second speaker above sees the language as a resource that is 'still there', even if she has not used it regularly. Informant IF03 expounds on this belief in greater detail in the following account. Whilst the force with which she does so is unusual in the dataset more generally, what is most remarkable is the way in which she convinces her friend (IF04) of how reasonable and common-sense this position is:

IF03	I like knowing that I have got the language
SD	Okay yeah
IF03	It's not important for me to be able to speak it every day and I don't know if I want to have it in my world every day
SD	Yeah
IF03	Maybe it's because I know it's so separate and so cliquey that I just wouldn't want to be part of that kind of thing anyway [. . .] But it doesn't- it wouldn't bother me- I wouldn't be fussed about using it every day in everyday language [. . .] I have it and I like having it cos it's like a little personal thing that you have that not everybody has
IF04	I haven't thought of it like that before- I guess there's so much pressure and so much kind of learning it to use it in a Gaelic world you know?
SD	Yeah
IF04	And stuff- but you know what's wrong with just having it?

Informant IF03 therefore appears to regard it as a matter of pride to 'have' Gaelic as an icon of personal identity and a 'little personal thing' that distinguishes her from others (see section 5.3.1, below). The language is not especially seen as being useful for communication 'every day', and in fact she states that she 'wouldn't want to be part' of the Gaelic community because of its perceived cliquiness (compare section 5.1.3). In response, informant IF04, her friend and flatmate, seems to be persuaded by her reasoning, and defends the position of 'just having it', as opposed to using the language 'in a Gaelic world'. In this way, it may be seen that certain language ideologies appear to spread rather surreptitiously, taking root through discursive constructions even as they are negotiated by speakers (see also Kroskrity 2000b; Boudreau and Dubois 2007). The apparent common sense of this ideology, however, positing that using Gaelic is less important than 'having' the language in the first place, is called starkly into question by the speaker in the following account:

IF01	Tha mise ag ràdh gu bheil mi caran fileanta (.) gu bheil mi (.) comasach Gàidhlig a bhruidhinn (.) ach chan eil mi ga cleachda' **so** mar sin chan eil mi **really** fileanta, no chan eil **really** comas agam [. . .] Tha daoine ag ràdh gum b' urrainn dhaibh Gàidhlig a bhruidhinn (.) mar na bràthraichean agam- ach chan eil iad ga cleachdadh- tha- is urrainn dhaibh/leughadh Gàidhlig/ach **you know** dìreach mar mi-fhìn tha iad air faclan eh (.) tha iad air /diochuimneachadh /faclan ach=
	I say that I'm kind of fluent (.) that I am (.) able to speak Gaelic (.) but I don't use it **so** *I'm therefore not* **really** *fluent, or I don't* **really** *have ability [. . .] People say that they could speak Gaelic (.) like my brothers- but they don't use it- they can read Gaelic but* **you know** *just like me they've- they've forgotten words but*

SD	=Mm hmm
IF01	Chan urrainn dhaibh a cleachda' (.) chan urrainn dhòmhsa **really** /g/a cleach- dadh **either** erm (.) cuideachd
	*they can't use it (.) I can't **really** use it **either** erm (.) as well*

Despite stating that she often claims to be a fluent speaker, informant IF01 reports that she forgets words, as do her brothers, from having used the language so seldom. As such, she argues, people who say they can speak Gaelic but who do not actually use it will find themselves in the same position, unable to use the language when they wish to do so. The above extracts exemplify two competing discourses advanced by different speakers: whilst some participants readily associate the attrition of their Gaelic language skills with their disuse of the language, for others, the discourse of 'having Gaelic' appears to counter the belief that using it regularly is important or necessary for maintaining abilities in the language. Tellingly, many of those who advanced the former position blamed their disuse of Gaelic on a lack of opportunity to speak it, bringing us to the final ideology of Gaelic language use that I discuss here.

5.1.5 'Opportunity' and choice in Gaelic use

The last set of beliefs in relation to Gaelic use concerns the complementary ideologies of opportunity and choice to use the language, discourses of which are frequently deployed to rationalise speakers' current linguistic practices. An ideology of opportunity is visible in the following extract, for example:

LF08	I've no:t got the opportunity if you like to speak it as much
SD	Yeah [[uh huh]
LF08	[[Em] (.) which is a shame because (1.7) you know I do kinda miss (1.1) miss em (1.8) being <u>able</u> to do- to speak it to outside people in different environments [. . .] it's a shame that I don't get to (.) to use it as often as I would like

Here a lack of opportunity to use Gaelic is considered the chief cause of the informant's disuse of the language. Her description of this scenario as a 'shame' and her feeling of 'missing' it resonate clearly with the ideology of regret or guilt discussed above (section 5.1.1). Yet any sense of personal culpability or guilt is absent from this excerpt; rather, it is the lack of opportunity to speak Gaelic that is seen to account for the situation. In the following extract, speakers' lack of opportunity to speak the language is identified as a key deficiency in the Gaelic community:

IF02	[B]u chòir comas a bhith aig daoine ach às aonais na cothroman (.) cha bhi comasan aig daoine
	People should have ability but without the opportunities (.) people won't have abilities
SD	Hmm
IF02	Tha mi smaoineachadh gu bheil (.) sin a dhìth- tha tuilleadh chothroman a dhìth air daoine gus a' Ghàidhlig a chleachdadh fiù 's dhèanainnsa feum air cothroman

Gàidhlig a chleachdadh [. . .] chan eil uimhir dhe chothroman ann 's dòcha a' dol dhan a' bhùth 's bruidhinn ri daoine ann an Gàidhlig
> *I think that (.) that's lacking- more opportunities for people to use Gaelic are lacking- even I could use [more] opportunities to use Gaelic [. . .] there aren't that many opportunities perhaps to go to the shop and to speak to people in Gaelic*

Even for the above informant, then, raised with Gaelic at home and now working in a Gaelic profession, opportunities to use the language are described to be lacking. Specifically, using Gaelic in shops in the Lowland city where she now lives is mentioned as a domain that might benefit from greater Gaelic opportunity. By contrast, the following speaker maintains that even in this urban Lowland context, opportunities to speak the language can be found by anyone who is truly intent on using Gaelic:

IF07	Tha mi smaoineachadh ma tha thu ag iarraidh Gàidhlig=
	I think if people want Gaelic=
SD	=Hmm?=
IF07	=Tha mi smaoineachadh (.) ma tha cuideigin (.) gu fìrinneach ag iarraidh a bhith beò ann an dòigh Ghàidhlig=
	=I think (.) if someone (.) truly wants to live in a Gaelic way=
SD	=Seadh
	=Yeah
IF07	Gum faigh iad iad- fiù 's gun /a/ smaoineachadh mu dheidhinn
	That they'll get it- even without thinking about it

Informant IF07, another speaker raised with Gaelic at home, uses the language significantly less than IF02 in the present day. Rather than blaming a lack of opportunities, however – which she argues there are plenty of – she draws on the ideology of choice when explaining why she uses the language this way:

IF07	Tha mi a' cleachdadh /a' Ghàidhlig/ em (.) ann an dòigh (3.0) ((sighs)) tha e faireachdainn rudeigin àraid- tha mi ceangal Gàidhlig gu mòr ri bhith beag- ri bhith òg [. . .] 's e dìreach a bhith dol air ais- 's e faireachdainn gu bheil thu dol air ais
	I use Gaelic em (.) in a way (3.0) ((sighs)) it feels a bit strange- I associate Gaelic with being small- with being young [. . .] it's just going backwards- it feels like you're going back
SD	Hmm (.) Seach air adhart? [[Seach a' dol air adhart?]
	Instead of forward? [[Instead of going forward?]
IF07	[[Seach air adhart] agus a' dol air ais (.) 's dòcha a dh'àiteigin nach- b' fheàrr leat gluasad air adhart no b' fheàrr leat a bhith nad inbheach- tha mi smaoineachadh
	[Instead of forward] and going back (.) perhaps to somewhere you don't- you'd prefer to move on or you'd prefer to be an adult- I think

Using Gaelic only rarely in the present day is therefore referred to very clearly as a choice on the part of this participant, who strongly associates using Gaelic with being a child. The long pause (3.0 s) and sigh that she produces at the start of the utterance betray a sense of negative affect for the speaker, who describes that she would rather 'move on' (*gluasad air adhart*) from such childhood language practices. As such, the decision not to use Gaelic in the present day is depicted as a rational choice for informant IF07. In a similar manner, informant IF04 – who currently uses Gaelic frequently in her working life – nevertheless states that continued commitment to using the language is dependent on her own future choices and decisions:

IF04   I personally have no qualms in saying I: I want to do with my life what I <u>want</u> to do and I'm not gonna stay within the Gaelic world just [[for the sake of Gaelic]
SD   [[For the sake of Gaelic yeah]
IF04   I won't- (.) my interests- at the moment I'm doing Gaelic primary teaching (.) and (2.5) I won't hide the fact that I don't necessarily want to be a Gaelic primary school teacher- I'm not doing it because (.) because I feel so passionately about working in Gaelic and keeping Gaelic alive although it's very important to me (.) but I'm far more interested in music and things so if that comes up I'm gonna go- I'm not gonna stay in something just for the sake of Gaelic

As such, choice is again seen as a key factor in the participant's engagement with the language, at present and in the future. Her current chosen career path is just that – a choice – and she therefore states that her commitment to using Gaelic in a professional context may not be permanent. IF04's future use of Gaelic is subject to other choices and opportunities that may present themselves in future. Yet the active choice to use Gaelic extensively after school seems mostly restricted to individuals raised with the language at home, or in Gaelic-speaking communities. Many former GME students report prioritising other life choices over Gaelic, as described by the following informant:

LM02   [P]riorities have come- have come into my life in terms ay (.) like at the moment my work's kind of (.) full [. . .] I don't think we'll ever get to the level which would make it easy for an individual to leave Gaelic-medium education (.) and to maintain (.) eh, the need to- to <u>need</u> to have the language [. . .] But I mean to be honest it needs people like me to decide against <u>all</u> the priorities I've got
SD   ((laughs))
LM02   to do it (.) and it doesn't sound like I'm going to be doing that any time soon

Questions of priority and need are therefore central to this account of Gaelic language use in the present day. Choices that this informant has made after school in terms of his professional life have been made with little consideration of Gaelic, and he maintains that the 'need to have the language' has fallen away since school. He states that making Gaelic an important aspect of his day-to-day life would mean choosing to go 'against all the priorities' that he now has in his adult life. Questions of choice and opportunity are therefore central to the ideologies of Gaelic language use

UNDERLYING LANGUAGE USE: IDEOLOGIES AND ATTITUDES   121

that interviewees express while explaining and rationalising their current language practices. I argue that each of the ideological themes that I have outlined above concerning Gaelic use tends to reinforce rationales pertaining to speakers' limited use of Gaelic, and to militate against more extensive engagement with the language in day-to-day life.

5.2 Ideologies of Gaelic II: Language and identities

Four main themes can be discerned in respect of Gaelic and sociocultural identities in the dataset as a whole: the first relates to the relevance of Gaelic to participants' sense of individuality and personal identity (section 5.2.1.), while the second specifically concerns Gaelic identity, and informants' associations with the label 'Gael' (*Gàidheal*; section 5.2.2.). The third section analyses participants' ideas and beliefs concerning Gaelic as a bounded and regional, 'Highlands and Islands' language (5.2.3), and, relatedly, the possibly rival status of Scots as a national language beyond this region. Lastly, the fifth subsection addresses discourses of ideologies in relation to Gaelic and national identities, as well as accounts concerning the relation of Gaelic to the wider political context of Scotland (5.2.5).

5.2.1 Gaelic and personal identity

Even without necessarily using Gaelic frequently in their day-to-day lives, many informants maintain that the language continues to be an important facet of their personal identity. This is often reported by informants to be a rather vague and intangible identification with the language, partly reflected in the ways in which participants relate their beliefs and feelings in this regard, and keys to speech acts such as hesitation and emphasis (Hymes 1974: 57):

> LM03   I think for me anyway it's an important- (.) an important thing to be able to- to speak Gaelic and it kinda em (.) forms a quite a large part of you in some way [. . .] It played a huge part in terms of my own background in terms of growing up and I suppose the person that I am now

Hesitation is indicated with self-interruption and pauses toward the start of the above speech act, whilst the informant reflects on the importance of the language to him personally. Although he may in fact use Gaelic only rarely today (compare the extract in section 4.1.3), informant LM03 states that having the ability to speak the language is important in itself, and that as such it 'forms quite a large part' of him. This belief in the continued importance of Gaelic to personal identity draws partly on the ideology of 'having' Gaelic discussed in section 5.1.4 of this chapter. Yet the informant's use of the phrase 'in some way' reflects the rather vague sense in which the language continues to be an important aspect of his personal identity. While he states that it 'played a huge part' in terms of his background, he is more circumspect in respect of the continued extent of its relevance in the present day; use of the phrase 'I suppose' perhaps adds to the sense of qualification here. The juxtaposition of the definite and continued importance of Gaelic to personal identity with relative disuse of the language is also apparent in the following two extracts:

> LF05 It's (.) a very important part of me- I would <u>always</u> put that above (2.4) <u>any</u>thing [. . .] it's something that I'd definitely say (2.2) [[defines me]
> SD   [[Yeah]
> LF05 Not defines me but is: part of who I am and my day-to-day life

> SD   Would you have said personally that Gaelic's an important part of your sense of self- your personal identity?
> IF05 Yes it is actually
> SD   Uh huh
> IF05 I always considered it quite important even if I don't use it that much (.) because it's a way to distinguish myself

The specific emphasis placed on 'always' and 'anything' in the first extract conveys a definite sense of continued, symbolic importance for Gaelic in the informant's life; indeed, she even states that the language 'defines' her in this way. Yet the long pauses she produces in reporting this (2.4 s and 2.2 s), and her immediate retraction of the latter point may reflect an apparent sense of paradox in reporting only limited use of the language but claiming it as central to one's sense of self. Similarly, speaker IF05 draws attention to this paradox when she states that Gaelic remains important to her as 'a way to distinguish' herself, even though she does not use it 'that much' in the present day. A sense of pride in having the language is further expounded upon in answer to my question in the following excerpt:

> SD   A bheil thu pròiseil gu bheil a' Ghàidhlig agad?
>   *Are you proud that you can speak Gaelic?*
> LF02 O gu dearbh fhèin tha- tha um (.) 's e: aon dha na rudan as inntinn/each/ mu mo dheidhinn tha mi a' smaoineachadh- nuair a tha mi a' bruidhinn ri cuideigin bidh mi ag ràdh 'tha Gàidhlig agam' fhios 'ad- 'o tha sin dìreach sgoinneil!'
>   *Oh yes indeed- yes um (.) it's: one of the most interesting things about me I think- when I'm speaking to someone I say 'I speak Gaelic' you know- 'oh that's just brilliant!'*

For many informants, therefore, the Gaelic language is a source of pride and personal distinctiveness in adulthood, whether or not they speak the language frequently in the present day. Yet the paradox referred to above is described in slightly different terms by the following informant, who is elsewhere rather critical of Gaelic generally:

> LM07 I mean it sort of sounds hypocritical to say that (.) I <u>do</u> have an appreciation for the romance of the thing given the absolutely risible attention I have paid to it and the neglect I've treated it with um you know despite being given a free language basically um (.) along with the (x) (.) uh but I mean yeah sure (.) it (1.2)

SD	It's- it's=
LM07	=I feel it's a part of my heritage in spite of the fact that I've mistreated it and I view- well what I've got left with <u>some</u> pride

Having used the language only very rarely in recent years, this participant reflects that it may be somewhat 'hypocritical' to claim, as he does, still to appreciate the 'romance' of Gaelic. Stating that he has treated the language with 'risible attention' and 'neglect', he claims to view what remains of his Gaelic 'with some pride', the emphasis here reflecting the rather limited degree to which he may feel this. Various roles are assigned to Gaelic as a facet of personal distinctiveness, therefore, with many former GME students claiming that it remains important in the absence of regular use of the language. But such feelings are generally described in a somewhat imprecise manner, with hesitation and uncertainty perhaps reflecting the difficulties that speakers experience when negotiating this apparently paradoxical aspect of their identity. Similarly paradoxical positions are apparent in informants' discussion of Gaelic in relation to their identification – or lack thereof – with the term Gael/ *Gàidheal*.

5.2.2 Gaels? – *Gàidheil?* Gaelic identity, culture and heritage

Informants who make little to no use of Gaelic in the present day tended not to use the term 'Gael/*Gàidheal*' – traditionally used in Gaelic to refer to someone who not only speaks the language but typically also claims ethnic and cultural identification with it – when describing their relationship with the language (see McCoy and Scott 2000). As in the following two excerpts, the discursive negotiation of the term often proceeded only upon my own explicit prompt:

SD	Would you call yourself a Gael?
IF06	Um wow um: (.) yeah I guess so
SD	Yeah
IF06	I- it's not something I would ever call myself but if I was asked the question I guess so yeah
SD	Yeah, but otherwise not specifically
IF06	It's not something that I really stro- I don't go around saying ((confrontational voice)) 'oh I'm a Gael' kind of thing

SD	Do you consider yourself a Gael for instance?
LM04	Eh (.) ((sighs)) och I mean (4.8) well kind of yeah
SD	Mm hmm
LM04	Em you know (.) I kinda come from that kinda heritage
SD	Yeah in terms of heritage uh huh
LM04	And I kind of (.) you know I've got more kind of (island links) the majority of like say my family [. . .] I would count myself primarily as Scottish
SD	Yeah
LM04	Em and (.) I don't know if I'd include Gaelic as part of that

Both the above participants express degrees of surprise and uncertainty when I broach the issue of being a Gael with them; it does not appear to be a category of identity with which they commonly associate, yet both answer tentatively in the affirmative, having reflected on the question, before going on to qualify and clarify this point. The first speaker states that she would never refer to herself in this way, appearing to view the label in rather defensive and confrontational terms. Similarly, while speaker LM04 claims the requisite 'heritage' to identify with the term, he sees himself 'primarily as Scottish' and appears rather uncertain as to how Gaelic relates to this identity category (see section 5.2.4, below). For both these speakers, association with the label 'Gael' appears to be somewhat problematic, though both initially answer 'yes' to my explicit question on this issue. Yet uncertainty and ambivalent association with the term is reported not only by participants who use Gaelic only rarely, as in the above cases. In both of the following accounts, respondents express a degree of uncertainty over the word, though both use Gaelic rather frequently in their working lives:

SD   An e Gàidheal a th' annad mar sin?
So are you a Gael then?

HF02   Dè th' ann an Gàidheal? ((laughs))
What is a Gael?

SD   Sin a' cheist aidh
That's the question yeah

HF02   Chanainn gur e (.) ach: em (.) **yeah** 's dòcha- chanainn gur e (.) mus deach mi dhan t-Sabhal Mhòr **you know** cha robh mi a' smaointinn orm fhìn mar Ghàidheal [. . .] feumaidh sinn an **definition** dè th' ann an Gàidheal 's dòcha a mhìneachadh an toiseach agus feumaidh sinn sin a fhreagairt tha mi smaointinn
I would say so (.) but: em (.) **yeah** *perhaps- I would say so (.) before I went to Sabhal Mòr* **you know** *I didn't think of myself as a Gael [. . .] we perhaps have to explain the* **definition** *what is a Gael at the start and we have to answer that I think*

LM06   Ged a rugadh mise ann an Sasainn (.) tha mis' gam fhaicinn fhìn mar Albannach gun teagamh (.) dìreach tha an teaghlach agam ann an sheo-sin far a bheil an (.) an dachaigh againn
Although I was born in England (.) I definitely see myself as a Scot (.) just my family is here- it's where (.) our home is

SD   So chan eil thu a' faireachdainn Sasannach idir
So you don't feel English at all

LM06   No chan eil chan eil
No *no no*
[. . .]

SD   [A]n e Gàidheal a th' annad mar sin?
Are you a Gael then?

LM06   ((laughs)) Chan e uill ((laughing)) cha chanainns' gur e Gàidheal a th' annam idir **no** (.) 's e Gall a th' annam
((laughs)) No well ((laughing)) I wouldn't say I'm a Gael at all **no** *(.) I'm a Gall [Lowlander]*

The first of the two speakers above therefore answers my question with another question, asking 'what is a Gael?' ('*dè th' ann an Gàidheal?*') in response to my prompt, before concluding tentatively that she is a Gael, but that further clarification of the term is needed generally. By contrast, speaker LM06 rejects the label outright, emphasising his identity as an *Albannach* (Scot) and *Gall* (Lowlander) while playing down any sense of affiliation with the terms *Gàidheal* (Gael) or *Sasannach* (English person). In both cases, however, discussion of the term 'Gael' is prompted by myself; it is not clear that either speaker would have even referred to the label without my own explicit mention of it. The few interviewees who offered their own interpretation of the word without my prompt tended not to identify strongly with the term or, indeed, dismissed it, as the above speaker did. In the following account, the label Gael is brought up without my asking an overt question, but the term is rejected out of hand by the informant:

IM01   San obair seo /tha/ mise (.) ann an dòigh (2.0) **you know** an ginealach ùr
       In this job I'm (.) in a way (2.0) **you know** *the new generation*

SD   Hmm

IM01   Ged nach eil mise a' smaoineachadh orm mar Ghàidheal airson /tha/ seòrsa **stigma attached** a tha mise faicinn
       Although I don't think of myself as a Gael because there's a kind of **stigma attached** *that I see*
       [. . .]

SD   An canadh tu mar sin gu bheil a' Ghàidhlig na pàirt chudromach de do chuid fhèin-aithne? (.) Nist thuirt thu nach robh thu a' faireachdainn mar Ghàidheal- mar gur e Gàidheal a th' annad=
       Yes [. . .] would you say that Gaelic is an important part of your identity? (.) Now you said that you didn't feel like a Gael- that you are a Gael=

IM01   =No tha mi a' tuigsinn /a' cheist/- tha- tha aig deireadh an latha cha/bhiodh mise/ a' faireachdainn mar- gum b' urrainn dhomh an obair seo a dhèanamh mura robh ceangal agamsa ris a' Ghàidhlig [. . .] **I mean** aig deireadh an latha chan e **evangelist** a th' annam anns a' Ghàidhlig [. . .] cha do smaoinich mi riamh gum bi nam oifigear leasachaidh na Gàidhlig agus ma bhruidhneas tu ris na tidsearan a bh' agam chanadh iad an aon rud [. . .] a thaobh fèin /aithneachadh/ tha mise smaoineachadh- chan e Gàidheal a th' annam idir idir
       =**No** *I understand the question- yes- yes at the end of the day I wouldn't feel like- that I could do this job unless I had a connection with Gaelic [. . .]* **I mean** *at the end of the day I'm not an* **evangelist** *in Gaelic [. . .] I never thought I'd be a Gaelic development officer and if you speak to the teachers I had they'd say the same thing [. . .] in terms of identity I think- I'm not a Gael at all*

Therefore, whilst seeing himself as belonging to a new generation ('*ginealach ùr*') of Gaelic speakers, participant IM01 rejects the term Gael, stating that neither he nor his GME teachers imagined that he would get the job he currently has in Gaelic, and that he does not regard his work in Gaelic development as making him, or requiring him to be, an 'evangelist' for the language. Crucially, he states that he sees a kind of 'stigma' connected to the label Gael. Although he does not explain explicitly what he means by this, it is clear that this feeling militates against his identification with the category. Overall, therefore, very few informants related a strong sense of identification with the label Gael, with many expressing uncertainty over the meaning of the term, and most only making reference to the word when prompted by my own question in this respect. Indeed, a particularly fervent rejection of the identity is related by one of the speakers in the following account:

SD	What about the label Gael- is that something you identify with?
IF03	'Oh I'm a Gael'- no I'm not a Gael!
IF04	You could never say that! ((laughs))
IF03	Oh no!
IF04	Oh! Em:
IF03	Does anyone call themselves that- 'I'm a Gael'? [. . .] I don't know what constitutes that (3.1) in the Gaelic world ((laughs)) Planet Gael! [. . .] I quite like 'Teuchter' though
SD	You like that one?
IF03	I like that yeah- I'm a Teuchter 'yeah you're a bit teuchie' (.) I am a bit teuchie sometimes- I quite like that
SD	((laughs))
IF03	Gael's a bit (.)
IF04	You do know it's a derogatory term?=
IF03	=plaid and what do you call that big sword?=
SD	[[=Claymore?]=
IF04	[[=Sword?]=
IF03	=Claymore- that's what Gael reminds me of (.) big tartan plaid in a battle

While struggling to believe that anyone would identify with the term Gael – associating it with the stereotype of the Highland or Jacobite warrior – speaker IF03 is rather more positive about the terms 'Teuchter' and 'teuchie'. Historically, these have been pejorative terms of abuse for Highlanders in the Lowlands – as is pointed out here by her friend. Interestingly, four informants in total referred positively to using this term as a descriptor of themselves, and none used it in a pejorative sense. Its formerly negative connotations therefore seem to have less force in the present day. While such vigorous rejection of the identity category 'Gael' is rare, a sense of ambivalence and uncertainty surrounding the term is discernible throughout the corpus. Neither do speakers in the dataset readily self-identify as 'Gaelic speakers', and again, the picture that emerges of Gaelic's role in informants' identity constructions is somewhat imprecise (see also Dunmore 2017, 2018).

5.2.3 National or regional language: 'Highlands and Islands' identity?

In contrast to the ambivalence around Gaelic identity described above, many informants expressed the belief that Gaelic indexed a principally regional identity, conveying an ideology that associates the language strongly with the Highlands and Islands of

Scotland. Such beliefs and feelings are broadly in line with attitudes to Gaelic at a national level (Paterson et al. 2014; West and Graham 2011). In particular, attitudes to Gaelic speakers' right to use the language in 'Gaelic-speaking areas' have been consistently and significantly more positive than those regarding provision and entitlements to use Gaelic in Scottish public life generally (Paterson et al. 2014: 11). In Gaelic-medium accounts within the dataset analysed here, participants often conveyed a sense that unnamed individuals were pushing or forcing ('*a' putadh*'/'*a' sparradh*') the language on people in areas of Scotland with limited Gaelic heritage. In similar terms, the belief that Gaelic is strongly rooted, and therefore more important, in a particular part of Scotland is advanced frequently throughout the corpus, as it is in the following excerpt:

> IF01   Tha mi a' smaointinn gu bheil e (.) er (.) gu bheil e gu math cudromach anns na: (.) sgìrean (.) far a bheil- far an <u>robh</u> Gàidhlig anns an eachdraidh aca (.) agus tha mi a' smaointinn gum biodh e math air Alba air fad ach chan eil mi a' smaointinn gum bu chòir dhaibh Gàidhlig a phuta' air na h-àiteachan (.) nach eil er (.) a' faireachdainn gu bheil iad ceangailte ris a' chànan [[**you know?**]
> *I think that it's (.) er (.) that it's quite important in the: (.) areas (.) where it's- where Gaelic was in their history (.) and I think that it would be good in all of Scotland but I don't think that they should force Gaelic on the places (.) that don't uh (.) feel that they're connected to the language [[**you know?**]*
>
> SD   [[Aidh]
>   *[[Yeah]*
>
> IF01   Tha mi a' smaointinn gu bheil e math (.) rudan a dhèanamh ach aig an aon àm (.) chan eil sinn ag iarraidh a bhith a' putadh Gàidhlig **you know?**
>   *I think that it's good (.) to do things but at the same time (.) we don't want to be forcing Gaelic* **you know?**

The speaker is mindful of a lack of connection to the language felt in parts of Scotland and argues that activists should therefore avoid forcing Gaelic ('*a' putadh Gàidhlig*') on these areas. Interestingly, this particular idea, of 'pushing' or 'forcing' Gaelic on parts of Scotland that are not perceived to have an historical connection to the language, is advanced more frequently by informants who opted to conduct the interview in Gaelic than in English. While it was expressed in different terms during English-medium interviews (such as 'keeping' Gaelic to where it was spoken historically and so on) this particular trope – *a' putadh/a' sparradh [na] Gàidhlig*, 'forcing Gaelic' on English (/Scots) speakers – is notable by its prevalence in Gaelic interviews.

1. SD   Bheil thu coimhead air a' Ghàidhlig mar chànan nàiseanta mar sin?
   Do you see Gaelic as a national language then?
2. IF11   (2.4) Em:: (.) ((sighs)) hhh- (.) ann an d:òigh tha [. . .] tha e gu math furasta dhòmhsa a ràdh- tha mise à xxx ((Western Isles)) tha mi às na h-Eileanan an Iar [. . .] tha mi ag obair air a' Ghàidhealtachd [. . .] tha Gàidhlig gu math (.) cudromach ann an shin- a's na h-àiteachan sin **so** tha e [[gu math]

		Em:: (.) ((sighs)) yyy- (.) in a w:ay yes [...] it's quite easy for me to say- I'm from xxx I'm from the Western Isles [...] I work in the Highlands [...] Gaelic is quite important there- in those places **so it's** [[quite]
3.	SD	[[Tha]
		[[Yes]
4.	IF11	furasta dhòmhsa a ràdh 'oh yeah tha Gàidhlig uabhasach cudromach' ach nuair a tha mise air a dhol sìos dhan a' Ghalltachd [...] chan eil (.) inbhe cho mòr aig a- aig a' chànan [...] ma tha sinne a' putadh a' chànain (.) air a' mhòr-chuid de dh'Alba chan eil iad dol a thuigs'
		easy for me to say 'oh yeah *Gaelic is very important' but when I've gone down to the Lowlands [...] the language doesn't have as much status [...] if we force the language (.) on the majority of Scotland they're not going to understand*

This participant is therefore seen to be noticeably hesitant reflecting on the status of Gaelic as a national language in turn 2 of the extract; she produces a long pause (2.4 s duration), elongates the consonant of the filler 'em', sighs and pauses again immediately after elongating the word-initial aspiration of 'tha' (*yes*) as 'hhh-'. She proceeds to make the qualification in turn 4 that she adopts this position with relative ease in the Highlands and Islands, but senses the language's more limited status in the Lowlands. She concludes in turn 4 that people in such places – constituting the majority of Scotland ('*a' mhòr-chuid de dh'Alba*') – will not understand if the language is forced on them by Gaelic speakers. Reservations and qualifications in attributing 'national language' status to Gaelic are similarly apparent in the following English excerpt, though the trope of 'forcing' the language is not used:

SD	[I]s it a national language d'you think?
IF13	(1.3) A national language? Hmm: (.) no
SD	No
IF13	I wouldn't say- I mean I think it should be- it is is it not? It is the national- it is the national language but I think a lot of people- I think at home you think 'oh yeah it is- everybody speaks it'
SD	Uh huh
IF13	But down here ((Lowlands)) I think so many people (1.1) are just like (.) ugh- not impressed or not- you know convinced

Again, the idea is expressed here that it is easy to imagine Gaelic to be important nationally when one is resident in Gaelic-speaking parts of Scotland, but that its lack of visibility elsewhere may count against a widespread appreciation of this. Similarly, the informant again hesitates when answering my question on whether Gaelic is a national language, pausing and initially responding 'no', before stating her belief that it should enjoy such status and wondering aloud whether it currently does so. Nevertheless, an appreciation of Gaelic as strongly indexical of a regional identity – and a perception that this position is comparatively straightforward and unproblematic– is discernible in the corpus as a whole. The following extract highlights this particular point:

IM02	I think it [i.e. Gaelic] is definitely a Highlands and Islands [[identity really]
SD	[[Yeah- that's how you see it?]
IM02	But then you've got people spread throughout the place [. . .] I think it gives you- you've got a real identity cos it's something different from where you're from
SD	Yeah
IM02	You know (.) you've got your identity with the Highlands and Islands and that

5.2.4 Albais/Scots language: A rival linguistic identity?

A possible rationale underlying many interviewees' preference for relating Gaelic to a regional, Highland identity may reflect historical arguments around the language. A surprising degree of uncertainty was expressed by many informants when reflecting on exactly where Gaelic was spoken in Scotland historically, and several entertain the impression that the language was traditionally confined to the Highlands and Islands, with the Scots language ('*Albais*' / '*Beurla Ghallda*') being widespread everywhere else (compare with the historical account in section 1.1 of this book). The belief that Gaelic is better conceived of as a language belonging and restricted to a specific region is advanced in the following account:

LM04	You know it would probably be good to keep Gaelic to where it was- well- where it was traditionally spoken I would say
SD	Mm hmm yeah
LM04	I mean there's parts of the country- I mean I'm not 100 per cent sure about Gaelic history but there's probably parts of the country where Gaelic was never spoken [. . .] I don't think of Gaelic as being a (.) you know a kind of (.) eh you know like the Scottish national language in a way
SD	No exactly
LM04	You know it's one of our- you know- there's other kinda- there's Scots and things as well [. . .] I'd say to kind of keep [Gaelic] to where it was traditionally spoken or where it was spoken in the past

While being unsure of exactly where Gaelic was traditionally spoken – not being '100 per cent sure about Gaelic history' – this informant expresses the belief that it would be beneficial 'to keep Gaelic' to such locales. Part of the reason that he does not regard Gaelic as 'the' (only) national language is the presence of 'Scots and things' elsewhere in the country. Similarly, the perceived strength of the Scots language is regarded by the following speaker as a reason not to promote Gaelic as a national language, again employing the ideological trope of '*a' sparradh*' (forcing) Gaelic:

HF03	Tha mi smaointinn g' eil sgìrean ann far a bheil Albais ga bruidhinn agus far nach eil 's dòcha Gàidhlig cho cudromach [. . .] cha chreid mi g' eil e ciallach a bhith eh a' sparradh (.) eh a' Ghàidhlig a's na h-àiteachan sin

	I think there are areas where Scots is spoken and where Gaelic is perhaps not as important [. . .] I don't think it's sensible to be eh forcing [. . .] eh Gaelic in those places
	[. . .]
SD	An e cànan nàiseanta a th' anns a' Ghàidhlig sa chiad àite? No an e cànan roinneil- a tha a' buntainn ris a' Ghàidhealtachd is dha na h-Eileanan?
	Is Gaelic a national language principally? Or is it a regional language- that belongs in the Highlands and Islands?
HF03	Tha mi smaointinn (.) gu bheil sin aig cridhe trioblaidean na Gàidhlig agus tha mi a' smaointinn leis a sin
	I think (.) that that's at the heart of the difficulties facing Gaelic and I think therefore
SD	Mm hmm=
HF03	=Tha mi a' smaointinn mas e cànan nàiseanta a bh' <u>ann</u> nach biodh sinn anns an t-suidheachadh a's a bheil sinn an-diugh (.) agus mar sin feumaidh mi a ràdh nach e [. . .] thathar a' faireachdainn gum bu chòir cànan nàiseanta a bhith ann ach cha chreid mi gu bheil e fìor
	=I think if it were a national language that we wouldn't be in the situation we're in today (.) and so I have to say that it's not a national language [. . .] it is felt that there should be a national language but I don't think it's true

Whilst the informant argues that it's unwise to 'force' Gaelic on parts of Scotland where Scots is spoken, therefore, she appears conversely to regard the fact that Gaelic is not currently a national language as a major cause of its current predicament. Yet, on the other hand, the belief that there ought to be a national language is rejected in any case, and speaker HF03 seems to argue that accommodating and respecting Scots in areas where it is spoken is sufficient reason not to promote Gaelic as a national language. The experience of actually offending Scots speakers by describing Gaelic in these terms was never referred to by informants, yet many appear eager to avoid such potential conflicts. By contrast, the following participant describes feeling a heightened sense that Gaelic is a national language, having been confronted by a Scots speaker's anti-Gaelic attitudes:

SD	Do you think of Gaelic as a national language?
LM01	(3.0) Yeah, well I did when I was talking about it with an- like a Scot person- somebody who speaks Scots
SD	Hmm
LM01	And they're totally against Gaelic
SD	Yeah
LM01	But there's a lot of like names are Gaelic and
SD	Yeah that's right a lot of place names and people's [[surnames]]
LM01	[[Surnames]]

Having paused to consider the question and his own feelings toward Gaelic – in response to a Scots speaker's negative view – the informant states his belief (after a long pause of 3 s duration) that Gaelic is a national language on the basis of the prevalence of Gaelic in Scottish place names and personal names. This rather controversial view of the two languages vying for status as national language was explicitly referred to only occasionally, but a discourse imagining a competitive relationship between the two varieties' appropriateness in different areas is notable in the extracts described above. This discourse seems particularly influential in determining participants' beliefs as to the relevance of Gaelic nationally.

As noted in Chapter 1, less circumscribed *Gesellschaft* conceptions of Gaelic and its role in Scottish identity may well be more widespread than was true in the past (Oliver 2002, 2006, 2010; Paterson et al. 2014). Nevertheless, an ideology that Gaelic may be conceived of more comfortably as a regional language, rooted strongly in the Highlands and Islands, is clearly discernible in the discourse of many speakers in the interview corpus. Many informants appear conscious of opposition to Gaelic among various groups in Scotland, and perceive a need to be sensitive to this and not to 'force' or 'push' the language on such groups. As such, the contested nature of the Gaelic language's place in Scotland is a theme that is frequently touched upon by participants. In the following section I consider the role that informants attribute to Gaelic in Scottish identity specifically.

5.2.5 Gaelic and Scottish identity: Language, nation and culture

The close association of language, nation and culture, a notion dating largely from the Romantic movement of the eighteenth and nineteenth centuries (see sections 1.1 and 2.1) is entertained by certain informants in respect of Gaelic in Scotland. Yet a larger proportion of participants view the relationship in more problematic terms, recalling the perceived opposition to Gaelic of various groups discussed above. Many interviewees frame this relationship within a discourse of inclusiveness, avoiding essentialist perspectives on the relevance of Gaelic to Scottish culture and identity; I return to this subtheme of discourse below. Firstly, however, I draw attention to views that give expression to romantic conceptions of the relationship between language and nation'.

LF06	The whole of Scotland should be speaking Gaelic [[uh huh]
SD	[[Yeah you think so?] Uh huh
LF06	Oh definitely (.) I do think every- everywhere in (.) Scotland should be speaking in Gaelic yeah [. . .] you go to Spain and when you go tae France and when you go tae any other of these places that've got other languages or two languages [. . .] we're so English
SD	That's right yeah
LF06	How's the Gaelic ever gonnae come out if everybody's only saying it in English you know?

Speaker LF06 alludes here to the perceived normality of bilingualism in continental Europe while envisaging a bilingual society across the entirety of Scotland. The use of additional languages in these contexts is contrasted with perceived English monolingualism in Scotland, a situation that is regarded as militating against Gaelic development. Furthermore, the speaker uses the romantic association of language and identity to describe this supposed dependence on the English language in terms of being 'English' as a consequence ('we're so English'). The view of Gaelic as the language of the Scots is expounded in similar terms in the following two accounts:

> LM09   I'm a big believer in (.) Scottish culture and [[Gaelic]
> SD   [[Yeah]
> LM09   and keeping our culture you know? [. . .] you need tae speak your own language- every country in the world (.) speaks their own language
> SD   Exactly- that's true
> LM09   And Gaelic's <u>our</u> language

> HF06   I play fiddle and do a lot for ceilidh bands and like I do Gaelic singing and that's such a big part of the whole musical heritage
> SD   Yeah of course
> HF06   And I guess Gaelic's a part of that- like you couldn't have the music without the language so: [. . .] I think it's really important (.) every country needs its own language you know?

In both these extracts, therefore, Gaelic is described as being Scotland's 'own language', and both speakers refer to the 'need' of every country to have such a national tongue. The rhetoric used in both cases is strikingly similar, and both allude to the importance of 'Scottish culture' in expressing the romantic ideology that language, culture and nation are inherently linked (see section 2.1.4). Yet this particular ideology, positing the supposedly intrinsic relation of Gaelic to Scottish culture, is advanced only by a relatively small number of informants. At the opposite end of the ideological spectrum, alternative beliefs as to the place of the language in Scotland are expressed:

> LM07   I mean I: don't think that Gaelic is a national language cos you know it's not it's- it's Irish
> SD   Hmm
> LM07   A bunch of Irish people came and settled the west coast
> SD   Yeah
> LM07   I mean that's <u>fine</u> eh I'm happy for it to: be- well I was- yeah I mean I'm happy for it to be on the Scottish Parliament website or whatever=
> SD   =Yeah
> LM07   But you know let's not pretend that it's a real loss that Edinburgh is not speaking Gaelic [. . .] that was never the case and it doesn't make sense to pretend otherwise

Such extreme views of the marginal role of Gaelic in Scottish culture – and indeed of its supposed status as 'Irish' – are related only very rarely in the interview corpus. Nevertheless, the expression of such relatively extreme views by an adult who was educated primarily through the language may come something of a surprise. The prevalence of such beliefs should not be overstated, therefore, and the majority of informants expressed generally positive views as to the connection of Gaelic to

Scottish national identity. Informants nevertheless tend to avoid perspectives that posit a straightforward connection between the language and their national identities. With reference to the overall question of language and national identity, interview participants generally express ideas and beliefs that lie somewhere between the two positions outlined above. More nuanced language ideologies are generally reflected in the dataset, participants frequently observing that Gaelic remains important as 'part' of Scotland's identity:

> SD   Just to ask a bit about how Gaelic relates to Scottish culture generally (.) sort of- how (.) significant a part do you think it plays?
> LM08   I think it's massive
> SD   Hmm
> LM08   I think (.) eh: (.) I think it's underestimated how important (.) it is to (.) tourism and things like that [. . .] I think I would <u>like</u> it to be more national but (.) just now it's- I mean it's definitely more west coast isn't it so [. . .] It doesn't make me more like (.) more Scottish it's just (.) <u>part</u> of Scotland

In this way speaker LM08 avoids assuming an essentialist stance on the importance of Gaelic to Scottish identity; while regarding the language as a 'massive' part of Scottish culture and important to the tourist industry, he associates the language with the western periphery and denies that his own relationship to the language makes him in any way 'more Scottish'. The informant states that he would like the language to 'be more national', however, and informants frequently convey a sense that Gaelic is deserving of wider recognition and celebration as part of Scottish culture than it currently enjoys. The avoidance of essentialist ideologies in relation to Gaelic and Scottish culture is indicated even more explicitly by certain other interviewees, however.

> IF01   Tha mi a' smaointinn gu bheil [Gàidhlig] gu math cudromach a chionn 's gu / bheil e/ pàirt dhen eachdraidh againn erm [. . .] tha e cudromach ach (.) san latha an-diugh tha (.) **you know** tha a h-uile sìon eile cudromach cuideachd [. . .] tha mi (.) dìreach cho em (.) eagallach nach eil e dol a bhith an (.) **what's the word?** (.) **kinda (.) I dunno fit in- fit in correctly with all the other cultural things that have happened since then**
>   *I think Gaelic is quite important because it's part of our history erm [. . .] it is important but (.) in the present day (.) you know everything else is important too [. . .] I'm (.) just so em (.) worried that it's not going to be (.) **what's the word?** (.) **kinda (.) I dunno fit in- fit in correctly with all the other cultural things that have happened since then***
> SD   Yeah okay
> IF01   Because it's constantly evolving isn't it?

Informant IF01therefore relates a sense of anxiety that Gaelic may be promoted as a facet of Scottish culture to the exclusion of other aspects of modern Scotland's multicultural society. She switches to English to convey her fears that the language might not 'fit in correctly' with more recent additions to that culture, and appears to associate the language strongly with history. Her use of code-switching in this way may represent an example of 'double-voicing' through language alternation, using English to relate a potentially controversial or problematic ideology in an 'other voice' (see Bakhtin 1986; Dunmore and Smith-Christmas 2015). Whereas a more essentialist position might attribute a pre-eminent and straightforward role to Gaelic in Scottish culture, the above informant is eager to avoid such a stance, switching to English to explain her sense of unease in this respect. Similarly, in the following account the interviewee appears intent on avoiding an essentialist stance, whilst reflecting on the potential benefits of recognising Gaelic as a national language:

> LM05 The history with Gaelic and its place in Scotland is quite mixed (.) and its place (.) I don't know (.) I see it as- yeah it definitely goes into the- the big pot of Scottishness [. . .] it's not a pre-requisite to being Scottish- I think there's- there are various factors that go in there
> SD Sure
> LM05 But it's- yeah it counts for quite a lot [. . .] it's not as straightforward as just a comparison with Welsh

The speaker alludes here to the Welsh context, where the language is perceived to enjoy a 'straightforward' and uncontroversial relationship to national identity. In the following account this sense is again reflected with regard to both Welsh and Irish Gaelic:

> IF05 If it was considered more of a whole of Scotland thing it would stand more of a chance [. . .] well that's what [Irish] Gaelic's done
> SD Yeah
> IF05 like- Irish, so why can't they do it here? [. . .] I think Gaelic is important to the Scottish culture but I don't think it's so important that to go independent- that that would be a major selling point

Once again, therefore, this informant appears eager to avoid assuming an essentialist ideology on the importance of Gaelic to Scottish culture; Gaelic in Scotland is not seen to have 'the same standing' as Irish in Ireland or Welsh in Wales, where each is felt to be an uncontroversial facet of national identity. In truth, the status of Welsh and Irish as national languages may be significantly more contested in those contexts than informants in these excerpts may appreciate (see, for example, Ó Riagáin 1997, 2001; Williams 2008, 2013). It is important to note that many interviewees take care not to state a straightforward connection between Gaelic and Scottish identity, largely because they believe the situation to be more complicated. Rather, the Gaelic language is more generally held to be a 'part' of Scotland that may retain some symbolic value, as discussed in the following extract:

> HF03 T]ha mi smaointinn gur e- leis gu bheil tòrr cultar agus dualchas (.) an cois na Gàidhlig a tha na bhuannachd do dh'Alba [. . .] tha mi smaointinn gu bheil e cudromach do dh'Alba air fad mar shamhla (.) mar a tha thu air ràdh agus: eh mar phàirt de /f/èin-aithne Alba air fad

>   *I think it's- because there's lots of culture and tradition (.) attached to Gaelic that's beneficial to Scotland [. . .] I think it's important to all of Scotland as a symbol (.) as you've said and: eh as a part of all Scotland's identity*
>   [. . .]
> SD   [A] bheil na Gàidheil – aig a bheil a' Ghàidhlig – nas Albannaiche na an fheadhainn aig nach eil Gàidhlig, an canadh tu?
>   *Are the Gaels- who can speak Gaelic- more Scottish than those who can't, would you say?*
> HF03 Cha chanainn air dòigh sam bith
>   *No I wouldn't at all*
> SD   Mm hmm (.) chan eil
>   *Mm hmm (.) no*
> HF03 **Absolutely not** chan eil
>   *no*

This speaker therefore feels that Gaelic retains a degree of importance as a symbol of Scotland's identity at the national level. Yet my intentionally essentialist suggestion that Gaelic-speaking Gaels may be considered more Scottish ('*nas Albannaiche*') than anyone else is rejected emphatically, with the informant switching to English to underscore her opposition to this proposition. Throughout the interview corpus, informants generally appear anxious to sidestep discourses that attribute a predominant role to the Gaelic language in the discussion of Scottish identity, viewing it more comfortably as a regional, 'Highland and Islands' language (section 5.2.3). While a few do express an ideology asserting the language's symbolic value, a majority of informants frame the discussion in terms of inclusiveness and the heterogeneity, with Gaelic regarded as just another a part of this. In this way, Gaelic appears to be iconised in some interviewees' ideologies as a symbol of Scottish identity in the discourse of many former GME students (Bucholtz and Hall 2004: 380; Kroskrity 2004: 507), whilst not being clearly indexical of this identity (see section 2.1).

The ten categories of language ideologies that I have so far discussed in this chapter can be seen to contribute in various ways to the picture of limited language use presented in Chapter 4. In section 5.1, I outlined five key ideologies of Gaelic language use that are apparent in interviewees' accounts; importantly, the ideologies speakers conveyed in terms of using more Gaelic often appeared to rationalise the language practices they reported in Chapter 4. Section 5.2 addressed ideologies of Gaelic and identities, which were often reported in a rather imprecise manner; while the language was regarded as important at some levels of informants' identities, a generally weak association with the label 'Gael/*Gàidheal*' was reported. A belief that Gaelic indexes a regional 'Highlands and Islands' identity more meaningfully than a national 'Scottish' identity was widely expressed, with many informants clearly eager to avoid being perceived as essentialist in their outlook on the importance of the language to Scotland as a whole. Overall, the rather mixed picture of language ideologies among former GME students tends to rationalise and reinforce informants' (mostly limited) Gaelic language practices, as reported in Chapter 4. To further refine these findings, I turn again now to the quantitative analysis of online questionnaires to bring a measure of data triangulation to bear on the results discussed here.

5.3 Gaelic language attitudes

In the final section of the online questionnaire, respondents were invited to indicate the degree to which they agreed or disagreed with 18 attitudinal statements concerning Gaelic. Nine statements concern the relevance of the language to sociocultural identities and 3 deal with perceptions of the Gaelic community, while the remaining 6 concern attitudes to GME itself. Responses to these 18 statements are shown in Tables 5.1–5.5, below.

5.3.1 Identities and attitudes

As the first nine attitudinal propositions concern the perceived relevance of Gaelic to social identities, respondents were first asked to select all the national identity categories that they felt applied to them, out of a choice of 'Scottish', 'British', 'Irish', 'English' and 'Welsh', with a further option of 'Other', which invited participants to state the identity they felt. Responses to this question are shown in Table 5.1.

In total, 95 of the 112 respondents (84.8%) selected only one national identity, while 13 selected two identities (11.6%) and 4 chose three (3.6%). Of the 95 who chose just one, 88 selected only 'Scottish' (78.6%), while 5 selected only 'British' (4.5%). Additionally, 1 individual entered 'Eileanach' (Islander) as their only national identity (0.9%), while another entered 'Gael'. The remaining 5 (4.5%) who entered either 'Eileanach' or 'Gael' did so in combination with other national identities (that is, Scottish or British), as did the 5 further respondents who selected 'English', 'Irish' or 'French'. Therefore a sense of Scottish identity was most strongly felt in the dataset, with 105 respondents indicating an affiliation with this national identity (93.8%), and 88 choosing it as their only national identity (78.6%). These findings parallel results reported in the 2012 Scottish Social Attitudes Survey, which found that 69% of Scots chose 'Scottish' as their national identity when forced to pick just one, compared to 20% who chose British (Park et al. 2013: 143–4).

Questionnaire participants' responses to attitudinal statements concerning Gaelic and identities are shown in Table 5.2.

An extremely high level of 'strong' agreement with the first proposition shown here, that Gaelic is important for the Highlands and Islands region (at 84.8%), is therefore notably higher than for the second, which proposes that Gaelic is important

Table 5.1 National identity

National identity	Scottish	British	English	Irish	Other: Gael	Other: Eileanach	Other: French
N	105	22	2	2	4	3	1
%	93.8	19.6	1.8	1.8	3.6	2.7	0.9

Table 5.2 Attitudes to Gaelic and Scottish identity

Attitudinal statement	Strongly disagree N (%)	Disagree N (%)	Neither agree or disagree N (%)	Agree N (%)	Strongly agree N (%)
'Gaelic is important for the Highlands and Islands'	0 (0)	1 (0.9)	1 (0.9)	15 (13.4)	95 (84.8)
'Gaelic is important for the whole of Scotland'	3 (2.7)	7 (6.3)	7 (6.3)	31 (27.7)	64 (57.1)
'Scotland would lose its separate identity if Gaelic died out'	10 (8.9)	13 (11.6)	9 (8.0)	30 (26.8)	50 (44.6)
'Gaelic is irrelevant to most people in Scotland'	31 (27.7)	30 (26.8)	12 (10.7)	27 (24.1)	12 (10.7)

for Scotland as a whole (57.1%; see section 5.2.4, above). By way of comparison, findings from the 2012 Scottish Social Attitudes Survey showed that 76% of Scots agreed that Gaelic was 'very' or 'fairly' important to the cultural heritage of Scotland as a whole, compared to 86% who agreed that the language was important to the cultural heritage of the Highlands and Islands (Paterson et al. 2014). Attitudes reflected here recall discourses that were frequently conveyed in interviews on the supposed relevance of Gaelic to regional, as opposed to national, identity (see section 5.2).

Nevertheless, overall levels of support for both statements – as well as for the third, concerning the potential loss of Scotland's distinctive identity – remain very high, at 98.2%, 84.8% and 71.4%, respectively. By contrast, only rather moderate disagreement is expressed for the fourth statement, that Gaelic is irrelevant to most Scots, with 54.5% disagreeing overall, but 34.8% agreeing. Responses to this proposition therefore recall expressions of reservation regarding the promotion of Gaelic that were frequently given in interviews regarding the language's relevance throughout Scotland, and concerns about 'pushing' (*a' putadh/a' sparradh*) the language on certain areas (see section 5.2.3, above). Similarly, in Table 5.3, attitudes expressed in questionnaires closely match language ideologies that were discussed in earlier sections of this chapter.

As can be seen in Table 5.3, overall support for the first two statements is extremely high, at 98.2% and 86.6% respectively, although strong agreement with a sense of pride in Gaelic (85.7%) outstrips that for Gaelic's perceived relevance to informants' Scottish identity (62.5%). A sense that Gaelic is only important for respondents' identity as Gaels is rejected by the majority; 66.1% disagree with this statement overall, while 13.4% agree and 20.5% express no opinion. Indeed, low levels of agreement with this proposition may recall mixed and largely ambivalent attitudes to the label 'Gael' that were reported in interviews (section 5.2.2).

Respondents are more evenly split with regard to the fourth statement, that no 'real' Scot can oppose Gaelic promotion, with 33.9% disagreeing and 45.5% agreeing; a proportion of 20.5% again express no opinion. Divided responses to this statement once again recall some of the ideologies discussed earlier in this chapter, particularly

Table 5.3 Attitudes to Gaelic and personal, cultural and national identities

Attitudinal statement	Strongly disagree N (%)	Disagree N (%)	Neither agree or disagree N (%)	Agree N (%)	Strongly agree N (%)
'I am proud to be able to speak Gaelic'	0 (0)	2 (1.7)	0 (0)	14 (12.5)	96 (85.7)
'Being a Gaelic speaker is an important part of my own Scottish identity'	4 (3.6)	4 (3.6)	7 (6.3)	23 (20.5)	74 (66.1)
'Gaelic is only relevant to my identity as a Gael'	41 (36.6)	33 (29.5)	23 (20.5)	11 (9.8)	4 (3.6)
'No real Scot can oppose the promotion of Gaelic'	19 (17.0)	19 (17.0)	23 (20.5)	27 (24.1)	24 (21.4)
'Being a Gaelic speaker is an important part of my British identity'	30 (26.8)	7 (6.3)	21 (18.8)	16 (14.3)	38 (33.9)

that of not 'forcing' Gaelic on parts of Scotland where people are perceived to be against it (section 5.2.3). Lastly in Table 5.3, attitudes appear to be fairly divided on the question of Gaelic's significance to British identity, with 18.8% of no opinion either way, 33% disagreeing that Gaelic is important for this and 48.2% agreeing. But relatively high levels of support for this proposition should be interpreted in combination with most informants' stated lack of British identity, as reported in Table 5.1; we may compare the fact that over a third of participants (33.9%) strongly agreed that being a Gaelic speaker was important to their British identity with the proportion who indicated they had a British identity at all (19.6%).

5.3.2 Attitudes to Gaelic language and community

As may be seen in Table 5.4, respondents expressed agreement by a slight majority that Gaelic is 'a dying language', with 45.5% agreeing and 42.9% disagreeing. By contrast, agreement that Gaelic is 'useful for job opportunities' is overwhelming at 99.1%,

Table 5.4 Attitudes to the Gaelic community

Attitudinal statement	Strongly disagree N (%)	Disagree N (%)	Neither agree nor disagree N (%)	Agree N (%)	Strongly agree N (%)
'Gaelic is a dying language'	20 (17.9)	28 (25.0)	13 (11.6)	36 (32.1)	15 (13.4)
'Gaelic is useful for job opportunities'	0 (0.0)	1 (0.9)	0 (0.0)	41 (36.6)	70 (62.5)
'Gaelic speakers are inward-looking'	34 (30.4)	18 (16.1)	31 (27.7)	24 (21.4)	5 (4.5)

and 62.5% strongly agreeing. A higher proportion of questionnaire respondents than anticipated – 41.9% – indicated that they used at least 'equal' amounts of Gaelic at work in Figure 4.3 (section 4.4, above); the finding that very nearly all informants agree that Gaelic is 'useful for job opportunities' is similarly unexpected. The figure may reflect a belief that recent developments in Gaelic revitalisation (such as the 2005 Act, 2008 establishment of BBC Alba and continuing recruitment drives for GME teachers) have greatly increased job opportunities in Gaelic, a view that was voiced by a minority of interviewees.

Nevertheless, strong support for this attitudinal statement appears somewhat anomalous. By contrast, divided opinions as to the status of Gaelic speakers as 'inward-looking' – with 46.4% disagreeing, 25.9% agreeing and 27.7% being of no opinion – seems relatively easier to explain. The supposed cliquiness, judgementalism and linguistic 'snobbery' that some interviewees reported to exist (section 5.2) is recalled in the finding that 53.6% of questionnaire respondents do not disagree with this statement. The high proportion of unsure responses may indicate that the sweeping statement that 'Gaelic speakers are inward-looking' is too general to elicit high levels of explicit support, but may alternatively indicate implicit agreement with the general sentiment.

5.3.3 Attitudes to GME

Finally on the questionnaire, respondents were asked to indicate their level of support for six statements pertaining to GME generally. As can be seen in Table 5.5,

Table 5.5 Attitudes to GME and intergenerational transmission

Attitudinal statement	Strongly disagree N (%)	Disagree N (%)	Neither agree or disagree N (%)	Agree N (%)	Strongly agree N (%)
'GME was a valuable experience for me'	1 (0.9)	4 (3.6)	1 (0.9)	18 (16.1)	88 (78.6)
'GME is important for creating new generations of speakers'	0 (0.0)	4 (3.6)	2 (1.8)	24 (21.4)	82 (73.2)
'In the future I would consider enrolling my own children in GME'	4 (3.6)	0 (0.0)	5 (4.5)	13 (11.6)	90 (80.4)
'In the future I would consider raising my own children through Gaelic at home'	3 (2.7)	8 (7.1)	10 (8.9)	14 (12.5)	77 (68.8)
'It is more important for Gaelic-speaking parents to pass their language on to children than to send them to GM schools or units'	7 (6.3)	15 (13.4)	22 (19.6)	26 (23.2)	42 (37.5)
'GME made it easier for me to learn other languages'	4 (3.6)	7 (6.3)	22 (19.6)	32 (28.6)	47 (42.0)

agreement with the first two propositions – that GME was a valuable experience for the respondent personally, and is important for creating new speakers generally – is overwhelming, at 94.6% in both cases.

Similarly, support for the third and fourth statements – that respondents would consider GME for their own children, and would also consider raising them through Gaelic at home – is extremely high, at 92.0% and 81.3%, respectively. Very high levels of support for the system generally may therefore be interpreted from these data, a situation that is again mirrored closely in the interview corpus generally. Support for potentially enrolling children in GME was also expressed frequently in interviews, although strong agreement here that GME is important for creating new generations of speakers – at 73.2% – is rather different from the more nuanced sense of the system's role that was more commonly related in interviews.

A total of 60.7% agreed with the fifth statement in Table 5.5, that 'it is more important for Gaelic-speaking parents to pass their language on to children' than to rely on GME. While strong agreement was lower than for other statements on GME – at 37.5%, with 19.6% neither agreeing nor disagreeing, and the same proportion again disagreeing – overall support is nevertheless very high. A higher level of support was expressed in relation to the final statement, that GME made it easier for former students to learn other languages, although 19.6% of respondents again expressed no opinion. Overall agreement with the statement, at 70.5%, is again very high, especially as only 31 individuals (27.7%) claimed elsewhere on the questionnaire actually to be able to speak an additional language. It therefore seems possible that respondents may have answered this question in relation to the perceived (and well-documented) benefits of GME in its most general terms, rather than their own personal experiences.

5.4 Concluding remarks and triangulation of language ideologies and attitudes

Language ideologies that participants expressed in interviews appeared in many instances to rationalise the language use patterns observed in Chapter 4, particularly in respect of interviewees' somewhat limited identification with the language in cultural terms (sections 5.2.2 to 5.2.4). This facet of participants' identities is further reflected in questionnaire responses (section 5.3). At other times, however, the language ideologies that interviewees' convey appear inconsistent with the usage patterns they described, a common finding in much research on language ideologies in contexts of language shift. For example, interviewees frequently conveyed a sense of guilt concerning their present lack of Gaelic use, and a desire to use Gaelic differently in future (section 5.1.1). Similarly, interviewees frequently described a desire to pass the language on to children in the future, expressing an ideology that Gaelic speakers have a duty or responsibility to do so (5.1.2). This feeling is similarly reflected in the finding of high levels of support for GME among questionnaire participants (section 5.3.3). Taken together, the qualitative and quantitative analyses presented in this chapter demonstrate clearly the attitudinal and ideological underpinnings of former GME students' linguistic practices.

6

Bilingual Life After School? Linguistic Practice and Ideologies in Action

This final chapter draws together the principal research findings presented in Chapters 4 and 5, above, providing a synthesis of key conclusions in respect of the overarching research questions initially outlined in section 1.1. The discussion presented will relate these findings to previously formulated theories of language revitalisation, and the possible role of education in reversing language shift (as discussed in Chapters 2 and 3). The principal research questions of this investigation, as outlined at the beginning of the book, comprised the following:

- What role does Gaelic play in the day-to-day lives of former Gaelic-medium students who started in GME during the first decade of its availability, and how and when do they use the language?
- What sets of beliefs and language ideologies do these Gaelic-medium educated adults express in relation to Gaelic?
- How do these beliefs and ideologies relate to their actual language practices, to their attitudes concerning the language, and to future prospects for the maintenance of Gaelic?

Each of the principal research questions has been addressed in the qualitative and quantitative analyses presented, and the triangulation of these two datasets provided an invaluable means by which to cross-check the validity of conclusions made through each analytic approach. The three sections of this final analytic chapter correspond broadly to the three principal research questions listed above. In response to the first, overarching research objective – assessing the role that Gaelic may play in former GME students' lives at present, and in particular how and when they use the language – I provide a summary in section 6.1 of informants' present-day Gaelic use (section 6.1.1). This section also summarises participants' reported abilities in the language (section 6.1.2), as well as their various experiences of Gaelic language socialisation during childhood (section 6.1.3).

These two considerations – current ability and past socialisation – appeared to bear the most striking relations to participants' present engagement with Gaelic. In response to the second principal research question – concerning former GME students' beliefs and language ideologies – section 6.2 draws together findings from the qualitative and quantitative analyses on informants' ideologies and attitudes in relation firstly to Gaelic language use (section 6.2.1), secondly to the relation of Gaelic to sociocultural identities (6.2.2), and lastly on GME as an education system generally (section 6.2.3). Finally, section 6.3 draws together the principal conclusions summarised in sections 6.1 to 6.2 and provides a concise summary of the study's overall conclusions, with a view to assessing how participants' beliefs, attitudes and ideologies concerning Gaelic relate to their current language practices, and to future prospects for the maintenance of Gaelic in Scotland.

6.1 Language use among Gaelic-medium educated adults: Past, present and future prospects

This section summarises the principal findings concerning Gaelic language use by participants in the investigation, considering the picture of participants' present-day Gaelic use (section 6.1.1), reported abilities (6.1.2), and experiences of Gaelic language socialisation during childhood (6.1.3) that is provided by the qualitative and quantitative analyses. As demonstrated in the empirical chapters above, these three issues are clearly closely related, and the secondary issues of abilities and socialisation experiences shed light on the question of Gaelic language use. I initially draw attention in the first section of discussion presented here to the issue of precisely how and when participants in the sample use the Gaelic language at present.

6.1.1 Present Gaelic language use

The majority of participants' social use of Gaelic, particularly with peers such as friends, siblings and partners, is reported to be limited across the interview and questionnaire datasets (see sections 4.1, 4.4). In the qualitative analysis, participants who were not socialised in Gaelic within the home during childhood reported particularly limited Gaelic use, providing support for Fishman's (1991, 2001b, 2013) theoretical cautioning about the limitations of the school environment in RLS, and for fostering minority language use outside of the formal domain of education. A total of 36 of all 46 interviewees described making low to limited use of Gaelic at present (4.1.2), two-thirds of whom (24) reported the very lowest levels of Gaelic use (4.1.3). Interview participants within the intermediate group tended not to use the language to a substantial degree in social interaction, although this group constituted the broadest category in terms of the heterogeneity of language practices reported.

Revealingly, two Gaelic language practices that were frequently related across the interview corpus were the occasional use of Gaelic, in informants' own words, as a 'secret code' – so as not to be understood by strangers (section 4.1.4) – and 'informal' use of Gaelic, characterised as extensive code-mixing with English (4.1.5). As discussed in section 4.1, a relatively superficial and limited use of the language, in terms of participants' engagement with Gaelic in their day-to-day lives, was interpreted from extracts describing these two language practices. In particular, the types of language alternation interviewees commonly referred to in section 4.1.5 appear qualitatively different to the kinds of code-switching observed either among traditional Gaelic speakers in heartland areas, or in bilingual communities outside of Scotland (see section 4.1.5; Smith-Christmas 2012, 2013; Gafaranga 2007, 2009).

The relatively few interviewees in the category of high overall Gaelic use are a notable exception to this general pattern. All 10 participants in this group use Gaelic in the course of their day-to-day work or studies, a finding that parallels Hodges' (2009) identification of Welsh-medium employment as a key domain for minority language use by individuals reporting generally higher levels of engagement with that language, after having completed Welsh-medium education. Notably in the present study, individuals' participation in Gaelic employment or study, and socialisation in Gaelic at home in childhood both correlate with higher social use of the language, such as with friends, siblings and partners outside of the more formal domains associated with work (section 4.1, 4.4). The apparent importance of home Gaelic language socialisation during childhood to former GME students' continued Gaelic language use lends support to Fishman's (1991, 2001a, 2001b, 2013) continual reassertion of the limitations of school-based interventions on behalf of minority language maintenance.

Yet, conversely, the key role that Gaelic employment appears to play in the day-to-day Gaelic language use of participants who reported a high overall level of Gaelic use may challenge Fishman's (2013: 493) characterisation of the workplace as a higher-order context, largely detached from and irrelevant to those of the home–community–neighbourhood. Crucially in this regard, the access to social networks of (informal) Gaelic-speaking peer groups that Gaelic workplaces may offer adults (see section 4.1.1) is a question that may have a key bearing on future rates of intergenerational transmission by this group. Nevertheless, the finding that only 10 of the 46 interviewees reported being so employed gives further support to Fishman's (1991, 2001b) general theoretical premise concerning the limitations of education in ethnolinguistic reproduction, and prospective rates of intergenerational transmission by high users of Gaelic in that group are unclear at present. The question of what will occur in subsequent social and linguistic stages of the bilingual lives of such high users presents an important lacuna for researchers seeking to address issues of Gaelic language maintenance and regeneration.

A much greater proportion of questionnaire respondents than interviewees reported using Gaelic at work or university, with 41.9% claiming to use at least 'equal' Gaelic and English in these contexts (and 6.3% claiming 'only Gaelic'). While a similar proportion (41.1%) claimed to use 'only English' at work or university, the proportion claiming to work or study (at least partly) in Gaelic clearly outstrips that within the interview corpus, in which only 10 individuals (21.7%) reported doing so. In this connection, we recall Edwards's (2009: 62) emphasis on the importance of 'domains of necessity' – including the school and workplace – for minority language maintenance efforts, since they tend generally to embrace the most central aspects of speakers' day-to-day existences.

Further analysis of questionnaire participants' language practices tends to support Fishman's cautious approach to the workplace as a focus of language regeneration efforts. Here we may recall his assertion that provision for endangered minority languages within the 'institutions of modernity' will do little for languages that are no longer reproduced organically in the home (1991: 406). The formal domains associated with work appear to predominate in questionnaire respondents' Gaelic use generally, with the language used considerably less in the home–family context. Although 47.3% of questionnaire respondents claimed to have 'at least one' Gaelic conversation every day (17% claiming to do so weekly, and 35.8% less than weekly), this is clearly not a very demanding criterion of use. More detailed questions on the contexts in which respondents claimed to use Gaelic revealed a less encouraging picture from a language revitalisation perspective (section 4.4). For example, 73.2% of questionnaire respondents claimed to use 'only' or 'mostly' English in the home, revealing a rather more doubtful perspective on future Gaelic maintenance. Crucially, correlations were consistently observed between Gaelic language use and reported levels of childhood socialisation in Gaelic at home, as well as continuity with GME and Gaelic study generally.

Overall in section 4.4, however, questionnaire informants' present use of Gaelic with family members was reported to be low, due firstly to the fact that only 41.1% claimed to have a mother who could speak Gaelic, while 35.7% had a father who could do so, and 26.8% had grandparents who could. Secondly, respondents with Gaelic-speaking family members reported widely varying levels of Gaelic use with them. For instance, a third (32.6%) of respondents with a Gaelic-speaking mother claimed to use only or mostly English with her, while 27.5% of those with a Gaelic-speaking father used mostly or only English with him. Crucially in this respect, whilst 60.7% claimed to have siblings who could speak Gaelic (probably indicative of parental choice of GME for multiple children), only one-quarter of these (25.0%) claimed to use at least 'equal' Gaelic with them, with the rest using 'only' or 'mostly' English.

Even more revealingly in terms of respondents' social use of Gaelic – and likely prospects for intergenerational transmission of Gaelic by graduates of GME – a mere 10.7% claimed that their partner or spouse could speak the language. Furthermore, 41.7% of this group reported using 'only' or 'mostly' English with their Gaelic-speaking partner. Crucially for the prospects of transmission of Gaelic by this group, only 9 of the 23 questionnaire respondents with children reported using any Gaelic with them (39.1%), and 4 of these respondents reported using 'mostly' English with their child.

Low levels of social use of Gaelic are further confirmed by the finding that only 20.5% of questionnaire informants reported using at least 'equal' amounts of Gaelic in conversations with their friends. Although 40.2% claimed to use at least 'equal' Gaelic with friends who are able to speak the language, it is nevertheless clear that English predominates in participants' social interactions. Relatedly, whilst telephone conversation, internet and social media use each plays an increasingly prominent role in social communication today, only 32.1% of respondents claim to use at least 'equal' Gaelic and English with Gaelic-speaking friends in phone conversations, 25.0% in social media exchanges, and 24.1% for SMS/text messages. Gaelic use declines even further in terms of participants' use of passive skills in leisure time, 22.3% claiming to make at least 'equal' use of Gaelic when listening to music and radio, and 14.3% using at least 'equal' amounts of Gaelic when watching television. This falls further to 11.6% when reading books, 6.3% on social media, and 8.0% on other internet sites.

Nevertheless, the finding that Gaelic continues to be used, even to these relatively limited degrees, as a communicative medium in the private and personal lives of a minority of my sample of Gaelic-medium educated adults is a significant one. Romaine's (2006: 443) assertion of the need, in many instances of language shift, to reconceptualise what we mean by language maintenance seems pertinent here. It may be that in seeking to address the overarching question of bilingual life among former Gaelic-medium students, the present investigation arrives inevitably at questions of post-vernacular language use, and the significance attached to Gaelic as a language that is no longer spoken in the daily existences of many past GME students. In a sense, therefore, the conclusions presented in Chapters 4 and 5 may in fact pertain to degrees of bilingual afterlife, subsequent to past immersion students' leaving school. It is clear that Gaelic does retain a role in the lives of a considerable proportion of informants, even if often only a symbolic one, or when viewed through the prism of past experience and the development of a sense of self. Crucially in this regard, reported abilities and socialisation in Gaelic appeared to bear an important relation to the extent to which such bilingual (after-)life was contingent on informants' actual use of the language at present.

6.1.2 Language abilities

With important implications for participants' maintenance of bilingualism after school, consistent correlations were observed between reported Gaelic language use and abilities in section 4.4 of the quantitative analysis. On the other hand, the fact that 21 participants (45.7%) chose to carry out the interview in Gaelic – irrespective of their reported Gaelic use generally – may reflect genuinely higher levels of continued ability than use among the interview sample. Interviewees' responses in respect of their Gaelic language abilities – and the degree to which past linguistic proficiencies might be recovered in future – seemed to provide anecdotal support for the dormant language hypothesis (Bardovi-Harlig and Stringer 2010: 8), though a great deal of detailed linguistic research would be needed to shed light on the nature of speakers' actual proficiencies. The fact that the sample analysed in this book was purposive and self-selected must also be borne in mind here, and considerably lower levels of language ability might be found among a larger and more representative sample of Gaelic-medium educated adults.

In section 4.4, 69.6% of questionnaire respondents reported that they were 'fluent' in Gaelic, while a further 13.4% reported that they could 'speak a fair amount'. At the lower end of the ability spectrum, 11.6% reported that they could speak 'some' Gaelic and 5.4% claimed to be able to 'speak a small amount of Gaelic', while no single participant reported hardly being able to speak Gaelic at all. Most questionnaire respondents also reported very high levels of Gaelic ability on a scale of 0–10 for each linguistic skill, with mean scores of 8.0 for speaking, 7.7 for reading, 7.1 for writing and 8.7 for understanding the language.

Nevertheless, it is notable that the equivalent scores for English were 1.8 points higher for speaking, 2.1 higher for reading, 2.4 for writing and 1.2 for understanding. Notable correlations were found between higher professed Gaelic ability and Gaelic use in general, at work and at home (section 4.4.4). The importance of these two issues in participants' maintenance of bilingual practices and abilities is an issue in need of further investigation, though insight from the qualitative analysis sheds further light, particularly in respect of Gaelic socialisation at home.

6.1.3 Language socialisation

Relatively high levels of Gaelic language socialisation were reported in interviews; 15 interviewees (32.6%) reported growing up in homes in which both parents – or single parents without a partner – spoke Gaelic to them, 9 of whom were from Gaelic-speaking communities in Skye and the Western Isles. A further 11 (23.9%) reported growing up in homes where one parent spoke the language to them. Although 43.5% of interviewees and 48.2% of questionnaire respondents reported growing up in homes in which neither parent could speak the language, these proportions are likely to be considerably smaller than among all students who started in GME during the period in question, again reflecting self-report bias in the purposive sample (see section 3.3.2). On the other hand, and crucially for the considerations of this survey, only 4 interview participants can be described as 'new speakers' of Gaelic (section 4.2.3): that is to say, speakers for whom Gaelic was not a primary language of socialisation in childhood, but who nevertheless continue to use the language frequently in the present day (O'Rourke and Ramallo 2011, 2013; McLeod et al. 2014; Dunmore 2017).

The finding that only 4 of the 20 interviewees with no parental background in Gaelic continue to make substantial use of the language may have important implications for the practicability of creating new speakers through GME. This finding is particularly striking when it is considered that 2 of these 4 reported growing up in communities where the language was widely used during their childhood, in contrast to the sociolinguistic setting of most formerly Gaelic communities today (see Munro et al. 2010; Will 2012). Many interviewees acknowledged the importance of GME as a way of supporting intergenerational transmission at home, and reported feeling more connected to Gaelic and Highland culture through having received GME (section 4.3.2).

Yet, conversely, interviewees who make limited use of Gaelic today often reported past experiences of negative affect in the system, particularly in respect of feeling 'segregated' from English-medium peers at school (section 4.3.3). Whilst some useful research on the social profiles and language practices of new speakers of Gaelic in urban central Scotland has been conducted (see McLeod et al. 2014), a good deal of work remains to be done on this threshold issue, particularly from the perspective of national language policy. Not least in this regard, the connection of new Gaelic speakerhood and GME, and the apparently somewhat limited role of the formal education system in creating new generations of Gaelic speakers is a question in clear need of further in-depth research.

Both qualitative and quantitative analyses suggest that professed socialisation in Gaelic at home during childhood tends to accompany higher reported levels of Gaelic use, although it should be noted once again that the proportion who reported such socialisation is likely to have been larger amongst interviewees than would be true of the wider population of Gaelic-medium educated adults. Similarly among questionnaire respondents, relatively high levels of socialisation in Gaelic at home and in the community were again reported. Some 21.4% claimed that more Gaelic than English was used in the home in which they were raised, with a further 10.7% claiming it was used to an equal degree (section 4.4).

By comparison, 14.3% of questionnaire respondents claimed that more Gaelic than English was used in the wider community they grew up in, and 9.8% claimed the languages were used equally. As interpreted from the qualitative analysis of interviews, statistical analysis of questionnaire responses confirmed notable correlations between socialisation and continued use of Gaelic with different interlocutors, and between socialisation and higher overall use of the language at home and work, suggestive of the roles that home exposure to and immersion in Gaelic may play in GME students' maintenance of the language in the long term.

6.2 Language ideologies and attitudes: Factors underlying linguistic practice

The second research objective identified in section 1.1 of the introductory chapter was to assess the sets of beliefs and language ideologies that Gaelic-medium educated adults express in relation to the Gaelic language. The language ideologies that were most frequently conveyed by interviewees provide invaluable data for understanding the language use patterns that were described in Chapter 4. Similarly, questionnaire participants' responses to eighteen attitudinal statements regarding the Gaelic language and community provide further important insights in this regard, and allow for cross-comparison with results from the qualitative analysis. Taken together, these two sets of data were used as a means to triangulate findings with a view to assessing the final research question, on the relation of participants' beliefs and ideologies to their professed Gaelic language use, and the implications of this relationship for the language's future prospects (see section 6.3, below).

6.2.1 Ideologies of Gaelic language use

In many cases, the language ideologies that participants expressed appeared to underpin or rationalise the language use patterns observed in Chapter 4 (see also Silverstein 1979: 193; Kroskrity 2004: 496). In light of the data presented in Chapter 5, Makihara's (2010: 44–5) statement that language ideologies often appear to have an important role in determining the rate and direction of language shift in minority language contexts therefore seems particularly apt. At other times, however, the language ideologies that interview participants convey appear inconsistent with the usage patterns they described, a common finding in much research on language ideologies in contexts of language shift (see Dauenhauer and Dauenhauer 1998: 62). For instance, interviewees frequently expressed a sense of regret and guilt concerning their present lack of Gaelic use, and a desire to use Gaelic differently in future (section 5.1.1). Nevertheless, beliefs and feelings of this nature appear, to this point at least, to have been insufficient motivation for participants actually to change their language practices in respect of Gaelic use in key domains. Language ideologies of this kind, reflecting a sense in which informants feel they should try to speak more Gaelic, are likely to derive at least in part from their experiences of GME. As such, Gaelic-medium educated adults' reproduction of language ideologies of Gaelic use – mediated through their interpretation and experience of ideological content that they may initially have encountered in the bilingual classroom (see Jaffe 2009: 395) – seems incongruous to their actual language practices currently.

Similarly, interviewees frequently described a desire to pass the language on to children in the future, conveying an ideology that Gaelic speakers have a duty or responsibility to do so (5.1.2). In spite of this, none of the 10 participants in the first category of high overall Gaelic use currently have children (section 4.1.1), and those participants with children in the second, intermediate usage category tended generally to report only limited use of the language with their sons or daughters currently (4.1.2). This finding demonstrates the manner in which ideologies and beliefs about the ways in which languages ought to be used are often culturally conditioned, and may not in fact be grounded in actual linguistic practice (see Silverstein 1979; Boudreau and Dubois 2007). Among questionnaire respondents, only 9 of the 23 participants with children reported using any Gaelic with them at present (39.1%), and 4 of these 9 respondents reported using 'mostly' English with their child. In light of these findings, and from responses within the interview corpus, the prospect of research participants' actually transmitting the language to children in the future seems somewhat unlikely, particularly given their limited Gaelic language use with spouses and partners (section 4.1.2).

Two rather different language ideologies seemed to militate against interviewees' greater use of Gaelic. I drew attention in section 5.1.4 to a frequently stated belief that it was possible to have Gaelic and to value the language as part of oneself without actually using it from day to day. Relatedly, many interviewees expressed a complementary ideology of opportunity and choice to use Gaelic (section 5.1.5) when explaining their present disuse of the language. Whilst describing a dearth of opportunity to use the language in their lives on the one hand, speakers also described their choice (not) to use the language as a decisive factor in this regard, with many claiming to have important priorities over speaking Gaelic at present. Interviewees often described a sense of discomfort with the 'snobbery' and judgement that they felt to exist in the Gaelic community (section 5.1.3), and a widespread belief that Gaelic speakers – whether learners or traditional speakers – tended to look down on others' Gaelic language was a clear theme that emerged in the interview corpus.

Crucially in this connection, Romaine's (2006: 445) emphasis on the ways in which linguistic perception in bilingual communities is often ideologically enmeshed with other sociocultural perceptions provides valuable insight. Whether or not the kinds of linguistic snobbery and judgmentalism to which participants referred are in fact widespread within the Gaelic community, it is clear that these traits are widely perceived to be an unwelcome characteristic of that community. This appears to impact in turn upon the willingness of former Gaelic-medium students to interact with other Gaelic speakers, or to use the language in their daily lives generally. Divided attitudes to the Gaelic community were also reflected in the responses of questionnaire respondents to the suggestion that 'Gaelic speakers are inward-looking', with only 46.4% disagreeing. By comparison, 25.9% agreed, with 27.7% of no opinion. Although quite general, the wording of this statement was quite strong compared to others on the questionnaire, and the finding that 53.6% of respondents did not disagree with it is noteworthy. The supposed judgementalism and 'snobbery' that some interviewees reported to exist in Gaelic communities may underlie the divided attitudes reflected here, although further research would be required to inform this hypothesis.

6.2.2 Gaelic and sociocultural identities

The qualitative analysis demonstrated that participants considered Gaelic to bear an important relation to their identities at several layers of their social lives and cultural identifications. Firstly, the significance of the language for participants' personal identity was commonly conveyed throughout the corpus (section 5.2.1). Likewise, questionnaire respondents agreed overwhelmingly that they were 'proud to be able to speak Gaelic', with 98.2% in total agreeing, and 85.7% doing so 'strongly'. The importance of Gaelic to the Highlands and Islands was also frequently related in interviews, and an ideology that Gaelic may be conceived of more comfortably as a regional language, rooted strongly in this area specifically, was clearly discernible (section 5.2.3). This sense of a regional identity was often framed within the frequently occurring trope of not forcing or pushing Gaelic (*putadh/sparradh na Gàidhlig*) on people and areas perceived not to have a connection to the language. In this regard, it was telling that only 33.9% of questionnaire respondents agreed that 'No real Scot can oppose the promotion of Gaelic', with 44.5% disagreeing.

More generally, interviewees often appeared eager to avoid discourses that attribute a predominant role to Gaelic in the discussion of Scottish identity, with many expressing awareness of Scots and a perceived need for sensitivity to speakers of that variety in the discussion of Scottish national identity (5.2.3 to 5.24). Uncertainty over the status of Gaelic as a national language was also reflected in the finding that 84.8% of questionnaire respondents agreed that 'Gaelic is important for the Highlands and Islands', compared to 57.1% who agreed that 'Gaelic is important for the whole of Scotland'. Nevertheless, 71.4% agreed that 'Scotland would lose its separate identity if Gaelic died out', and only 34.8% agreed that 'Gaelic is irrelevant to most people in Scotland.' Results from both the quantitative and qualitative analyses are therefore comparable to positive attitudes to Gaelic in Scottish identity found among the wider public, such as those recently reported in recent volumes of the Scottish Social Attitudes Survey (Paterson et al. 2014). By way of comparison, and in contrast to these surveys of the general public, 86.6% of questionnaire respondents agreed that 'Being a Gaelic speaker is an important part of my own Scottish identity' (62.5% agreeing 'strongly'). Questionnaire informants, in common with interviewees, were therefore considerably more comfortable attributing a role to Gaelic in their own Scottish identity than suggesting it was a national language for all of Scotland. In the long term, the goal of fostering a more self-confident identification with the Gaelic language among GME students may rest in large part upon better communicating the importance of the language to Scottish heritage and identity generally (see section 1.1). Clearly, this objective touches on issues of political will and ideology at the level of national policy-making, and the existence of such goodwill or a supportive language ideology within government currently is far from clear.

The qualitative analysis found widespread indifference to the label 'Gael' in interview participants' identity constructions, and whilst a vehement rejection of the identity category Gael was rare (though notably present) in the corpus, a sense of ambivalence and uncertainty surrounding the term is clearly discernible (section 5.2.2). On the questionnaire, 66.1% of respondents disagreed that 'Gaelic is only relevant to my identity as a Gael', with only 13.4% agreeing. These findings are broadly comparable to results in Oliver's research concerning high-school students' self-identification as Gaels (2002, 2006). A total of 48.2% of questionnaire participants agreed that 'Being a Gaelic speaker is an important part of my British identity', with 33.0% disagreeing. In the interview data, many informants appeared to attach some significance to Gaelic in their rejection of British identity, though most regarded the language in less overtly political terms (see section 5.2.5). A feeling of British identity was very rarely reported in the interview corpus, and the relevance of the language to identity constructions in this regard remains a question in need of further research.

The beliefs and language ideologies that interview participants expressed in relation to Gaelic therefore pertained to ten thematic categories, five of which concerned language use as such, and five touching on its relevance for sociocultural identities. The attitudinal propositions that were designed to elicit responses on the online questionnaire similarly drew mostly on these overarching themes. The combination of the qualitative and quantitative approaches represented an invaluable means by which to cross-check and triangulate research findings in response to the second research question outlined in section 1.1 of this book. Whilst a number of the ideologies of Gaelic language use that were reported in interviews appeared to rationalise and reinforce the language use patterns that were observed, other sets of beliefs that participants expressed seem contradictory to these.

The specific place of Gaelic in Scottish national identity – the category of cultural affiliation that informants were much the most comfortable professing – seems to be a matter of some debate for participants in the present study, with many reluctant to define the relationship in unproblematic terms. Conversely, a weak association or even hostile attitude toward the label 'Gael' predominated in many interviewees' discussions of their cultural identities, and the relevance of Gaelic to contemporary speakers' identities beyond the idiosyncrasies of personal distinctiveness is a question in need of further in-depth research.

6.2.3 Attitudes to GME

Although support for GME as a system was generally strong amongst interview participants, only a negligible number mentioned the benefits that GME might have for revitalising Gaelic in Scotland. By comparison, questionnaire respondents expressed overwhelming support (94.6%) for the proposition that 'GME is important for creating new generations' of speakers of the language. Divided opinions as to the success of revitalisation efforts appeared to be reflected in responses to the proposition that 'Gaelic is a dying language', with 45.5% agreeing and 42.9% disagreeing. Relatedly, support for the idea of enrolling children in GME was generally high among interviewees.

Support for the statement that 'GME was a valuable experience' for the respondent was overwhelming at 94.6%, while 92.0% of respondents also agreed that they would consider GME for their own children (compared to 81.3% who would consider raising children through Gaelic at home). Informants' belief in the benefits of GME is also reflected in the overwhelming 99.1% agreement with the statement that 'Gaelic is useful for job opportunities', which may appear once again to reflect self-report bias in the purposive sample, though further research would be needed to confirm this. Nevertheless, 60.7% agreed that 'it is more important for Gaelic-speaking parents to pass their language on to children than to send them to GM schools or units', with 19.6% neither agreeing nor disagreeing, and the same proportion again disagreeing. This general support for the idea of passing Gaelic on therefore seems to parallel language ideologies in the interview corpus that expressed a sense of responsibility to transmit the language to children in future and, simultaneously, to conflict with the Gaelic usage patterns reported by the minority of respondents with children at present (see section 4.4). This kind of mismatch between language practices and ideologies recalls theoretical definitions of language ideologies outlined in section 2.1 (see Dauenhauer and Dauenhauer 1998: 62; Boudreau and Dubois 2007: 104).

6.3 Conclusions: Bilingual life and the relationship of linguistic practice and ideology

The final research objective outlined at the start of the present investigation was to address the issue of how participants' beliefs and ideologies may relate to their actual language practices, attitudes and, crucially, future prospects for the maintenance of Gaelic. A thorough discussion of the apparent relationships between informants' language practices and ideologies, and between language ideologies and attitudes, has been provided in the preceding section (6.2). Whilst certain language ideologies that were expressed in interviews seemed to rationalise and thereby reinforce the language use patterns that most informants reported (section 4.1; see also Silverstein 1979: 193), others – such as the ideology of guilt at current disuse, or the responsibility to speak more Gaelic – seemed somewhat contradictory to those patterns (see Dauenhauer and Dauenhauer 1998: 62). By contrast, the language ideologies that were most frequently advanced by the 46 interviewees generally corresponded closely to language attitudes reflected in responses by the 112 questionnaire participants to eighteen attitudinal propositions concerning Gaelic language, community and culture.

I draw attention in this final section to the prospects for Gaelic language maintenance and intergenerational transmission amongst research participants that may be inferred from the analyses presented in Chapters 4 and 5 of this book. A key finding of the investigation outlined in this monograph is the relatively low levels of Gaelic language use recorded among a majority of participants in both qualitative and quantitative analyses. This was particularly true of social use of Gaelic with peers – notably friends, siblings and partners – which was weak throughout the interview corpus and questionnaire dataset. In themselves, current patterns of reported Gaelic use with peers can hardly be theorised to correspond directly to likely prospects for the successful transmission of the language to children in future, and in the absence of large numbers of current parents in either the qualitative or the quantitative datasets, it is difficult to offer a concrete conclusion in this respect.

Nevertheless, one might infer from the generally low levels of Gaelic language use that most participants reported – and the limited use with children reported by (the relatively few) parents in both datasets – that the majority of participants would struggle to provide a Gaelic-rich home environment for potential children in future, in spite of their beliefs and best intentions in this regard (see section 5.1.2). As Ó hIfearnáin (2013a: 349) has indicated, whilst the relevance of Fishman's (1991, 2001a, 2001b) principal theoretical stance regarding the centrality of intergenerational transmission to language revitalisation initiatives remains largely unchallenged, intergenerational transmission processes, as such, remain relatively poorly understood. In order to address this limitation adequately in respect of former GME students under investigation here, longitudinal and ethnographic research charting the subsequent language practices of participants would be required, considering potential changes in participants' language practices as greater numbers of individuals in the sample start families of their own. In spite of this, it may nevertheless be stated that the prospects for intergenerational transmission by the majority of the 130 informants in both analyses undertaken for this book clearly appear limited.

For participants who reported higher levels of Gaelic language use in their day-to-day lives, employment or study in the language formed a crucial social structure for linguistic practices, and the more formal domains associated with work predominated in their Gaelic use. The qualitative analysis nevertheless demonstrated that participation in Gaelic employment or study appeared also to facilitate access to networks in which the language is used socially. The 10 interviewees within this group therefore seem to be the most likely potential sources of intergenerational transmission amongst the cohort under investigation here, though none of them have children of their own as yet. Further characteristics of participants who reported higher levels of current Gaelic use in both analyses were higher professed levels of Gaelic ability, and reported experiences of socialisation in the language at home. The relation of both of these factors to higher levels of Gaelic language use was substantiated in the statistical analysis, which found frequent correlations attesting to their interrelationship (section 4.4).

Additionally, the statistical analysis demonstrated that continuation with GME into secondary school was linked to higher levels of present-day Gaelic use. Higher levels of ability, socialisation and continuation with Gaelic study therefore appear to accompany greater use of the language, as might be expected. Nevertheless, the influence of each of these factors on former GME students' Gaelic use, and the relationship of each to the other, are questions in clear need of further research. In particular, fine-grained ethnographic and longitudinal research would yield invaluable data on the relationship of these variables to Gaelic language use in school years, after GME, and further along, when greater proportions of GME leavers have started families of their own.

While generally positive attitudes to Gaelic – and very supportive attitudes to GME – were reported by informants in the qualitative and quantitative portions of the investigation, language ideologies that emerged in the semi-structured interviews go some way to explaining the low levels of Gaelic language use reported by the majority of participants in the survey. Certain language ideologies expressed in this regard appeared contradictory to participants' current language practices, however, particularly those that indicated a sense of guilt and regret at reported lack of Gaelic use, and a sense of responsibility to pass the language on to the next generation. By contrast, widespread perceptions of the existence of linguistic snobbery in the Gaelic community, a sense of appreciation for 'having' the language whilst not regularly speaking it, and having other compelling life priorities over Gaelic each seemed to rationalise informants' limited use of the language.

In spite of this, participants conveyed a strong sense of pride in speaking Gaelic in both datasets, and the importance of the language to informants' personal identity was clear from both analyses. Association with the traditional identity category 'Gael' appeared weak throughout, however, and the continued salience of a distinctive Gaelic identity to young Gaelic speakers' social lives is a question in need of further research (see also Dunmore 2017, 2018). Conversely, perceptions of Gaelic as a national language were conflicted, and its relevance to Scottish identity was widely questioned in both interviews and questionnaire responses.

In many respects, conclusions presented in this book in respect of limited present Gaelic use may come as little surprise to other researchers who have investigated the delivery and impact of GME since the late 1980s. Certainly, the majority of research participants themselves claimed informally not to expect many of their old classmates to speak the language in the present day. Fishman's (1991, 2001a, 2001b, 2013) theories of RLS would predict exactly this outcome, and from that perspective, the results may come as little surprise to researchers who adopt a similar theoretical stance to Fishman. Significantly, however, this book provides robust empirical evidence for the first time of the likely long-term social and linguistic outcomes, not only of GME, but also of minority language 'immersion revitalisation' education (after García 2009: 128) in comparable contexts throughout the world. In that respect, this monograph represents an important contribution to the fields of applied and educational linguistics, and the sociology of language more generally. For parents, teachers and policymakers who initially campaigned for the system's establishment, who were responsible for its delivery over the past thirty years, or who continue to promote the development of GME as a means of creating new speakers, the generally limited Gaelic language use that former Gaelic-medium students report in this investigation is likely to be a source of considerable disappointment and frustration.

Nevertheless, the findings presented in this book should be beneficial for the development of evidence-based language policy in Scotland, as well as in other contexts of language shift internationally. In policy terms, an over-reliance on the education system as a means of creating new speakers of minority languages – who will use the language extensively in later life and transmit the language to their children without difficulty – should clearly be avoided. The analyses presented above demonstrated convincingly for the first time that the fact of receiving GME is, in and of itself, unlikely to bolster students' frequent use of the language outside of the classroom setting subsequently, when formal schooling is 'over and done with' (Fishman 2001b: 470). Nevertheless, the finding that continuation with GME into secondary-level education correlates consistently with higher levels of reported Gaelic use and ability should demonstrate to policymakers the crucial importance of securing continuity in the provision of bilingual education throughout the education system (see O'Hanlon 2012). The results outlined in the empirical chapters of this book also lend support to Edwards's (2013: 13) re-assertion of the need to recognise a qualitative distinction between the bilingual profiles of adult speakers who were socialised into Gaelic in communities where the language was widely spoken, and those who may not have had that opportunity and who acquire Gaelic either mostly or entirely through the education system.

The results outlined in this book provide clear evidence for the first time of longer-term social and linguistic outcomes among adults who received GME, regarding both their current and potential future engagement with the language socially, and the values and beliefs they hold in relation to it. This evidence should be of value for the development of policy in relation to the provision of GME as an education system, as well as to the creation of new spaces for the use of Gaelic in society at large. As Dorian (2011: 468) has observed, the long-term success of current efforts to revitalise Gaelic in Scotland remains in large part to be seen, and the evidence provided in the present study tends to support her view that the relatively favourable position of the Gaelic language is precarious at present. The evidence-based appraisal of the effectiveness of GME for securing the revitalisation of Gaelic provided in this book should impact on official understandings and policy priorities for language maintenance at home and abroad. In particular, the research presented in this book has demonstrated the limited degree to which the education system can be relied upon for equipping and enabling students to lead a truly bilingual life after school.

Bibliography

Alén Garabato, C., and H. Boyer (2005), 'Scolarisation ne vaut pas normalisation sociolinguistique', in H. Boyer (ed.), *De l'école occitane à l'enseignement public: Vécu et représentations sociolinguistiques. Une enquête auprès d'un groupe d'ex-calondrons*, Paris: L'Harmattan, pp. 29–76.
An Comunn Gaidhealach (1936), *Report of Special Committee on the Teaching of Gaelic in Schools and Colleges*, Glasgow: An Comunn Gaidhealach.
Andersen, R. W. (1982), 'Determining the linguistic attributes of language attrition', in R. D. Lambert and B. F. Freed (eds), *The Loss of Language Skills*, Rowley, MA: Newbury House, pp. 83–118.
Anderson, B. R. O. (1991), *Imagined Communities: Reflections on the Origin and Spread of Nationalism*, 2nd edn, London: Verso.
Azurmendi, M., and I. Martinez de Luna (2011), 'Success–failure continuum of Euskara in the Basque Country', in J. A. Fishman and O. García (eds), *Handbook of Language and Ethnic Identity: The Success–Failure Continuum in Language and Ethnic Identity Efforts (Vol. II)*, Oxford: Oxford University Press, pp. 323–48.
Baker, C. (1992), *Attitudes and Language*, Clevedon: Multilingual Matters.
Baker, C. (2006), 'Psycho-sociological analysis in language policy', in T. Ricento (ed.), *An Introduction to Language Policy*, Oxford: Blackwell, pp. 210–28.
Baker, C. (2007), *A Parents' and Teachers' Guide to Bilingualism*, 3rd edn, Clevedon: Multilingual Matters.
Baker, C. (2011), *Foundations of Bilingual Education and Bilingualism*, 5th edn, Clevedon: Multilingual Matters.
Baker, C., and O. García (eds) (2007), *Bilingual Education: An Introductory Reader*, Clevedon: Multilingual Matters.
Baker, C., and C. L. Griffith (1983), 'Provision of materials and tests for Welsh-speaking pupils with learning difficulties: A national survey', *Educational Research*, 25: 60–70.
Bakhtin, M. M. (1986), *Speech Genres and Other Late Essays*, transl. and ed. C. Emerson, M. Holquist and V. W. McGee, Austin: University of Texas Press.

Baldauf, R. B. (2005), 'Coordinating government and community support for community language teaching in Australia: Overview with special attention to New South Wales', *International Journal of Bilingual Education and Bilingualism*, 8: 132–44.

Bale, J. (2010), 'International comparative perspectives on heritage language education policy research', *Annual Review of Applied Linguistics*, 30: 42–65.

Bardovi-Harlig, K., and D. Stringer (2010), 'Variables in second language attrition: Advancing the state of the art', *Studies in Second Language Acquisition*, 32: 1–45.

Barrow, G. W. S. (1989), 'The lost Gàidhealtachd of medieval Scotland', in W. Gillies (ed.), *Scotland and Gaelic / Alba agus a' Ghàidhlig*, Edinburgh: Edinburgh University Press, pp. 67–88.

Barry, B. (2001), *Culture and Equality: An Egalitarian Critique of Multiculturalism*, Cambridge: Polity Press.

Bayley, R., and S. R. Schecter (2003), 'Introduction: Toward a dynamic model of language socialization', in R. Bayley and S. R. Schecter (eds), *Language Socialization in Bilingual and Multilingual Societies*, Clevedon: Multilingual Matters, pp. 1–8.

Bechhofer, F., and D. McCrone (2014), 'What makes a Gael? Identity, language and ancestry in the Scottish Gàidhealtachd', *Identities: Global Studies in Culture and Power*, 2014: 1–21.

Bialystok, E., and B. Miller (1999), 'The problem of age in second language acquisition: Influences from language, task, and structure', *Bilingualism: Language and Cognition*, 2: 127–45.

Birdsong, D. (2004), 'Second language acquisition and ultimate attainment', in A. Davies and C. Elder (eds), *The Handbook of Applied Linguistics*, Oxford: Blackwell, pp. 82–105.

Birdsong, D. (2009), 'Age and the end state of second language acquisition', in W. Ritchie and T. Bhatia (eds), *New Handbook of Second Language Acquisition*, London: Emerald, pp. 401–20.

Birdsong, D., and M. Molis (2001), 'On the evidence for maturational effects in second language acquisition', *Journal of Memory and Language*, 44: 235–49.

Bòrd na Gàidhlig (2007), *The National Plan for Gaelic 2007–2012*, Inverness: Bòrd na Gàidhlig.

Bòrd na Gàidhlig (2012a), *Dàta Foghlam Gàidhlig 2011–12 [Gaelic Education Data 2011–12]*, Inverness: Bòrd na Gàidhlig, <http://www.gaidhlig.org.uk/Downloads/Data% 20Foghlaim%202011-12%20Am%20Follais%20Gaidhlig.pdf> (last accessed 10 Mar. 2013).

Bòrd na Gàidhlig (2012b), *National Gaelic Language Plan, 2012–2017*, Inverness: Bòrd na Gàidhlig.

Bòrd na Gàidhlig (2013), 'Census Points to Positive Future for Gaelic', <http://www.gaidhlig.org.uk/bord/en/news/article.php?ID=458> (last accessed 1 Oct. 2013).

Bòrd na Gàidhlig (2014), 'Gaelic Education Helps Reverse Decline of the Gaelic Language', <http://www.gaidhlig.org.uk/bord/en/news/article.php?ID=474> (last accessed 9 Jul. 2014).

Bòrd na Gàidhlig (2017), *Draft National Gaelic Language Plan 2017–2022*, Inverness: Bòrd na Gàidhlig, <http://www.gaidhlig.scot/ wp-content/uploads/2017/02/national-gaelic-language-plan2017-22-en.pdf> (last accessed 9 Aug. 2018).

Bòrd na Gàidhlig (2018), *National Gaelic Language Plan 2018–2023*, Inverness: Bòrd na Gàidhlig, <http://www.gaidhlig.scot/wp-content/uploads/2018/03/BnG-NGLP-18-23.pdf> (last accessed 9 Aug. 2018).
Boudreau, A., and L. Dubois (2007), 'Français, acadien, acadjonne: Competing discourses on language preservation along the shores of the Baie Sainte-Marie', in A. Duchêne and M. Heller (eds), *Discourses of Endangerment: Ideology and Interest in the Defence of Languages*, London: Continuum, pp. 98–120.
Bourdieu, P. (1990), *The Logic of Practice*, transl. R. Price, Stanford, CA: Stanford University Press.
Bourdieu, P. (1991), *Language and Symbolic Power*, transl. G. Raymond and M. Adamson, Cambridge: Polity Press.
Boyer, H. (ed.) (2005), *De l'école occitane à l'enseignement public: Vécu et représentations sociolinguistiques. Une enquête auprès d'un groupe d'ex-calondrons*, Paris: L'Harmattan.
Broudic, F. (2010), *L'Enseignement du et en breton. Rapport à Monsieur le Recteur de l'Académie de Rennes*, Brest: Emgleo Breiz.
Bucholtz, M., and K. Hall (2004), 'Language and identity', in A. Duranti (ed.), *A Companion to Linguistic Anthropology*, Oxford: Blackwell, pp. 369–94.
Bucholtz, M., and K. Hall (2005), 'Identity and interaction: A sociocultural linguistic approach', *Discourse Studies*, 7: 585–614.
Butler, Y. G. (2013), 'Bilingualism/multilingualism and second-language acquisition', in T. K. Bhatia and W. C. Ritchie (eds), *The Handbook of Bilingualism and Multilingualism*, 2nd edn, Oxford: Blackwell, pp. 109–36.
Cameron, D. (2001), *Working with Spoken Discourse*, London: Sage.
Campbell, I., with M. MacLeod, M. Danson and D. Chalmers (2008), 'Measuring the Gaelic Labour Market: Current and Future Potential – Final Report, Stage 2', Report for Highlands and Islands Enterprise, Skills Development Scotland and Bòrd na Gàidhlig, Inverness: Hecla Consulting.
Campbell, K. (1983), 'Gaelic', in J. D. McClure (ed.), *Minority Languages in Central Scotland*, Aberdeen: Association for Scottish Literary Studies, pp. 11–14.
Canagarajah, S. (2006), 'Ethnographic methods in language policy', in T. Ricento (ed.), *An Introduction to Language Policy*, Oxford: Blackwell, pp. 153–69.
Canale, M., and M. Swain (1980), 'Theoretical bases of communicative approaches to language teaching and testing', *Applied Linguistics*, 1: 1–47.
Cavanaugh, J. (2013), 'Language ideologies and language attitudes', in P. Auer, J. Caro Reina and G. Kaufmann (eds), *Language Variation: European Perspectives IV*, Amsterdam: John Benjamins, pp. 45–55.
Cenoz, J. (2001), 'Basque in Spain and France', in G. Extra and D. Gorter (eds), *The Other Languages of Europe: Demographic, Sociolinguistic and Educational Perspectives*, Clevedon: Multilingual Matters, pp. 45–57.
Cenoz, J. (2009), *Towards Multilingual Education: Basque Education Research from an International Perspective*, Clevedon: Multilingual Matters.
Charmaz, K. (2002). 'Qualitative interviewing and grounded theory analysis', in J. F Gubrium and J. A. Holstein (eds), *Handbook of Interview Research: Context and Method*, Thousand Oaks, CA: Sage, pp. 777–96.

Clancy, T. O. (2011), 'Gaelic in medieval Scotland: Advent and expansion', *Proceedings of the British Academy*, 167: 349–92.

Clark, J. L. D., and E. H. Jorden (1984), *A Study of Language Attrition in Former U.S. Students of Japanese and Implications for Design of Curriculum and Teaching Materials: Final Project Report*, <http://www.eric.ed.gov> (last accessed 1 Mar. 2016).

Coady, M., and M. Ó Laoire (2002), 'Mismatches in language policy and practice in education: The case of Gaelscoileanna in the Republic of Ireland', *Language Policy*, 1: 143–58.

Cochran, E. (2008), 'Language Use and Attitudes among Adolescents in Gaelic-Medium Education'. Unpublished MPhil thesis, University of Edinburgh.

Cohen, A. D. (1975), 'Forgetting a second language', *Language Learning*, 25: 127–38.

Comunn na Gàidhlig (1989), *Gaelic Progress Report 1982–1988*, Inverness: Comunn na Gàidhlig.

Cole, A., and C. Williams (2004), 'Institutions, identities and lesser-used languages in Wales and Brittany', *Regional and Federal Studies*, 14: 554–79.

Costa, J. (2017), *Revitalising Language in Provence: A Critical Approach*, Oxford: Blackwell and Philological Society.

Council of Europe (2014), 'European Charter for Regional or Minority Languages – Fourth Report of the Committee of Experts in Respect of the United Kingdom', <https://wcd.coe.int/ViewDoc.jsp?Ref=CM%282013%29150andLanguage=lan EnglishandSite=CMand BackColorInternet=C3C3C3andBackColorIntranet=ED B021andBackColorLogged=F5D383#P134_16648> (last accessed 16 Jan. 2016).

Coupland N., H. Bishop, A. Williams, B. Evans and P. Garrett (2005), 'Affiliation, engagement, language use and vitality: Secondary school students' subjective orientations to Welsh and Welshness', *International Journal of Bilingual Education and Bilingualism*, 8: 1–24.

Crago, M. B., B. Annahatak and L. Ningiuruvik (1993), 'Changing patterns of language socialization in Inuit homes', *Anthropology and Education Quarterly*, 24: 205–23.

Crystal, D. (2000), *Language Death*, Cambridge: Cambridge University Press.

Dauenhauer, N. M., and R. Dauenhauer (1998), 'Technical, emotional, and ideological issues in reversing language shift: Examples from Southeast Alaska', in L. A. Grenoble and L. J. Whaley (eds), *Endangered Languages: Current Issues and Future Prospects*, Cambridge: Cambridge University Press, pp. 57–98.

de Corne, H. (2010), 'Indigenous language education policy: Supporting community-controlled immersion in Canada and the US', *Language Policy*, 9: 115–41.

de Courcy, M. (2005), 'Policy challenges for bilingual and immersion education in Australia: Literacy and language choices for users of Aboriginal languages, Auslan, and Italian', *International Journal of Bilingual Education and Bilingualism*, 8: 178–87.

De Houwer, A. (2007), 'Parental language input patterns and children's bilingual use', *Applied Psycholinguistics*, 28: 411–24.

Dementi-Leonard, B., and P. Gilmore (1999), 'Language revitalization and identity in social context: A community-based Athabascan language preservation project in western interior Alaska', *Anthropology and Education Quarterly*, 30: 37–55.

Devine, T. M. (1994), *Clanship to Crofter's War*, Manchester: Manchester University Press.

Dorian, N. (1981), *Language Death: The Life Cycle of a Scottish Gaelic Dialect*, Philadelphia: University of Pennsylvania Press.

Dorian, N. (1987), 'The value of language-maintenance efforts which are unlikely to succeed', *International Journal of the Sociology of Language*, 68: 57–67.

Dorian, N. (1993), 'A response to Ladefoged's Other View of Endangered Languages', *Language*, 69: 575–9.

Dorian, N. (2010), 'Linguistic and ethnographic fieldwork', in J. A. Fishman and O. García (eds), *Handbook of Language and Ethnic Identity: Disciplinary and Regional Perspectives (Vol. I)*, 2nd edn, Oxford: Oxford University Press, pp. 89–106.

Dorian, N. (2011), 'The ambiguous arithmetic of language maintenance and revitalization', in J. A. Fishman and O. García (eds), *Handbook of Language and Ethnic Identity: The Success–Failure Continuum in Language and Ethnic Identity Efforts (Vol. II)*, Oxford: Oxford University Press, pp. 461–71.

Dörnyei, Z. (2005), *The Psychology of the Language Learner: Individual Differences in Second Language Acquisition*, Mahwah, NJ: Lawrence Erlbaum.

Dressler R. A. H. (2012), 'Simultaneous and Sequential Bilinguals in a German Bilingual Program'. Unpublished PhD thesis, University of Calgary.

Duchêne, A., and M. Heller (eds) (2007), *Discourses of Endangerment: Ideology and Interest in the Defence of Languages*, London: Continuum.

Duchêne, A., and M. Heller (eds) (2012), *Language in Late Capitalism: Pride and Profit*, London: Routledge.

Duff, P. A. (2010), 'Language socialization into academic discourse communities', *Annual Review of Applied Lingustics*, 30: 169–92.

Duff, P. A., and D. Li (2009), 'Indigenous, minority, and heritage language education in Canada: Policies, contexts, and issues', *The Canadian Modern Language Review*, 66: 1–8.

Dumville, D. N. (2002), 'Ireland and North Britain in the earlier Middle Ages: Contexts for *Míniugud Senchasa Fher nAlban*', in C. Ó Baoill and N. R. McGuire (eds), *Rannsachadh na Gàidhlig 2000*, Aberdeen: An Clò Gaidhealach, pp. 185–212.

Dunbar, R. (2001), 'Minority language rights regimes: An analytical framework, Scotland, and emerging European norms', *International and Comparative Law Quarterly*, 50: 90–120.

Dunbar, R. (2006), 'Gaelic in Scotland: The legal and institutional framework', in W. McLeod (ed.), *Revitalising Gaelic in Scotland: Policy, Planning and Public Discourse*, Edinburgh: Dunedin Academic Press, pp. 1–23.

Dunmore, S. (2017), 'Immersion education outcomes and the Gaelic community: Identities and language ideologies among Gaelic medium-educated adults in Scotland', *Journal of Multilingual and Multicultural Development*, 38: 726–41.

Dunmore, S. (2018), 'New Gaelic speakers, new Gaels? Language ideologies and ethnolinguistic continuity among Gaelic-medium educated adults', in C. Smith-Christmas, N. Ó Murchadha, M. Hornsby and M. Moriarty (eds), *New Speakers of Minority Languages: Linguistic Practice and Ideology*, Basingstoke: Palgrave, pp. 23–44.

Dunmore, S. and C. Smith-Christmas (2015), 'Voicing the "other": Code-switching in discourses of Gaelic language ideology', in E. Torgersen, S. Hårstad, B. Maehlum and U. Røyneland (eds), *Language Variation: European Perspectives V*, Amsterdam: John Benjamins, pp. 86–97.

Dunn, C. M., and A. G. Robertson (1989), 'Gaelic in education', in W. Gillies (ed.), *Scotland and Gaelic/Alba agus a' Ghàidhlig*, Edinburgh: Edinburgh University Press, pp. 44–55.

Duranti, A. (1997), *Linguistic Anthropology*, Cambridge: Cambridge University Press.

Durkacz, V. E. (1983), *The Decline of the Celtic Languages*, Edinburgh: John Donald.

Eastman, C. (1984), 'Language, ethnic identity and change', in J. Edwards (ed.), *Linguistic Minorities, Policies and Pluralism*, London: Academic Press, pp. 259–76.

Echeverria, B. (2003), 'Schooling, language, and ethnic identity in the Basque Autonomous Community', *Anthropology and Education Quarterly*, 34: 351–72.

Edwards, J. R. (ed.) (1984a), *Linguistic Minorities, Policies and Pluralism*, London: Academic Press.

Edwards, J. R. (1984b), 'Language, diversity and identity', in J. Edwards (ed.), *Linguistic Minorities, Policies and Pluralism*, London: Academic Press, pp. 277–310.

Edwards, J. R. (2004), 'Language minorities', in A. Davies and C. Elder (eds), *The Handbook of Applied Linguistics*, Oxford: Blackwell, pp. 451–75.

Edwards, J. R. (2009), *Language and Identity*, Cambridge: Cambridge University Press.

Edwards, J. R. (2010a), *Minority Languages and Group Identity: Cases and Categories*, Amsterdam: John Benjamins.

Edwards, J. R. (2010b), *Language Diversity in the Classroom*, Clevedon: Multilingual Matters.

Edwards, J. R. (2013), 'Bilingualism and multilingualism: Some central concepts', in T. K. Bhatia and W. C. Ritchie (eds), *The Handbook of Bilingualism and Multilingualism*, 2nd edn, Oxford: Blackwell, pp. 5–25.

Edwards, V. and L. P. Newcombe (2005), 'When school is not enough: New initiatives in intergenerational language transmission in Wales', *International Journal of Bilingual Education and Bilingualism*, 8: 298–312.

Ellis, R. (2004), 'Individual differences in second language learning', in A. Davies and C. Elder (eds), *The Handbook of Applied Linguistics*, Oxford: Blackwell, pp. 525–51.

Elorza, I., and I. Muñoa (2008), 'Promoting the minority language through integrated plurilingual language planning: The case of the ikastolas', in J. Cenoz (ed.), *Teaching Through Basque: Achievements and Challenges*, Clevedon: Multilingual Matters, pp. 85–101.

Ethnologue (2017), *Languages of the World*, <http://www.ethnologue.com> (last accessed 2 Mar. 2017).

Eusko Jauriaritza/Basque Government (2013), *Fifth Sociolinguistic Survey 2011*, Donostia-San Sebastian: Basque Government.

Ewing, K. P. (2006), 'Revealing and concealing: Interpersonal dynamics and the negotiation of identity in the interview', *Ethos*, 34: 89–122.

Ferguson, G. (2006), *Language Planning and Education*, Edinburgh: Edinburgh University Press.

Fetterman, D. M. (1998), *Ethnography: Step by Step*, 2nd edn, London: Sage.

Fishman, J. A. (1972), *Language in Socio-Cultural Change*, Stanford, CA: Stanford University Press.

Fishman, J. A. (1991), *Reversing Language Shift: Theoretical and Empirical Foundations of Assistance to Threatened Languages*, Clevedon: Multilingual Matters.

Fishman, J. A. (ed.) (2001a), *Can Threatened Languages Be Saved? Reversing Language Shift Revisited: A 21st Century Perspective*, Clevedon: Multilingual Matters.

Fishman, J. A. (2001b),'From theory to practice (and vice versa): Review, reconsideration, and reiteration', in J. Fishman (ed.), *Can Threatened Languages Be Saved? Reversing Language Shift Revisited: A 21st Century Perspective*, Clevedon: Multilingual Matters, pp. 451–83.

Fishman, J. A. (2010), 'Sociolinguistics: Language and ethnic identity in context', in J. A. Fishman and O. García (eds), *Handbook of Language and Ethnic Identity: Disciplinary and Regional Perspectives (Vol. I)*, 2nd edn, Oxford: Oxford University Press, pp. xxiii–xxxv.

Fishman, J. A. (2013), 'Language maintenance, language shift, and reversing language shift', in T. K. Bhatia and W. C. Ritchie (eds), *The Handbook of Bilingualism and Multilingualism*, 2nd edn, Oxford: Blackwell, pp. 466–94.

Flege, J. E. (1999), 'Age of learning and second-language speech', in D. Birdsong (ed.), *Second Language Acquisition and the Critical Period Hypothesis*, Mahwah, NJ: Erlbaum.

Flege, J. E., G. H. Yeni-Komshian and S. Liu (1999), 'Age constraints on second-language acquisition', *Journal of Memory and Language*, 41: 78–104.

Fleming, A., and R. Debski (2007), 'The use of Irish in networked communications: A study of schoolchildren in different language settings', *Journal of Multilingual and Multicultural Development*, 28: 85–101.

Forsey, M. G. (2010), 'Ethnography as participant listening', *Ethnography*, 11: 558–72.

Fraser, A. (1989), 'Gaelic in Primary Education: A Study of the Development of Gaelic Bilingual Education in Urban Contexts'. Unpublished PhD thesis, University of Glasgow.

Friedman, D. A. (2010), 'Becoming national: Classroom language socialization and political identities in the age of globalization', *Annual Review of Applied Linguistics*, 30: 193–210.

Gaelscoileanna Teo (2013), *Irish-Medium Education Outside the Gaeltacht 2012–2013*, Dublin: Gaelscoileanna Teo, <http://www.gaelscoileanna.ie/en/about/statistics/> (last accessed 25 Jan. 2016).

Gafaranga, J. (2007), *Talk in Two Languages*, Basingstoke: Palgrave Macmillan.

Gafaranga, J. (2009), 'The conversation analytic approach to code-switching', in B. E. Bullock and A. Jacqueline (eds), *The Cambridge Handbook of Linguistic Code-Switching*, Cambridge: Cambridge University Press.

Gal, S. (1993), 'Diversity and contestation in linguistic ideologies: German speakers in Hungary', *Language in Society*, 22: 337–59.

Gal, S., and K. Woolard (1995), 'Constructing languages and publics: Authority and representation', *Pragmatics*, 5: 129–38.

García, O. (2009), *Bilingual Education in the 21st Century: A Global Perspective*, Oxford: Blackwell.
García, O., and L. Wei (2014), *Translanguaging: Language, Bilingualism and Education*, Basingstoke: Palgrave Macmillan.
Gardner, R. C. (1982), 'Social factors in language retention', in R. D. Lambert and B. F. Freed (eds), *The Loss of Language Skills*, Rowley, MA: Newbury House, pp. 24–43.
Gardner, R. C. (1985), *Social Psychology and Second Language Learning: The Role of Attitude and Motivation*, London: Edward Arnold.
Gardner, R. C. (2010), *Motivation and Second Language Acquisition*, Bern: Peter Lang.
Gardner, R. C., and W. E. Lambert (1959), 'Motivational variables in second language acquisition', *Canadian Journal of Psychology*, 13: 266–72.
Gardner, R. C., and W. E. Lambert (1972), *Attitudes and Motivation in Second Language Learning*, Rowley, MA: Newbury House.
Garrett, P. B. (2007), 'Language socialization and the (re)production of bilingual subjectivities', in M. Heller (ed.), *Bilingualism: A Social Approach*, London: Palgrave Macmillan, pp. 233–56.
Garrett, P. D., and P. Baquedano-López (2002), 'Language socialization: Reproduction and continuity, transformation and change', *Annual Review of Anthropology*, 31: 339–61.
Gellner, E. (2006), *Nations and Nationalism*, 2nd edn (Oxford: Blackwell).
Glaser, B. G., and A. L. Strauss (1967), *The Discovery of Grounded Theory: Strategies for Qualitative Research*, Chicago: Aldine.
Glaser, K. (2006), 'Reimagining the Gaelic community: Ethnicity, hybridity, politics and communication', in W. McLeod (ed.), *Revitalising Gaelic in Scotland: Policy, Planning and Public Discourse*, Edinburgh: Dunedin Academic Press, pp. 169–84.
Glaser, K. (2007), *Minority Languages and Cultural Diversity in Europe: Gaelic and Sorbian Perspectives*, Clevedon: Multilingual Matters.
Grant, J. H. (1983), 'An Investigation into the Feasibility of Establishing Gaelic/English Bilingual Schools on the Mainland of Scotland'. Unpublished MPhil dissertation, University of Glasgow.
Gubrium, J. F., and J. A. Holstein (eds) (2002), *Handbook of Interview Research: Context and Method*, Thousand Oaks, CA: Sage.
Hamel, J., S. Dufour and D. Fortin (1993), *Case Study Methods*, London: Sage.
Hammersley, M., and P. P. Atkinson (2007), *Ethnography: Principles in Practice*, 3rd edn, London: Routledge.
Harley, B. (1994), 'After immersion: Maintaining the momentum', *Journal of Multilingual and Multicultural Development*, 15: 229–44.
Harley, B., and M. Swain (1984), 'The interlanguage of immersion students and its implications for second language teaching', in A. Davies, C. Criper and A. P. R. Howatt (eds), *Interlanguage*, Edinburgh: Edinburgh University Press, pp. 291–311.
Harris, J., and Murtagh, L. (1999), *Teaching and Learning Irish in Primary School*, Dublin: Institiúid Teangeolaíochta Éireann [Irish Linguistic Institute].

Harrison, B., and R. Papa (2005), 'The development of an Indigenous knowledge program in a New Zealand Maori-language immersion school', *Anthropology and Education Quarterly*, 36: 57–72.
Haugen, E. (1974), *The Ecology of Language*, Stanford, CA: Stanford University Press.
Hearn, J. (2008), 'What's wrong with Domination?', *Journal of Power*, 1: 37–49.
Hearn, J. (2012), *Theorizing Power*, Basingstoke: Palgrave Macmillan.
Heller, M. (2006), *Linguistic Minorities and Modernity: A Sociolinguistic Ethnography*, 2nd edn, London: Continuum.
Heller, M. (ed.) (2007a), *Bilingualism: A Social Approach*, London: Palgrave Macmillan.
Heller, M. (2007b), 'Bilingualism as ideology and practice', in M. Heller (ed.), *Bilingualism: A Social Approach*, London: Palgrave Macmillan, pp. 1–24.
Heller, M. (2010), *Paths to Postnationalism: A Critical Ethnography of Language and Identity*, Oxford: Oxford University Press.
Henze, R., and K. A. Davis (1999), 'Authenticity and identity: Lessons from Indigenous language education', *Anthropology and Education Quarterly*, 30: 3–21.
Herder, J. G. von (1960) [1772], *Sprachphilosophische Schriften*, Hamburg: Felix Meiner.
Her Majesty's Government (1986), *The Grants for Gaelic Language Education (Scotland) Regulations 1986*, Edinburgh: Scottish Office.
Her Majesty's Inspectorate of Education (1989), *Some Recent Developments in Gaelic Education*, Livingston: HMIE.
Her Majesty's Inspectorate of Education (2005), *Improving Achievement in Gaelic*, Livingston: HMIE.
Her Majesty's Inspectorate of Education (2011), *Gaelic Education: Building on the Successes, Addressing the Barriers*, Livingston: HMIE.
Hinton, L., and J. Ahlers (1999), 'The issue of "authenticity" in California language restoration', *Anthropology and Education Quarterly*, 30: 56–67.
Hoare, R. (2000), 'Linguistic competence and regional identity in Brittany: Attitudes and perceptions of identity', *Journal of Multilingual and Multicultural Development*, 21: 324–46.
Hobsbawm, E. J. (1992), *Nations and Nationalism since 1780: Programme, Myth, Reality*, 2nd edn, Cambridge: Cambridge University Press.
Hodges, R. (2009), 'Welsh language use among young people in the Rhymney Valley', *Contemporary Wales*, 22: 16–35.
Hornberger, N. (ed.) (2008), *Can Schools Save Indigenous Languages? Policy and Practice on Four Continents*, Hampshire: Palgrave Macmillan.
Hroch, M. (1985), *Social Preconditions of National Revival in Europe*, Cambridge: Cambridge University Press.
Huguet, A., and E. Llurda (2001), 'Language attitudes of school children in two Catalan/Spanish bilingual communities', *International Journal of Bilingual Education and Bilingualism*, 4: 267–82.
Hunter, J. (1976), *The Making of the Crofting Community*, Edinburgh: John Donald.
Hyltenstam, K., and N. Abrahamsson (2000), 'Who can become native-like in a second language? All, some, or none? On the maturational constraints controversy in second language acquisition', *Studia Linguistica*, 54: 150–66.

Hymes, D. (1972), 'On communicative competence', in J. B. Pride and J. Holmes (eds), *Sociolinguistics: Selected Readings*, Harmondsworth: Penguin, pp. 269–93.

Hymes, D. (1974), *Foundations in Sociolinguistics: An Ethnographic Approach*, London: Tavistock.

Irvine, J. T. (1989), 'When talk isn't cheap: Language and political economy', *American Ethnologist*, 16: 248–67.

Irvine, J. T., and S. Gal (2000), 'Language ideology and linguistic differentiation', in P. Kroskrity (ed.), *Regimes of Language: Ideologies, Polities, and Identities*, Santa Fe, NM: School of American Research Press, pp. 35–84.

Jaffe, A. (1999), *Ideologies in Action: Language Politics on Corsica*, Berlin: Mouton de Gruyter.

Jaffe, A. (2007a), 'Discourses of endangerment: Contexts and consequences of essentializing discourses', in A. Duchêne and M. Heller (eds), *Discourses of Endangerment: Ideology and Interest in the Defence of Languages*, London: Continuum, pp. 57–75.

Jaffe, A. (2007b), 'Minority language movements', in M. Heller (ed.), *Bilingualism: A Social Approach*, London: Palgrave Macmillan, pp. 50–95.

Jaffe, A. (2009), 'The production and reproduction of language ideologies in practice', in N. Coupland and A. Jaworski (eds), *The New Sociolinguistics Reader*, Basingstoke: Palgrave Macmillan, pp. 390–404.

Johnstone, B., J. Andrus and A. E. Danielson (2006), 'Mobility, indexicality, and the enregisterment of "Pittsburghese"', *Journal of English Linguistics*, 34: 77–104.

Johnstone, R. (2001), *Immersion in a Second or Additional Language at School: Evidence from International Research*, Stirling: Scottish Centre for Teaching and Research.

Jones, M. C. (1998), *Language Obsolescence and Revitalization: Linguistic Change in Two Sociolinguistically Contrasting Welsh Communities*, Oxford: Oxford University Press.

Jones, R., and C. Williams (2009), 'The sociolinguistic context of Welsh', in M. Ball and N. Müller (eds), *The Celtic Languages*, 2nd edn, Abingdon: Routledge, pp. 650–711.

Joseph, J. E. (2004), *Language and Identity: National, Ethnic, Religious*, Basingstoke: Houndmills.

Joseph, J. E. (2010), 'Identity', in C. Llamas and D. Watt (eds), *Language and Identities* (Edinburgh: Edinburgh University Press), pp. 9–17.

King, K. A. (2000), 'Language ideologies and heritage language education', *International Journal of Bilingual Education and Bilingualism*, 3: 167–84.

King, K. A. (2001), *Language Revitalization Processes and Prospects: Quichua in the Ecuadorian Andes*, Clevedon: Multilingual Matters.

King, K. A., N. Schilling-Estes, L. Fogle, J. Lou and B. Soukup (eds) (2008), *Sustaining Linguistic Diversity: Endangered and Minority Languages and Varieties* (Washington, DC: Georgetown University Press).

Köhler, W. (2009), *Bretonisch und Französisch im Süd-Finistère – Ein facettenreicher Sprachkonflikt*, Hechingen: Libertas.

Kondo-Brown, K. (2010), 'Curriculum development for advancing heritage language competence: Recent research, current practices, and a future agenda', *Annual Review of Applied Linguistics*, 30: 24–41.

Köpke, B., and M.S. Schmid (2004), 'First language attrition: The next phase', in M. S. Schmid, B. Köpke, M. Keijzer and L. Weilemar (eds), *First Language Attrition: Interdisciplinary Perspectives on Methodological Issues*, Amsterdam: John Benjamins, pp. 1–43.

Kramsch, C. (2004), 'Language, thought, and culture', in A. Davies and C. Elder (eds), *The Handbook of Applied Linguistics*, Oxford: Blackwell, pp. 235–61.

Krashen, S. (1982), *Principles and Practice in Second Language Learning*, Oxford: Pergamon.

Krauss, M. (1992), 'The world's languages in crisis', *Language*, 68: 4–10.

Krombach, H. (1995), 'The dialectic of identity: From individual to nation', *ASEN Bulletin No. 10*, London: London School of Economics, pp. 42–4.

Kroskrity, P. V. (ed.) (2000a), *Regimes of Language: Ideologies, Polities, and Identities*, Santa Fe, NM: School of American Research Press.

Kroskrity, P. V. (2000b), 'Regimenting languages: Language ideological perspectives', in P. Kroskrity (ed.), *Regimes of Language: Ideologies, Polities, and Identities*, Santa Fe, NM: School of American Research Press, pp. 1–34.

Kroskrity, P. V. (2000c), 'Language ideologies in the expression and representation of Arizona Tewa ethnic identity', in P. Kroskrity (ed.), *Regimes of Language: Ideologies, Polities, and Identities*, Santa Fe, NM: School of American Research Press, pp. 329–60.

Kroskrity, P. V. (2004), 'Language ideologies', in A. Duranti (ed.), *A Companion to Linguistic Anthropology*, Oxford: Blackwell, pp. 496–517.

Kruideiner, B., and R. Clement (1986), *The Effect of Context on the Composition and Role of Orientations in Second Language Acquisition*, Quebec: International Centre for Research on Bilingualism.

Kulick, D., and B. B. Schieffelin (2004), 'Language socialization', in A. Duranti (ed.), *A Companion to Linguistic Anthropology*, Oxford: Blackwell, pp. 349–68.

Kumar, K. (2003), *The Making of English National Identity*, Cambridge: Cambridge University Press.

Ladefoged, P. (1992), 'Another view of endangered languages', *Language*, 68: 809–11.

La Fontaine, J. S. (1985), 'Person and individual: Some anthropological reflections', in M. Carrithers, S. Collins and S. Lukes (eds), *The Category of the Person*, Cambridge: Cambridge University Press, pp. 123–40.

Laihonen, P. (2008), 'Language ideologies in interviews: A conversation analysis approach', *Journal of Sociolinguistics*, 12: 668–93.

Lambert, R. D. (1989), 'Language attrition', *Review of Applied Linguistics*, 83–4: 177–86.

Lambert, R. D., and B. F. Freed (eds) (1982), *The Loss of Language Skills*, Rowley, MA: Newbury House.

Lambert, R. D., and G. R. Tucker (1972), *Bilingual Education of Children: The St. Lambert Experiment*, Rowley, MA: Newbury House.

Landgraf, S. (2013), 'Cànain agus Cultar ann am Foghlam tro Mheadhan na Gàidhlig: Neartan, Duilgheadasan agus am Buaidh air Comasan is Seasamhan Cànain na h-Òigridh'. Unpublished PhD thesis, University of Aberdeen/University of the Highlands and Islands.

Lazaraton, A. (2003), 'Evaluative criteria for qualitative research in applied linguistics: Whose criteria and whose research?', *The Modern Language Journal*, 87: 1–12.
Littlewood, W. (2004), 'Second language learning', in A. Davies and C. Elder (eds), *The Handbook of Applied Linguistics*, Oxford: Blackwell, pp. 501–24.
Long, M. (1985), 'Input and second language acquisition theory', in S. M. Grass and C. G. Madden (eds), *Input in Second Language Acquisition*, Rowley, MA: Newbury House, pp. 377–93.
Lowe, D. (1985), 'Life is one big yawn in any language', *Glasgow Herald*, 10 October, p. 14.
Lukes, S. (2005), *Power: A Radical View*, 2nd edn, Basingstoke: Palgrave Macmillan.
Mac an Tàilleir, I. (2010), '1901–2001: A' Ghàidhlig anns a' Chunntas-shluaigh', in G. Munro and I. Mac an Tàilleir (eds), *Coimhearsnachd na Gàidhlig an-diugh/Gaelic Communities Today*, Edinburgh: Dunedin Academic Press, pp. 19–34.
MacCaluim, A. (2007), *Reversing Language Shift: The Social Identity and Role of Scottish Gaelic Learners*, Belfast: Cló Ollscoil na Banríona.
McCarty, T. L. (2003), 'Revitalising Indigenous languages in homogenising times', *Comparative Education*, 39: 147–63.
McCarty, T. L. (2013), *Language Planning and Policy in Native America: History, Theory, Praxis*, Clevedon: Multilingual Matters.
McCarty, T. L., M. E. Romero-Little and O. Zepeda (2008), 'Indigenous language policies in social practice: The case of Navajo', in K. A. King, N. Schilling-Estes, L. Fogle, J. Lou and B. Soukup (eds), *Sustaining Linguistic Diversity: Endangered and Minority Languages and Varieties*, Washington, DC: Georgetown University Press, pp. 159–72.
McCoy, G., with M. Scott (eds), (2000), *Aithne na nGael: Gaelic Identities*, Belfast: ULTACH Trust.
McCrone, D. (1998), *The Sociology of Nationalism: Tomorrow's Ancestors*, London: Routledge.
McCrone, D. (2001), *Understanding Scotland: The Sociology of a Nation*, 2nd edn, London: Routledge.
Macdonald, S. (1997), *Reimagining Culture: Histories, Identities and the Gaelic Renaissance*, Oxford: Berg.
Macdonald, S. (1999), 'The Gaelic renaissance and Scotland's identities', *Scottish Affairs*, 26: 100–18.
Mac Donnacha, S., F. Ní Chualáin, A. Ní Shéaghdha and T. Ní Mhainín (2005), *Staid Reatha na Scoileanna Gaeltachta 2004*, Dublin: An Chomhairle um Oideachas Gaeltachta agus Gaelscolaíochta.
McEwan-Fujita, E. (2003), 'Gaelic in Scotland, Scotland in Europe: Minority Language Revitalization in the Age of Neoliberialism'. Unpublished PhD thesis, University of Chicago.
McEwan-Fujita, E. (2010a), 'Ideology, affect, and socialization in language shift and revitalization: The experiences of adults learning Gaelic in the Western Isles of Scotland', *Language in Society*, 39: 27–64.

McEwan-Fujita, E. (2010b), 'Ideologies and experiences of literacy in interactions between adult Gaelic learners and first-language Gaelic speakers in Scotland', *Scottish Gaelic Studies*, 26: 87–114.

McEwan-Fujita, E. (2010c), 'Sociolinguistic ethnography of Gaelic communities', in M. Watson and M. Macleod (eds), *Edinburgh Companion to the Gaelic Language*, Edinburgh: Edinburgh University Press, pp. 172–217.

MacFarlane, A., and M. Wesche (1995), 'Immersion outcomes: Beyond language proficiency', *The Canadian Modern Language Review*, 51: 250–74.

MacGregor, M. D. (2006), 'The statutes of Iona: Text and context', *Innes Review*, 57: 111–81.

MacGregor, M. D. (2009), 'Gaelic barbarity and Scottish identity in the later Middle Ages', in D. Broun and M. D. MacGregor (eds), *Mìorun Mòr nan Gall, 'The Great Ill-Will of the Lowlander'? Lowland Perceptions of the Highlands, Medieval and Modern*, Glasgow: Centre for Scottish and Celtic Studies, University of Glasgow, pp. 7–48.

MacGregor, V. (2009), 'GME at Tollcross Primary School'. Unpublished manuscript, Tollcross Primary School, Edinburgh.

MacIlleChiar, I. (1985), 'Gaelic-medium schools—why? and when?', in J. Hulbert (ed.), *Gaelic: Looking to the Future*, Dundee: Andrew Fletcher Society, pp. 28–33.

MacKenzie, G. (2013), 'Minority Language Education, Cultural Transmission and Identities: A Sociological Profile of Former Gaelic-Medium Education (GME) Pupils in the Scottish Gàidhealtachd'. Unpublished MRes thesis, Napier University, Edinburgh.

MacKinnon, K. (1977), *Language, Education and Social Processes in a Gaelic Community*, London: Routledge and Kegan Paul.

MacKinnon, K. (1991), *Gaelic: A Past and Future Prospect*, Edinburgh: Saltire Society.

MacKinnon, K. (1993), 'Scottish Gaelic today: Social history and contemporary status', in M. Ball (ed.), *The Celtic Languages*, London: Routledge, pp. 491–535.

MacKinnon, K. (1994), *Gaelic in 1994: Report to the EU Euromosaic Project*, Black Isle: SGRUD Research.

MacKinnon, K. (2005), 'Gaelic-Medium Education 1985–2005: SGRÙD Research for Bòrd na Gàidhlig', <http://www.sgrud.org.uk/anfy/celtic/gaelic_medium_education85_05/page1.htm> (last accessed 14 Nov. 2017).

MacKinnon, K. (2009), 'Scottish Gaelic today: Social history and contemporary status', in M. Ball and N. Müller (eds), *The Celtic Languages*, 2nd edn, Abingdon: Routledge, pp. 587–649.

MacLeod, D. J. (2007), 'Sùil air ais', in M. NicNeacail and M. MacIomhair (eds), *Foghlam tro Mheadhan na Gàidhlig*, Edinburgh: Dunedin Academic Press, pp. 1–15.

MacLeod, D. J. (2009), 'Reversing the decline of Gaelic: The contribution of Gaelic-medium education', *Transactions of the Gaelic Society of Inverness*, 65: 228–43.

MacLeod, M. (2004a), 'Communicating culture in education: A study of curriculum change in the Outer Hebrides', in U. Kockel and M. Nic Craith (eds), *Communicating Cultures*, Münster: Lit.

MacLeod, M. (2004b), 'Teachers and change in the Western Isles'. Unpublished PhD thesis, University of Cambridge.

McLeod, W. (2003), 'Foghlam tro mheadhan na Gàidhlig ann an Alba', in M. Scott and R. Ní Bhaoill (eds), *Gaelic-Medium Education Provision: Northern Ireland, the Republic of Ireland, Scotland, and the Isle of Man*, Belfast: Cló Ollscoil na Banríona, pp. 104–32.

McLeod, W. (2005), 'Gaelic in Scotland: The impact of the Highland Clearances', in N. Crawhill and N. Ostler (eds), *Creating Outsiders: Endangered Languages, Migration and Marginalisation: Proceedings of the Ninth Conference of the Foundation for Endangered Languages*, Bath: Foundation for Endangered Languages, pp. 176–83.

McLeod, W. (2007), 'Foghlam tro mheadhan na Gàidhlig anns a' cho-theacsa eadar-nàiseanta', in M. NicNeacail and M. MacÌomhair (eds), *Foghlam tro Mheadhan na Gàidhlig*, Edinburgh: Dunedin Academic Press, pp. 16–38.

McLeod, W. (2014), 'Gaelic in contemporary Scotland: Contradictions, challenges and strategies', *Europa Ethnica*, 2014: 3–12.

McLeod, W., I. Pollock and A. MacCaluim (2010), 'Adult Gaelic Learning in Scotland: Opportunities, Motivations and Challenges', Edinburgh: Celtic and Scottish Studies, University of Edinburgh, <www.arts.ed.ac.uk/celtic/poil easaidh/> (last accessed 15 Oct. 2015).

McLeod, W., B. O'Rourke and S. Dunmore (2014), 'New Speakers of Gaelic in Edinburgh and Glasgow', Soillse Research Report, Sleat, Isle of Skye: Soillse.

Macleod, M. (1963), 'Gaelic in Highland education', *Transactions of the Gaelic Society of Inverness*, 43: 305–34.

Macleod, M. (2010), 'Language in society: 1800 to the modern day', in M. Watson and M. Macleod (eds), *The Edinburgh Companion to the Gaelic Language*, Edinburgh: Edinburgh University Press, pp. 22–45.

Macleod, M., M. MacLeod, A. Thirkell and D. Coyle (2014), 'Young Speakers' Use of Gaelic in the Primary Classroom: A Multi-Perspectival Pilot Study', Soillse research report, Sleat, Isle of Skye: Soille, <http://www.soillse.ac.uk/downloads/YoungSpeakers_Final.pdf> (last accessed 29 May 2017).

MacMillan, G. (2012), 'Comas cànain oileanaich a chaidh tro fhoghlam tro mheadhan na Gàidhlig gun Ghàidhlig san dachaigh', Paper presented at Rannsachadh na Gàidhlig 7, 21–3 Aug., University of Glasgow.

MacNeil, M. (1994), 'Immersion programmes employed in Gaelic-medium units in Scotland', *Journal of Multilingual and Multicultural Development*, 15: 245–52.

MacNeil, M., and B. Stradling (2000), *Emergent Identities and Bilingual Education: The Teenage Years*, Sleat, Isle of Skye: Lèirsinn Research Centre.

McPake, J., W. McLeod, F. O'Hanlon, M. Wilson and G. Fassetta (2013), 'Gaelic for Teachers: Design Options for a Sabbatical Course of Intensive Gaelic Language and Pedagogies for Qualified Teachers Wishing to Work in Gaelic Medium Classrooms', Report for Bòrd na Gàidhlig, Glasgow: University of Strathclyde.

Makihara, M. (2010), 'Anthropology', in J. A. Fishman and O. García (eds), *Handbook of Language and Ethnic Identity: Disciplinary and Regional Perspectives (Vol. I)*, 2nd edn, Oxford: Oxford University Press, pp. 32–48.

Makoni, S., and A. Pennycook (2007), *Disinventing and Reconstituting Languages*, Clevedon: Multilingual Matters.

Manuelito, K. (2005), 'The role of education in American Indian self-determination: Lessons from the Ramah Navajo Community School', *Anthropology and Education Quarterly*, 36: 73–87.

Márkus, G. (2017), *Conceiving a Nation: Scotland to AD 900*, Edinburgh: Edinburgh University Press.

May, S. (2005), 'Bilingual/Immersion education in Aotearoa/New Zealand: Setting the context', *International Journal of Bilingual Education and Bilingualism*, 8: 365–76.

May, S. (2012), *Language and Minority Rights: Ethnicity, Nationalism and the Politics of Language*, 2nd edn, Abingdon: Routledge.

May, S., and R. Hill (2005), 'Māori-medium education: Current issues and challenges', *International Journal of Bilingual Education and Bilingualism*, 8: 377–403.

Mendoza-Denton, N., and D. Osborne (2010), 'Two languages, two identities?', in C. Llamas and D. Watt (eds), *Language and Identities*, Edinburgh: Edinburgh University Press, pp. 113–22.

Mill, J. S. (1991) [1861], *On Liberty and Other Essays*, ed. by J. M. Gray, Oxford: Oxford University Press.

Milroy, L. (1987), *Language and Social Networks*, 2nd edn, Oxford: Blackwell.

Mitchell, R. (1992), 'The "independent" evaluation of bilingual primary education: A narrative account', in J. C. Alderson and A. Beretta (eds), *Evaluating Second Language Education*, Cambridge: Cambridge University Press, pp. 100–40.

Mitchell, R., D. McIntyre, M. MacDonald and J. McLennan (1987), *Report of an Independent Evaluation of the Western Isles' Bilingual Education Project*, Stirling: Department of Education, University of Stirling.

Mitchell, R., F. Myles and E. Marsden (2013), *Second Language Learning Theories*, 3rd edn, Abingdon: Routledge.

Moïse, C. (2007), 'Protecting French: The view from France', in A. Duchêne and M. Heller (eds), *Discourses of Endangerment: Ideology and Interest in the Defence of Languages*, London: Continuum, pp. 216–41.

Moriarty, M. (2010), 'The effects of language planning initiatives on the language attitudes and language practices of university students: A comparative study of Irish and Basque', *Language Problems and Language Planning*, 34: 141–57.

Morrison, M. F. (2006a), "A' Chiad Ghinealach: The Experience of Gaelic Medium Education in the Western Isles'. Unpublished PhD thesis, University of Glasgow.

Morrison, M. F. (2006b), "A' chiad ghinealach – the first generation: A survey of Gaelic-medium education in the Western Isles', in W. McLeod (ed.), *Revitalising Gaelic in Scotland: Policy, Planning and Public Discourse*, Edinburgh: Dunedin Academic Press, pp. 139–54.

Mulholland, G. (1981), *The Struggle for a Language: Gaelic in Education*, Edinburgh: Rank and File.

Müller, M. (2006),'Language use, language attitudes and Gaelic writing ability among secondary pupils in the Isle of Skye', in W. McLeod (ed.), *Revitalising Gaelic in Scotland: Policy, Planning and Public Discourse*, Edinburgh: Dunedin Academic Press, pp. 119–38.

Munro, G., I. Taylor and T. Armstrong (2010), 'The State of Gaelic in Shawbost: Language Attitudes and Abilities in Shawbost', Inverness: Bòrd na Gàidhlig,

<http://www.gaidhlig.org.uk/Downloads/The%20state%20of%20Gaelic%20in%20Shawbost.pdf> (last accessed 7 Aug. 2017).

Murray, J., and F. MacLeod (1981),'Sea change in the Western Isles of Scotland: The rise of locally relevant bilingual education', in J. P. Sher (ed.), *Rural Education in Urbanized Nations: Issues and Innovations*, Boulder, CO: Westview Press, pp. 235–54.

Murray, J., and C. Morrison (1984), *Bilingual Primary Education in the Western Isles, Scotland: Report of the Bilingual Education Project, 1975–81*, Stornoway: Acair.

Murtagh, L. (2003), 'Retention and attrition of Irish as a second language'. Unpublished PhD thesis, University of Groningen.

Murtagh, L. (2008), 'Out-of-school use of Irish, motivation and proficiency in immersion and subject-only post-primary programmes, *International Journal of Bilingual Education and Bilingualism*, 10: 428–53.

Nairn, T. (1997), *Faces of Nationalism: Janus Revisited*, London: Verso.

Nance, C. (2013), 'Phonetic Variation, Sound Change, and Identity in Scottish Gaelic'. Unpublished PhD thesis, University of Glasgow.

Nance, C. (2015), '"New" Scottish Gaelic speakers in Glasgow: A phonetic study of language revitalisation', *Language in Society*, 44: 553–79.

National Records of Scotland (2013a), 'Statistical Bulletin: 2011 Census – Key Results on Population, Ethnicity, Identity, Language, Religion, Health, Housing and Accommodation in Scotland – Release 2A', <http://www.scotlands census.gov.uk/documents/censusresults/release2a/StatsBulletin2A.pdf> (last accessed 26 Sep. 2016).

National Records of Scotland (2013b), Scotland Census 2011 – Education, <http://www.scotlandscensus.gov.uk/ods-visualiser/#view=educationChartand selectedWafers=0andselectedColumns=0,1,2,3,4andselectedRows=0,7,12,16> (last accessed 2 Dec. 2017).

Nettle, D., and S. Romaine (2000), *Vanishing Voices: The Extinction of the World's Languages*, Oxford: Oxford University Press.

Newcombe, L. P. (2007), *Social Context and Fluency in L2 Learners: The Case of Wales*, Clevedon: Multilingual Matters.

New Zealand Department of Education (2018), *Māori Language in Education*, <https://www.educationcounts.govt.nz/statistics/maori-education/maori-in-schooling/6040> (last accessed 11 Dec. 2018).

Nic a' Bhàird, R. (2007), 'A' stiùreadh an t-solarachaidh: Sealladh bho na sgoiltean', in M. NicNeacail and M. MacÌomhair (eds), *Foghlam tro mheadhan na Gàidhlig*, Edinburgh: Dunedin Academic Press, pp. 39–51.

Nic Craith, M. (2007), 'Rethinking language policies: challenges and opportunities', in C. Williams (ed.), *Language and Governance*, Cardiff: University of Wales Press, pp. 159–84.

Nicholls, C. (2005), 'Death by a thousand cuts: Indigenous language bilingual education programmes in the Northern Territory of Australia, 1972–1998', *International Journal of Bilingual Education and Bilingualism*, 8: 160–77.

NicNeacail, M., and M. MacÌomhair (eds) (2007), *Foghlam tro Mheadhan na Gàidhlig*, Edinburgh: Dunedin Academic Press.

Nix-Victorian, J. M. (2010), 'The Impact of Early French Immersion Education on Language Use Patterns and Language Attitude of Post-secondary Students'. Unpublished PhD Thesis, University of Louisiana at Lafayette.

Ó Baoill, C. (2010), 'A history of Gaelic to 1800', in M. Watson and M. Macleod (eds), *The Edinburgh Companion to the Gaelic Language*, Edinburgh: Edinburgh University Press, pp. 1–21.

Ó Baoill, D. (1999), 'Social cultural distance, integrational orientation and the learning of Irish', in A. Chambers and D. Ó Baoill (eds), *Intercultural Communication and Language Learning*, Dublin: Irish Association for Applied Linguistics, pp. 189–200.

Ó Baoill, D. (2007), 'Origins of Irish-medium education: The dynamic core of language revitalisation in Northern Ireland', *International Journal of Bilingual Education and Bilingualism*, 10: 410–27.

Ochs, E. (1979), 'Transcription as theory', in E. Ochs and B. B. Schieffelin (eds), *Developmental Pragmatics*, New York: Academic Press, pp. 43–72.

Ochs, E. (1993), 'Constructing social identity: A language socialization perspective', *Research on Language and Social Interaction*, 26: 287–306.

Ó Duibhir, P. (2009), 'A comparison of Irish immersion students' attitudes and motivation to Irish in the Republic of Ireland and Northern Ireland', *Proceedings of the BAAL Annual Conference*, Newcastle: Newcastle University, pp. 113–16.

Ó Duibhir, P. (2018), *Immersion Education: Lessons from a Minority Language Context*, Clevedon: Multilingual Matters.

Ó Giollagáin, C. S. Mac Donnacha, F. Ní Chualáin, A. Ní Shéaghdha and M. O'Brien (2007), 'Comprehensive Linguistic Study of the Use of Irish in the Gaeltacht: Principal Findings and Recommendations', Report for the Department of Rural, Community and Gaeltacht Affairs, Dublin: Stationery Office.

Ó hAineiféin, D. (2008), *An Tumoideachas in Éirinn/Immersion Education in Ireland*, Dublin: Coiscéim/Conradh na Gaeilge.

O'Hanlon, F. (2010), 'Gaelic-medium primary education in Scotland: Towards a new taxonomy?', in G. Munro and I. Mac an Tàilleir (eds), *Coimhearsnachd na Gàidhlig an-diugh/Gaelic Communities Today*, Edinburgh: Dunedin Academic Press, pp. 99–115.

O'Hanlon, F. (2012), 'Lost in Transition? Celtic Language Revitalization in Scotland and Wales: The Primary to Secondary School Stage'. Unpublished PhD thesis, University of Edinburgh.

O'Hanlon, F., W. McLeod and L. Paterson (2010), 'Gaelic-Medium Education in Scotland: Choice and Attainment at the Primary and Early Secondary School Stages', Report for Bòrd na Gàidhlig, <https://www.research.ed.ac.uk/portal/files/3275316/Gaelic_medium_education_in_Scotland.O_Hanlon.McLeod.Paterson.pdf> (last accessed 5 Mar. 2017).

O'Hanlon, F., L. Paterson and W. McLeod (2012), 'Language Models in Gaelic-Medium Pre-school, Primary and Secondary Education', report for Soillse/Scottish Government, <http://www.parant.org.uk/pdfs/Modailean_Canain_ann_am_Foghlam_Ro-sgoile_Bunsgoile_agus_ard-sgoile_Meadhain_Ghaidhlig.pdf> (last accessed 20 Jan. 2016).

Ó hIfearnáin, T. (2007), 'Raising children to be bilingual in the Gaeltacht: Language preference and practice', *International Journal of Bilingual Education and Bilingualism*, 10: 510–28.

Ó hIfearnáin, T. (2008), 'Endangering language vitality through institutional development: Ideology, authority, and official standard Irish in the Gaeltacht', in K. A. King, N. Schilling-Estes, L. Fogle, J. Lou and B. Soukup (eds), *Sustaining Linguistic Diversity: Endangered and Minority Languages and Varieties*, Washington, DC: Georgetown University Press, pp. 113–28.

Ó hIfearnáin, T. (2011), 'Breton language maintenance and regeneration in regional education policy', in C. Norrby and J. Hajek (eds), *Uniformity and Diversity in Language Policy*, Clevedon: Multilingual Matters, pp. 93–106.

Ó hIfearnáin, T. (2013a),'Family language policy, first language Irish speaker attitudes and community-based response to language shift', *Journal of Multilingual and Multicultural Development*, 34: 348–65.

Ó hIfearnáin, T. (2013b), 'Institutional Breton language policy after language shift', *International Journal of the Sociology of Language*, 223: 117–35.

Oliver, J. (2002), 'Young People and Gaelic in Scotland: Identity Dynamics in a European Region'. Unpublished PhD thesis, University of Sheffield.

Oliver, J. (2005), 'Gaelic and identities in Scotland: Contexts and contingencies', *Scottish Affairs*, 51: 1–24.

Oliver, J. (2006), 'Where is Gaelic? Revitalisation, language, culture and identity', in W. McLeod (ed.), *Revitalising Gaelic in Scotland: Policy, Planning and Public Discourse*, Edinburgh: Dunedin Academic Press, pp. 155–68.

Oliver, J. (2010), 'The predicament? Planning for culture, communities and identities', in G. Munro and I. Mac an Tàilleir (eds), *Coimhearsnachd na Gàidhlig an-diugh / Gaelic Communities Today*, Edinburgh: Dunedin Academic Press, pp. 73–86.

Ó Muircheartaigh, J., and T. Hickey (2008), 'Academic outcome, anxiety and attitudes in early and late immersion in Ireland', *International Journal of Bilingual Education and Bilingualism*, 11: 558–76.

Ó Riagáin, P. (1997), *Language Policy and Social Reproduction: Ireland 1893–1993*, Oxford: Clarendon Press.

Ó Riagáin, P. (2001), 'Irish language production and reproduction 1981–1996', in J. Fishman (ed.), *Can Threatened Languages be Saved?*, Clevedon: Multilingual Matters, pp. 195–214.

O'Rourke, B., and F. Ramallo (2011), 'The native-non-native dichotomy in minority language contexts: Comparisons between Irish and Galician', *Language Problems and Language Planning*, 35: 139–59.

O'Rourke, B., and F. Ramallo (2013), 'Competing ideologies of linguistic authority amongst "new speakers" in contemporary Galicia', *Language in Society*, 42: 287–305.

Park, A., C. Bryson, E. Clery, J. Curtice and M. Phillips (eds) (2013), *British Social Attitudes: 30th Report*, London: NatCen Social Research.

Paterson, L. (2003), *Scottish Education in the Twentieth Century*, Edinburgh: Edinburgh University Press.

Paterson, L., F. O'Hanlon, R. Ormston and S. Reid (2014), 'Public attitudes to Gaelic and the debate about Scottish autonomy', *Regional and Federal Studies*, 2014: 1–22.
Pauwels, A. (2004), 'Language maintenance', in A. Davies and C. Elder (eds), *The Handbook of Applied Linguistics*, Oxford: Blackwell, pp. 719–37.
Peters, A. M., and S. T. Boggs (1986), 'Interactional routines as cultural influences upon language acquisition', in B. B. Schieffelin and E. Ochs (eds), *Language Socialization Across Cultures*, Cambridge: Cambridge University Press, pp. 80–96.
Phillipson, R., and T. Skutnabb-Kangas (2013), 'Linguistic imperialism and endangered languages', in T. K. Bhatia and W. C. Ritchie (eds), *The Handbook of Bilingualism and Multilingualism*, 2nd edn, Oxford: Blackwell, pp. 495–516.
Pierce, C. (1955), *Philosophical Writings of Pierce*, ed. by J. Buchler, New York: Dover.
Poland, B. D. (2002), 'Transcription quality', in J. F. Gubrium and J. A. Holstein (eds), *Handbook of Interview Research: Context and Method*, Thousand Oaks, CA: Sage, pp. 629–49.
Pollock, I. (2010), 'Learning from learners: Teachers in immersion classes', in G. Munro and I. Mac an Tàilleir (eds), *Coimhearsnachd na Gàidhlig an-diugh/Gaelic Communities Today*, Edinburgh: Dunedin Academic Press, pp. 117–25.
Potowski, K. (2007), *Language and Identity in a Dual Immersion School*, Clevedon: Multilingual Matters.
Pujolar, J. (2007), 'Bilingualism and the nation-state in the post-national era', in M. Heller (ed.), *Bilingualism: A Social Approach*, London: Palgrave Macmillan, pp. 71–95.
Reicher, S., and N. Hopkins (2001), *Self and Nation*, London: Sage.
Ricento, T. (2006), 'Methodological perspectives in language policy: An overview', in T. Ricento (ed.), *An Introduction to Language Policy*, Oxford: Blackwell, pp. 129–34.
Richards, E. (2007), *Debating the Highland Clearances*, Edinburgh: Edinburgh University Press.
Ritchie, J., J. Lewis and G. Elam (2003), 'Designing and selecting samples', in J. Ritchie and J. Lewis (eds), *Qualitative Research Practice: A Guide for Social Science Students and Researchers*, London: Sage, pp. 77–108.
Robasdan, B. (2006), 'Foghlam Gàidhlig: Bho linn gu linn', in W. McLeod (ed.), *Revitalising Gaelic in Scotland: Policy, Planning and Public Discourse*, Edinburgh: Dunedin Academic Press, pp. 87–118.
Roberts, A. (1991), 'Parental attitudes to Gaelic-medium education in the Western Isles of Scotland', *Journal of Multilingual and Multicultural Development*, 12: 253–69.
Robertson, B. (2001), 'Gaelic in Scotland', in G. Extra and D. Gorter (eds), *The Other Languages of Europe: Demographic, Sociolinguistic and Educational Perspectives*, Clevedon: Multilingual Matters, pp. 83–102.
Rogerson, J., and A. Gloyer (1995), 'Gaelic cultural revival or language decline?', *Scottish Geographical Magazine*, 111: 46–52.
Romaine, S. (2000), *Language in Society: An Introduction to Sociolinguistics*, 2nd edn, Oxford: Oxford University Press.
Romaine, S. (2006), 'Planning for the survival of linguistic diversity', *Language Policy*, 5: 441–73.

Romaine, S. (2008), 'Linguistic diversity, sustainability, and the future of the past', in K. King, N. Schilling-Estes, L. Fogle, J. Lou and B. Soukup (eds), *Sustaining Linguistic Diversity: Endangered and Minority Languages and Varieties*, Washington, DC: Georgetown University Press, pp. 7–21.

Romaine, S. (2013), 'The bilingual and multilingual community', in T. K. Bhatia and W. C. Ritchie (eds), *The Handbook of Bilingualism and Multilingualism*, 2nd edn, Oxford: Blackwell, pp. 445–65.

Roquette, M. L. (2005), 'Représentations sociales, pratiques et implication personelle: Un regard psychosocial sur l'expérience des Calandretas', in H. Boyer (ed.), *De l'école occitane à l'enseignement public: Vécu et représentations sociolinguistiques. Une enquête auprès d'un groupe d'ex-calondrons*, Paris: L'Harmattan, pp. 81–8.

Rumsey, A. (1990), 'Wording, meaning, and linguistic ideology', *American Anthropologist*, 92: 346–61.

Russell, R. A. (1999), 'Lexical maintenance and attrition in Japanese as a second language', in L. Hansen (ed.), *Second Language Attrition in Japanese Contexts*, Oxford: Oxford University Press, pp. 114–41.

Sapir, E. (1962), *Culture, Language, and Personality: Selected Essays*, ed. by D. Mandelbaum, Berkeley: University of California Press.

Saville-Troike, M. (2003), *The Ethnography of Communication: An Introduction*, 3rd edn, Oxford: Blackwell.

Scammell, K. (1985), 'Pre-school playgroups', in J. Hulbert (ed.), *Gaelic: Looking to the Future*, Dundee: Andrew Fletcher Society, pp. 21–27.

Schieffelin, B. B., and E. Ochs (1986a), 'Language socialization', *Annual Review of Anthropology*, 15: 163–91.

Schieffelin, B. B., and E. Ochs (eds) (1986b), *Language Socialization across Cultures*, Cambridge: Cambridge University Press.

Schieffelin B. B., K. A. Woolard and P. Kroskrity (eds) (1998), *Language Ideologies: Practice and Theory*, Oxford: Oxford University Press.

Schiffrin, D. (1996), 'Narrative as self-portrait: Sociolinguistic constructions of identity', *Language in Society*, 25: 167–203.

Schilling-Estes, N. (2004), 'Constructing ethnicity in interaction', *Journal of Sociolinguistics*, 8: 163–95.

Schmid, M. S. (2011), *Language Attrition*, Cambridge: Cambridge University Press.

Schmid, M. S., and K. de Bot (2004), 'Language attrition', in A. Davies and C. Elder (eds), *The Handbook of Applied Linguistics*, Oxford: Blackwell, pp. 210–34.

Schmid, M. S., B. Köpke and K. de Bot (2013), 'Language attrition as a complex, non-linear development', *International Journal of Bilingualism*, 17: 675–83.

Schmidt, R. (2007), 'Defending English in an English-dominant world: The ideology of the "Official English" movement in the United States', in A. Duchêne and M. Heller (eds), *Discourses of Endangerment: Ideology and Interest in the Defence of Languages*, London: Continuum, pp. 197–215.

Scottish Government (2011), *Curriculum for Excellence: Gaelic Excellence Group Report*, Edinburgh: Scottish Government, <http://www.scotland.gov.uk/Resource/Doc/91982/0114490.pdf> (last accessed 3 Jun. 2016).

Scottish Office Education Department (1950), *The Primary School in Scotland: A Memorandum for the Curriculum*, Edinburgh: HMSO.
Scottish Office Education Department (1951), *Education in Scotland in 1950: A Report for the Secretary of State for Scotland*, Edinburgh: HMSO.
Scottish Office Education Department (1965), *Primary Education in Scotland*, Edinburgh: HMSO.
Scottish Office Education Department (1993), *Curriculum and Assessment in Scotland National Guidelines: Gaelic 5–14*, Edinburgh: SOED.
Scottish Office Education Department (1994), *Provision for Gaelic Education in Scotland: A Report by HM Inspectors of Schools*, Edinburgh: SOED.
Selleck, C. (2013), 'Inclusive policy and exclusionary practice in secondary education in Wales', *International Journal of Bilingual Education and Bilingualism*, 16: 20–41.
Silverman, D. (2006), *Interpreting Qualitative Data*, 3rd edn, London: Sage.
Silverstein, M. (1979), 'Language structure and linguistic ideology', in R. Cline, W. Hanks and C. Hofbauer (eds), *The Elements: A Parasession on Linguistic Units and Levels*, Chicago: Chicago Linguistic Society, pp. 193–247.
Silverstein, M. (2000), 'Whorfianism and the linguistic imagination of nationality', in P. Kroskrity (ed.), *Regimes of Language: Ideologies, Polities, and Identities*, Santa Fe, NM: School of American Research Press, pp. 85–138.
Skutnabb-Kangas, T. (1988), 'Multilingualism and the education of minority children', in T. Skutnabb-Kangas and J. Cummins (eds), *Minority Education: From Shame to Struggle*, Clevedon: Multilingual Matters.
Skutnabb-Kangas, T. (2000), *Linguistic Genocide in Education – or Worldwide Diversity and Human Rights?*, London: Lawrence Erlbaum.
Smith, A. (2010), *Nationalism*, 2nd edn, Cambridge: Polity Press.
Smith-Christmas, C. (2012), 'I've lost it here *dè a bh' agam?*': Language Shift, Maintenance, and Code-Switching in a Bilingual Family'. Unpublished PhD thesis, University of Glasgow.
Smith-Christmas, C. (2013), 'Stance and code-switching: Gaelic–English bilinguals on the Isles of Skye and Harris', in P. Auer, J. Caro Reina and G. Kaufmann (eds), *Language Variation: European Perspectives IV*, Amsterdam: John Benjamins, pp. 229–45.
Smith-Christmas, C. (2015), *Family Language Policy: Maintaining an Endangered Language in the Home*, Basingstoke: Palgrave.
Snow, M. A. (1982), 'Graduates of the Culver City Spanish Immersion Program: A followup report', Paper presented at the Sixteenth Annual TESOL Convention, Honolulu, Hawaii.
Snow, M. A., A. M. Padilla and R. N. Campbell (1988), 'Factors influencing language retention of graduates of a Spanish immersion program', *Applied Linguistics*, 9:182–97.
Statistics for Wales (2013), *School Census Results: First Release*, <http://www.wales.gov.uk/docs/statistics/2013/130711-school-census-results-2013-en.pdf> (last accessed 28 Feb. 2018).
Statistics for Wales (2014), *2011 Census Data – Characteristics of Households in Wales*, <http://wales.gov.uk/docs/statistics/2014/140225-2011-census-characteristics-households-en.pdf> (last accessed 28 Jan. 2016).

Statistics New Zealand (2013), *2013 Census Quick Stats about Maori*, Wellington: Statistics New Zealand, <http://www.stats.govt.nz/Census/2013-census/profile-and-summary-reports/quickstats-about-maori-english.aspx> (last accessed 20 Jun. 2016).

Stockdale, A., B. MacGregor and G. Munro (2003), *Migration, Gaelic-Medium Education and Language Use*, Sleat, Isle of Skye: Ionad Nàiseanta na h-Imrich, Sabhal Mòr Ostaig, <http://www.ini.smo.uhi.ac.uk/projects/Migration_report.doc> (last accessed 20 Mar. 2016).

Stoessel, S. (2002), 'Investigating the role of social networks in language maintenance and shift', *International Journal of the Sociology of Language*, 153: 93–131.

Stradling, B., and M. MacNeil (2000), *Home and Community: Their Role in Enhancing the Gaelic Language Competencies of Children in Gaelic-Medium Education*, Sleat, Isle of Skye: Lèirsinn Research Centre.

Strubell, M. (1999), 'From language planning to language policies and language politics', in P. J. Weber (ed.), *Contact + Confli(c)t: Language Planning and Minorities*, Bonn: Dümmler, pp. 237–47.

Swain, M. (1995), 'Three functions of output in second language learning', in G. Cook and B. Seidlhofer (eds), *Principles and Practice in Applied Linguistics*, Oxford: Oxford University Press, pp. 234–50.

Swain, M. (1997), 'French immersion programs in Canada', in J. Cummins and D. Corson (eds), *Encyclopaedia of Language and Education: Vol. 5. Bilingual Education*, Dordrecht: Kluwer, pp. 261–70.

Swain, M., and R. K. Johnson (1997), 'Immersion education: A category within bilingual education', in R. K. Johnson and M. Swain (eds), *Immersion Education: International Perspectives*, Cambridge: Cambridge University Press, pp. 11–16.

Talmy, S. (2010), 'Qualitative interviews in applied linguistics: From research instrument to social practice', *Annual Review of Applied Linguistics*, 30: 128–48.

Taylor, C. (1989), *Sources of the Self: The Making of the Modern Identity*, Cambridge: Cambridge University Press.

Thomas, E. M., and D. B. Roberts (2011), 'Exploring bilinguals' social use of language inside and outside of the minority classroom', *Language and Education*, 25: 89–108.

Thompson, F. (1985), 'How strong the horsehair?', in J. Hulbert (ed.), *Gaelic: Looking to the Future*, Dundee: Andrew Fletcher Society, pp. 5–10.

Timms, C. T. (2012), 'Indigenous Language Revitalisation in Aotearoa New Zealand and Alba Scotland'. Unpublished PhD thesis, University of Otago.

Trabelsi, S. (1998), 'Langues minoritaires territoriales: Le rôle de la population bilingue dans la dissemination de la parole minoritaire'. Unpublished PhD thesis, Stendhal University, Grenoble.

Trudgill, P. (1974), *Sociolinguistics: An Introduction*, Harmondsworth: Penguin.

UNESCO (2003a), *Education in a Multilingual World*, UNESCO Education Position Paper, Paris: UNESCO.

UNESCO (2003b), *Language Vitality and Endangerment*, UNESCO Intangible Cultural Heritage Unit Ad Hoc Expert Group on Endangered Languages, Paris: UNESCO.

Usborne, E., J. Caouette, Q. Qumaaluk and D. M. Taylor (2009), 'Bilingual education in an Aboriginal context: Examining the transfer of language skills from Inuktitut to English or French', *International Journal of Bilingual Education and Bilingualism*, 12: 667–84.

Ushioda, E., and Z. Dörnyei (2009), 'Motivation, language identities and the L2 self: A theoretical overview', in Z. Dörnyei and E. Ushioda (eds), *Motivation, Language Identity and the L2 Self*, Clevedon: Multilingual Matters, pp. 1–8.

Valdés, G., S. V. González, D. L. García and P. Márquez (2008), 'Heritage languages and ideologies of language', in D. M. Brinton, O. Kagan and S. Bauckus (eds), *Heritage Language Education: A New Field Emerging*, New York: Routledge, pp. 107–30.

Von Humboldt, W. (1988) [1836], *On Language: The Diversity of Human Language Structure and its Influence on the Mental Development of Mankind*, transl. P. Heath, Cambridge: Cambridge University Press.

Walsh, J. and W. McLeod (2008), 'An overcoat wrapped around an invisible man? Language legislation and language revitalisation in Ireland and Scotland', *Language Policy*, 7: 21–46.

Warren, C. A. B. (2002), 'Qualitative interviewing', in J. F Gubrium and J. A. Holstein (eds), *Handbook of Interview Research: Context and Method*, Thousand Oaks, CA: Sage, pp. 83–120.

Watson-Gegeo, K. A. and D. W. Gegeo (1986), 'Calling-out and repeating routines in Kwara'ae children's language socialization', in B. B. Schieffelin and E. Ochs (eds), *Language Socialization Across Cultures*, Cambridge: Cambridge University Press, pp. 17–49.

Weiyun He, A. (2010), 'The heart of heritage: Sociocultural dimensions of heritage language learning', *Annual Review of Applied Linguistics*, 30: 66–82.

Welsh Assembly Government (2010), *Iaith Fyw, Iaith Byw – A Living Language: A Language for Living, A Strategy for the Welsh Language*, Cardiff: Welsh Assembly Government.

Welsh Language Board (2008), *The Welsh Language Surveys of 2004–06*, Cardiff: Welsh Language Board.

West, C., and A. Graham (2011), *Attitudes to the Gaelic Language*, Edinburgh: Scottish Government Social Research.

Whorf, B. L. (1956) [1940], *Language, Thought, and Reality: Selected Writings of Benjamin Lee Whorf*, ed. by J. B. Carroll, Cambridge, MA: MIT Press.

Will, V. (2012),'Why Kenny Can't *Can*: The Language Socialization Experiences of Gaelic-Medium Educated Children in Scotland'. Unpublished PhD thesis, University of Michigan.

Williams, C. H. (2008), *Linguistic Minorities in Democratic Context*, Basingstoke: Palgrave Macmillan.

Williams, C. H. (2010), 'The Celtic world', in J. A. Fishman and O. García (eds), *Handbook of Language and Ethnic Identity: Disciplinary and Regional Perspectives (Vol. I)*, 2nd edn, Oxford: Oxford University Press, pp. 237–54.

Williams, C. H. (2013), *Minority Language Promotion, Protection and Regulation: The Mask of Piety*, Basingstoke: Palgrave Macmillan.

Williams, G. (1992), *Sociolinguistics: A Sociological Critique*, London: Routledge.
Williams, I. W. (ed.) (2003), *Our Children's Language: The Welsh-Medium Schools of Wales 1939–2000*, Talybont: Y Lolfa.
Wilson, B. (1985), 'Gaelic primary education inaugurated in Glasgow', *Glasgow Herald*, 15 August, p. 14.
Withers, C. W. J. (1984), *Gaelic in Scotland 1698–1981: The Geographical History of a Language*, Edinburgh: J. Donald.
Withers, C. W. J. (1988), *Gaelic Scotland: The Transformation of a Culture Region*, London: Routledge.
Wong, L. (1999), 'Authenticity and the revitalization of Hawaiian', *Anthropology and Education Quarterly*, 30: 94–115.
Woolard, K. A. (1998), 'Introduction: Language ideology as a field of inquiry', in B. B. Schieffelin, K. A. Woolard and P. V. Kroskrity (eds), *Language Ideologies*, Oxford: Oxford University Press, pp. 3–47.
Woolard, K. A. (2007), 'Is there linguistic life after high school? Longitudinal changes in the bilingual repertoire in metropolitan Barcelona', *Language in Society*, 40: 617–48.
Woolard, K. A., and B. B. Schieffelin (1994), 'Language ideology', *Annual Review of Anthropology*, 23: 55–82.
Woolf, A. (2007), *From Pictland to Alba: 789–1070*, Edinburgh: Edinburgh University Press.
Wray, A., and A. Bloomer (2006), *Projects in Linguistics and Language Studies*, 3rd edn, Abingdon: Routledge.
Wright, S. C., D. M. Taylor and J. Macarthur (2000), 'Subtractive bilingualism and the survival of the Inuit language: Heritage- versus second-language education', *Journal of Educational Psychology*, 92: 63–84.
Wright, W. E. (2013), 'Bilingual education', in T. K. Bhatia and W. C. Ritchie (eds), *The Handbook of Bilingualism and Multilingualism*, 2nd edn, Oxford: Blackwell, pp. 598–623.
Yin, R. (2009), *Case Study Research: Design and Method*, 4th edn, London: Sage.
Zalbide, M., and J. Cenoz (2008), 'Bilingual education in the Basque Autonomous Community: Achievements and challenges', in J. Cenoz (ed.), *Teaching Through Basque: Achievements and Challenges*, Clevedon: Multilingual Matters, pp. 5–20.

Index

affect, 30
   negative, 83, 87–9, 110, 115, 120, 146
Aithris na Maidne, 55; *see also* Radio nan Gàidheal
Alba, 72, 127, 134, 139
   Kingdom of, 5; *see also* BBC Alba
An Comunn Gaidhealach, 44–5
An Là, 55; *see also* BBC Alba
ancestry, 19–20, 24; *see also* ethnicity; heritage
Anderson, Benedict, 24
Aotearoa/New Zealand, 40
applied linguistics, 14, 41, 153
Argyll, 5, 47, 54, 82, 91
Australia, 40

Baker, Colin, 29, 31, 36, 59
Basque language, 6, 37, 39
BBC Alba, 55, 93, 139
bilingualism, 7, 18, 20, 29, 32, 40–1, 46, 68, 131, 145
Bòrd na Gàidhlig, 2, 8, 10, 49
Bourdieu, Pierre, 13, 23, 27
Breton language, 38
Britain, 1, 2, 5, 6; *see also* identity: British
Brythonic, 5
Bucholtz, Mary, 21, 23
burghs, 1, 5

Cameron, Deborah, 60, 62–3
Canada, 30–1, 33–4, 39–40, 46
Catalan language, 34, 38–9
Cavanaugh, Jillian, 26
Celtic, 35

children *see* education; family; intergenerational transmission
choice, 13, 32, 49, 79–80, 100
   GME, 49–50, 98, 144
   ideology of, 109, 118–20, 148
Church of Scotland, 44
code-switching, 57, 61–3, 71, 73–5, 134, 142–3
Comhairle nan Eilean, 45
Comhairle nan Eilean Siar, 54, 91
communication, 4, 6, 12, 14, 34, 45, 59, 87, 103, 117, 144
   electronic, 55–6, 14, 102–4, 106–7, 144
   wider, 6, 22, 25; *see also* discourse; interaction
community, 4, 9, 10–14, 16, 20–8, 30–1, 34, 39–41, 45, 48–52, 60, 62, 75, 92–3, 107, 143, 148
   Basque Autonomous, 39
   Gaelic, 4–5, 7, 9, 27, 56–7, 61, 65, 71, 77–8, 80–3, 87–8, 93, 108, 110, 113–18, 120, 136, 138, 146–9, 151, 153–4
   imagined, 24
   Irish-speaking, 36–7
competence
   communicative, 28, 30, 60
   linguistic, 4, 13, 15, 22, 29, 31, 50, 80–1, 95
   pragmatic, 30
Comunn na Gàidhlig, 7, 46, 48
Costa, James, 4
Council of Europe, 49
Crystal, David, 14

culture, 4, 6, 13, 14, 17–28, 31–2, 41, 58–61, 123, 148
   Gaelic, 2, 3, 5–9, 49, 80, 82–7, 89, 137–8, 140, 142, 146, 151
   Indigenous, 39–40
   Scottish, 7–9, 131–5, 137–8
   Xish/Xian, 10–13, 22

diglossia, 11–12
discourse, 4, 20, 30, 43, 59–60, 65, 71–2, 109–10, 118, 121, 131, 135, 137, 149; *see also* communication; interaction; speaking
Diwan, 38
domain, 10, 12–15, 30, 33–4, 51–2, 104, 119, 148
   higher-order, 12, 34, 39, 71, 96, 142–4
   home, 12, 28, 51, 75, 82, 107
Dorian, Nancy, 9–10, 14, 23, 34, 52, 56, 154
Dörnyei, Zoltán, 31–2
Dunbar, Rob, 8, 10, 44, 47

Edinburgh, 10, 32, 48, 90–1, 132
education, 1, 3, 7, 10–12, 15, 18, 20, 27–9, 35, 43–5, 48, 46, 60, 90, 141–2, 146, 153–4
   Basque-medium, 39
   bilingual, 1, 3, 17, 29, 34, 40–1, 46, 60, 154
   French immersion, 29–31
   higher, 56, 66
   immersion revitalisation, 15–17, 29, 33–5, 39, 41, 49, 153
   Irish-medium, 36–8
   Māori-medium, 40–1
   Welsh-medium, 30, 33, 35–6, 143
Education (Scotland) Act 1872, 2, 7, 44
Education (Scotland) Act 1918, 7, 44–5
Edwards, John, 10–15, 18–22, 24–5, 30–2, 143, 154
employment, 11
   Gaelic, 66, 71, 75, 90, 152
   Welsh, 33, 143
English language, 2, 28–9, 31, 36–7, 41, 55–7, 61–3, 69–80, 87–90, 92–106, 110, 112, 114, 124–5, 128, 131–6, 142–8
   language shift to, 2, 5–8, 20, 28, 44–5, 49, 51; *see also* Scots language
Enlightenment, 6; *see also* improvement; modernity
essentialism, 22–3
ethnicity, 19–21, 25; *see also* identity: ethnic
ethnography, 4, 9, 57–60, 152–3; *see also* speaking: ethnography of

Ethnologue, 4
European Charter for Regional or Minority Languages, 49

Facebook, 55; *see also* communication: electronic
family, 39, 56, 67–72, 75, 79–86, 96–102, 111–12, 123–4; *see also* domain: home
family–neighbourhood–community nexus, 11–12, 15, 77, 144; *see also* intergenerational transmission
feminism, 23
Fishman, Joshua, 3–4, 9–15, 18, 20, 22, 25, 34–5, 52, 142–4, 153
fluency, 32–3, 35–6, 40, 45, 47, 50, 52, 68, 70, 77, 81, 93–5, 115–18, 145
Free Church of Scotland, 44

Gael *see Gàidheal*
Gaelic Language (Scotland) Act 2005, 7–8, 139
Gaelic renaissance, 7, 9
Gaelic-medium education (GME), 1–3, 10, 15–16, 23, 28–30, 42–56, 64, 65–7, 70–93, 96–8, 100–2, 106–8, 114, 120–5, 135–6, 139–40, 141–54; *see also* choice: GME; education: bilingual
Gaelscoileanna, 36–8; *see also* education: Irish-medium
Gaeltacht, 36–7
Gàidheal, 4–5, 52, 82, 115, 121, 123–5, 135–7, 150; *see also* identity: Gaelic
Gàidhealtachd, 5, 9; *see also* Highlands and Islands
Gal, Susan, 26–7
García, Ofelia, 18, 21, 35
Gardner, Robert, 29, 31
Gellner, Ernest, 24
Gemeinschaft, 9, 12, 52; *see also* community
Gesellschaft, 9, 12, 52, 131; *see also* society
Glasgow, 2, 9–10, 32, 46–8, 50, 52–4, 90–1, 114
guilt
   ideology of, 108–11, 118, 140, 148, 151, 153

habitus, 27
Hall, Kira, 21, 23
Haugen, Einar, 14, 18
Hawai'ian language, 39
Heller, Monica, 4, 13, 15, 18, 24–5
Her Majesty's Inspectorate of Education, 2, 48

INDEX

heritage, 6, 24, 34–5
  Gaelic, 51, 80, 123–4, 127, 132, 137
  Scottish, 8–9, 15; *see also* ethnicity; tradition
Highland Clearances, 2, 7; *see also* Enlightenment; improvement; inequality
Highland Council, 47, 54, 91
Highlands and Islands, 2, 44, 47, 54, 57–8, 81, 90, 121, 126
  Gaelic within, 5–9, 26, 44, 81–2, 103, 121, 128–37, 146, 149; *see also* Gàidhealtachd
Hobsbawm, Eric, 24
Hroch, Miroslav, 24
Hymes, Dell, 28, 30, 59–62, 64, 87

Iaith Fyw, 35
iconisation, 23, 27, 52, 135
identity, 3, 6, 8, 10, 17–28, 31, 41, 58, 61
  British, 136–8, 150
  cultural, 14, 17, 19, 21, 34, 39, 56
  ethnic, 10, 18–20, 22–3, 25, 27, 52
  Gaelic, 8–9, 49, 51–2, 121, 123–6, 135, 138, 149–50, 153
  heritage, 51, 123, 150
  Irish, 37
  national, 24–5, 130–4, 136, 150, 153
  personal, 117, 121–3, 138, 149
  regional, 52, 126–30, 135, 138, 149
  Scottish, 8–9, 27, 48, 52, 61, 124–5, 129, 131–8, 149–50
  social, 20–1, 61, 108
  Xian, 10, 22
idiom, 25, 50
ikastolak, 39; *see also* education: Basque-medium
improvement, 5–6
indexicality, 9, 27, 128, 135
Indigenous languages, 33, 35, 39–40
inequality, 13
Inglis, 1, 5; *see also* English language; Scots language
input, 30–3
  Gaelic language, 48, 89, 109
interaction, 17, 20–1, 27–8, 30, 36, 43, 47, 53, 56–65, 70, 72, 74–5, 79, 85, 100, 104, 105, 142, 144; *see also* communication; discourse
interaction hypothesis, 30
  intergenerational transmission, 3, 11–15, 40, 53, 59, 67, 75, 84, 97–102, 109, 111–12, 139, 144–6, 152; *see also* family; language socialisation

Inuktitut language, 28, 40
Inverness, 2, 45, 46, 54, 91
Inverness Society for Gaelic Schools, 44
Inverness-shire Gaelic Education Scheme, 45
Irvine, Judith, 27

Jaffe, Alexandra, 13, 23, 25, 27
Johnstone, Richard, 30–1, 33, 49, 51
judgement, 13
  ideology of, 113–15, 139, 148–9

King, Kendall, 26, 35
Krauss, Michael, 4
Kroskrity, Paul, 25–6

Ladefoged, Peter, 14
Lambert, Wallace, 29, 31
Language, 14
language acquisition, 11, 16, 18, 28–32, 36, 41
  English, 7, 41
  Gaelic, 2, 50, 64, 79, 83–4
  Welsh, 36
language alternation *see* code-switching
language attitudes, 2–3, 8, 20, 26, 29, 31, 33, 35, 37, 51
  Gaelic, 8, 51–2, 55–6, 64, 108, 111, 113, 127, 130, 136–40, 142, 147–9, 151–3
  parental, 48; *see also* language ideologies
language attrition, 13, 16, 28–9, 32–4, 37, 41, 110
  Gaelic, 110, 115–16, 118
  Irish, 33
language decline, 1, 10, 13, 22, 41
  Gaelic, 1–4, 7, 10, 44, 46, 86, 115–16, 145; *see also* language attrition; language shift
language ideologies, 2, 6, 8, 10–13, 16–18, 22–9, 34–5, 37, 41, 58, 153
  Gaelic, 2, 59, 64, 69, 108–11, 113, 115–21, 126, 129, 131–5, 137, 140–2, 147–51, 153
  Irish, 37
language loss; 1, 4, 10, 32, 109, 115; *see also* language attrition; language decline; language shift
language maintenance, 3, 10–13, 15, 21–2, 25, 29, 32–5, 40, 59
  Gaelic, 44, 48, 51, 68, 101, 107, 112, 141–7, 151–2, 154
  Indigenous, 39–40; *see also* reversing language shift
language planning *see* language policy

language policy, 1, 11, 12, 29, 15, 103, 146, 154
  Gaelic, 2, 15, 44, 46–9, 53, 65, 112, 150–4
  Irish, 37
  Scottish, 2, 5–6, 44, 146, 153–4
  Welsh, 35
language revitalisation, 1–4, 7, 10, 12–16, 23, 29, 34–5, 41
  Basque, 39
  Catalan, 34
  Gaelic, 7, 9, 44, 47– 9, 51–6, 65, 138, 141–4, 151–4
  Indigenous, 1–2, 39
  Irish, 37–8
  Welsh, 35–6; *see also* language maintenance; language policy; reversing language shift
language revival *see* language revitalisation
language shift, 4, 10–15, 20–2, 26, 35, 140–8, 154
  Gaelic–English, 5–7, 28, 46; *see also* language decline
language socialisation, 16–18, 27–9, 41
  Gaelic, 48, 50, 59, 65–7, 70, 75–89, 92–3, 97–102, 106–7, 114, 141–7, 152
  Welsh, 36; *see also* community; domain: home
language use, 4, 8, 13–16, 20–5, 27, 33–5, 41–3, 56, 60–2
  Breton, 38
  Catalan, 38
  Gaelic, 1–4, 16, 28, 48, 50–3, 57–9, 65–76, 85, 89, 93–106, 108–9, 113–15, 120, 135, 140–53
  Irish, 33
  Māori, 41
  Navajo, 39
  Welsh, 36–8; *see also* linguistic practice
learners, 9, 28, 30–1, 35
  Gaelic, 50, 81, 114–15, 148
  Irish, 37; *see also* language acquisition
linguistic anthropology, 17–19, 25–6, 41, 53, 59–60; *see also* sociolinguistics
linguistic practice, 3, 10, 13–15, 18, 20, 21–8, 34, 61
  Gaelic, 56, 69–75, 77, 83–5, 92–4, 96, 108–14, 118, 120–1, 135, 141–8, 151–3; *see also* language use
linguistic snobbery
  perceptions of, 108–9, 113, 115, 139, 148–9, 153
literacy, 11, 24, 84, 95

Lowlands, 1–2, 5, 7, 9, 46, 57–8, 61, 69, 76, 79–81, 90, 111, 119, 125–8

MacCaluim, Alasdair, 49
Macdonald, Sharon, 9
McEwan-Fujita, Emily, 28
MacKinnon, Kenneth, 2, 47, 49
McLeod, Wilson, 7, 8, 35, 51, 81
Makihara, Miki, 19–21, 25–6, 147
Māori language, 40–1
May, Stephen, 19, 22, 24, 40–1
Mill, John Stuart, 6, 25
Ministerial Advisory Group on Gaelic (MAGOG), 7
modernity, 4, 12, 15, 20, 23–4, 115, 133, 144
motivation, 8, 15, 33, 72, 109–10, 148
  instrumental, 31
  integrative, 31–2
  parental, 48–9, 51
  pupil, 35, 37
music, 80, 85–6, 104–7, 132, 145
multiculturalism, 23, 28, 133
multilingualism, 12, 18, 20, 27–8, ; *see also* bilingualism

National Gaelic Language Plan, 8, 15, 49
nationalism, 23–5, 27
  English, 24
  linguistic, 24
  Scottish, 24; *see also* Romanticism
native speakers, 31, 33, 40, 65, 75, 83, 88, 110, 113, 115, 148; *see also* tradition
Navajo language, 39
new speakers, 10, 15, 38, 65, 79–84, 89, 140, 146, 153–4; *see also* learners
Nic Craith, Máiréad, 4
Normans, 1, 5
Northumbrian, 1, 5; *see also* Inglis
Nova Scotia, 49

Occitan language, 38
Ochs, Elinor, 19, 21, 62
O'Hanlon, Fiona, 44, 46, 50–1
Ó hIfearnáin, Tadhg, 14–15, 36–8, 152
Oliver, James, 9, 52, 150
output, 30, 33

parents *see* family; intergenerational transmission; motivation: parental
Paterson, Lindsay, 9, 44
Pictish language, 5
Pierce, Charles, 27

plurilingualism, 19; *see also* bilingualism; multilingualism
policymakers *see* language policy
positionality, 20–1, 60
power, 13, 18, 25
practice *see* linguistic practice

Quebec, 28, 40; *see also* Canada; St Lambert experiment

radio *see* music; Radio nan Gàidheal
Radio nan Gàidheal, 55
repertoire
  bilingual, 36, 61; *see also* bilingualism
reversing language shift (RLS), 3, 10, 13, 22, 34, 75, 141; *see also* language revitalisation
revitalisation *see* language revitalisation
Romaine, Suzanne, 4, 11–14, 17, 20, 145, 148
Romanticism, 6, 24, 27, 131–2

Sabhal Mòr Ostaig, 79, 114, 124
St Lambert experiment, 29; *see also* education: French immersion
Sapir-Whorf Hypothesis, 19
school *see* education
Scots language, 1–2, 5, 61–2, 121, 127, 129–32, 149; *see also* English language; Inglis
Silverstein, Michael, 25
social media *see* communication: electronic; Facebook; Twitter
society, 9, 11, 14, 17, 19–20, 25, 52
  Gaelic, 1, 5–6, 154
  Scottish, 1–2, 8, 56, 131, 133
Society in Scotland for Propagating Christian Knowledge (SSPCK), 6–7
sociolinguistics, 1, 3, 11–13, 15, 17–18, 20, 30, 38, 58–9, 60, 62, 107, 146

sociology of language, 17, 24, 25, 58–9, 153
speaking, 27, 31, 32, 68, 71–2, 74–5, 93, 95, 99–100, 115–16, 146, 148, 153
  ethnography of, 3, 43, 59–65; *see also* communication; discourse
standard language, 12, 18, 25, 62
Statutes of Iona, 5
Strubell, Miquel, 15

television, 55, 93, 104–5, 145; *see also* BBC Alba
tradition, 4, 6, 9, 10, 12, 21, 25, 34, 44
  Gaelic, 9, 50, 85–6, 115, 123, 134–5, 143; *see also* heritage
transcription, 16, 43, 58, 60, 62–4
Twitter, 55; *see also* communication: electronic

UK census, 2–4, 9–10, 36, 46, 90
United Kingdom *see* Britain; identity: British
United Nations, 4
United States of America, 39
Ushioda, Ema, 32

von Herder, Johann Gottfried, 6, 24; *see also* Romanticism
von Humboldt, Wilhelm, 6, 24; *see also* Romanticism

Welsh Language Act 1993, 7
Western Isles, 15, 28, 43, 45–6 , 48–52, 54, 57, 76–80, 87, 88, 110, 146
Williams, Colin, 19, 20, 22
Williams, Glyn, 13
Withers, Charles, 5–6
Woolard, Kathryn, 26, 33–4, 38–9
Woolf, Alexander, 5

Xish language, 10–12, 22; *see also* Fishman: Joshua; identity: Xian

EU representative:
Easy Access System Europe
Mustamäe tee 50, 10621 Tallinn, Estonia
Gpsr.requests@easproject.com

www.ingramcontent.com/pod-product-compliance
Lightning Source LLC
Chambersburg PA
CBHW071845230426
43671CB00012B/2074